The Struggle for Indigenous Rights in Latin America

To the indigenous activists,
who are changing their worlds.

To Nelle Fuller,
*who has always believed in the justice
of Native American causes.*

The Struggle for Indigenous Rights in Latin America

Edited by

Nancy Grey Postero and Leon Zamosc

sussex
ACADEMIC
PRESS

BRIGHTON • PORTLAND

2 4 6 8 10 9 7 5 3 1

First published 2004 in Great Britain by
SUSSEX ACADEMIC PRESS
PO Box 2950
Brighton BN2 5SP

and in the United States of America by
SUSSEX ACADEMIC PRESS
920 NE 58th Ave   Suite 300
Portland, Oregon 97213–3786

British Library Cataloguing in Publication Data
A CIP catalogue record for this book is available from the British Library.

Library of Congress Cataloging-in-Publication Data
The struggle for indigenous rights in Latin America /
    edited by Nancy Grey Postero and Leon Zamosc.
      p.   cm.
    Includes bibliographical references and index.
    ISBN 1-84519-006-8 (hardcover : alk. paper)
    ISBN 1-84519-063-7 (pbk. : alk. paper)
      1. Indians—Civil rights. 2. Indigenous
peoples—Latin America—Civil rights. 3. Human
rights—Latin America. 4. Latin America—Politics
and government. 5. Latin America—Social policy.
I. Postero, Nancy Grey. II. Zamosc, León.
E65.S87 2004
323.1197′08—dc22
                                                        2004014037
                                                        CIP

Typeset and designed by G&G Editorial, Brighton
Printed by MPG Books Ltd, Bodmin, Cornwall
This book is printed on acid-free paper.

Contents

Contents

Preface and
Acknowledgments

This volume is the result of two years of collaboration. It began at the University of California in San Diego, in May of 2002, at a small research seminar convened by Leon Zamosc and Nancy Postero, under the auspices of UCSD's Center for Iberian and Latin American Studies. In that first meeting, we set up the framework and began our discussions about the diversity of indigenous struggles in Latin America. We thank CILAS and an anonymous sponsor for the resources necessary to bring us together.

A second, larger conference was held in Cochabamba, Bolivia, in May 2003, to include a wide variety of participants. We were very lucky to have had the opportunity to collaborate with two partner organizations in Bolivia, PROEIBAndes and CEIDIS. PROEIBAndes, *Programa de Formación en Educación Intercultural Bilingue Para los Países Andinos* is a two-year master's program for indigenous leaders. We thank PROEIB's directors, Luis Enrique López and Inge Sichra, and the conference co-ordinator, Fernando Garcés for encouraging the project and getting their wonderful and engaged students involved. Many of the professors and members of their board presented their work and acted as discussants on the panels. CEIDIS, *el Consorcio Sur Andino*, is made up of CESU, the *Centro de Estudios Superiores Universitarios*, and CENDA, *Centro de Comunicación y Desarollo Andino*. CEIDIS, and its director Pablo Regalsky, coordinated the meetings, and contributed papers based on recent intercultural work. We thank all of our Bolivian partners.

The Cochabamba meeting was especially fruitful because of the participation of indigenous leaders from countries across the region. This was made possible by OXFAM America, and its Lima-based director, Martin Scurrah, who provided funding for their presence. We are extremely grateful for their support. The invited guests – from Guatemala, Colombia, Ecuador, Venezuela, Peru, Chile, and Australia – brought an insider's perspective to the discussions. Engaging in this dialogue was the very reason for the second conference, and we believe the results were extremely valuable.

Preface and Acknowledgments

This book is a direct outcome of that meeting. All our authors presented their papers and incorporated the comments, critiques, and questions received from the participants. The first chapter, in particular, reflects many of the issues discussed in the plenary sessions. We hope that all the participants will find this book helpful in the continued analysis of these issues, which is made better through collective discussions. A Spanish edition of the material is soon to be published, to make it accessible to the majority of the conference participants.

The editors thank all those who took part in both conferences, and especially the authors whose chapters appear here. We are also grateful to Jessa Lewis for her help in translating materials, and to CILAS for its logistic assistance.

The Struggle for
Indigenous Rights
in Latin America

Indigenous Movements and the Indian Question in Latin America

Nancy Grey Postero and Leon Zamosc

Crawford Young's 1976 survey of race, ethnicity, and cultural pluralism in the "Third World" argued that in Latin America, class and nationalism were more important than Indian self-affirmation. "Indians *qua* Indians," he concluded, "are not collective actors in the national political arena" (C. Young 1976: 428, see also van der Berghe 1970, Mason 1970). Yet, even as Young was asserting the political marginalization of Indians, a change in attitudes among Latin American indigenous populations[1] was taking place. In the early twenty-first century, few would disagree that Indians *qua* Indians are among the most important social actors in the struggles over the future of Latin American democracies.

Throughout the 1980s and 1990s, native peoples across the continent organized, mobilized, and participated in national and international political processes to demand cultural recognition and political rights. In the 1980s, Nicaragua's Miskito, Suma, and Rama peoples were granted territorial autonomy (Diaz-Polanco 1997). In 1990, Bolivian Indians staged a massive and highly publicized march up the Andes to La Paz, demanding *Territorio y Dignidad* (territory and dignity). In 1992, indigenous organizations sponsored continent-wide demonstrations rejecting the celebration of the "discovery of America," commemorating instead "five hundred years of popular and indigenous resistance" (Assies *et al.* 2000, Hale 1994). January 1994 saw the startling emergence of the Zapatista army in Chiapas, Mexico, which challenged the corruption and neoliberal strategies of the PRI-run government. The struggle against neoliberalism has also been central to the evolution of

Ecuador's national indigenous organization, the *Confederación de Nacionalidades Indígenas del Ecuador* (CONAIE), which since its first Indigenous Uprising in 1990, has become an important protagonist in Ecuadorian politics.

The rise of indigenous movements has lead to important political and cultural changes. States have been forced to respond to them and their demands, which have included territory, autonomy, cultural recognition, and reforms to existing state structures (Assies *et al.* 2000). By challenging exclusionary nationalism and demanding to be recognized as members of the nation (Roper *et al.* 2003), indigenous groups are beginning to contribute to the democratization of Latin American governments, expanding political participation to previously excluded groups (Van Cott 1994: 22). Beyond opening up membership into the nation, these groups also bring new visions of the role of the state. As Varese points out, subaltern positions of discrimination and marginalization provide them within particular visions of nationhood, which may offer important alternative visions for the state and society as a result of their experiences (Varese 1996, see also Stephen 2002). In many countries, constitutional reforms now recognize the multi-ethnicity and pluri-culturalism of the populations. Indigenous people have been granted new forms of individual and collective rights. Assisted by international NGOs, many states now offer intercultural bilingual education and culturally appropriate development projects. While much remains to be done – native people are invariably among the poorest in all countries, and their lands and livelihoods are in constant danger – the Indian Question has definitively come to the forefront of political agendas across Latin America.

Celebrating the "return of the Indian" (Albó 1991), observers and advocates of social movements have chronicled the rise of indigenous organizations and explored the factors that account for their emergence. Searching for common trends across Latin America, these initial studies have raised important questions: First, how did people marginalized for centuries, exploited economically and discriminated racially, manage to make such an impact, and, second, why now? These questions have been subject to a variety of theoretical approaches. Yashar (1998, 1999), for instance, has suggested that the emergence of indigenous movements can be explained by examining a confluence of three important factors: the opportunities to organize provided by democratic liberalization; the incentives to organize in response to the effects of neoliberal reforms, especially the end of corporatist models of state-Indian relations; and the capacity to organize provided by trans-community networks of support. Others, like Kay Warren, have brought from anthropology concerns about indigenous representation and critical engagements questioning strategic essentializing (K. Warren 1998a, Warren and Jackson 2002). Studies have taken diverse approaches, from "neo-indigenista" scholarship to post-modern critiques of indigenous political programs. A further group of scholars, including Allison Brysk, has focused on the influence of transnational allies and the growing importance of what they call the "international indigenous movement" (Brysk 1994, 2000, Roper *et al.* 2003).

In these initial approaches, scholars have been instrumental in dispelling the myth that Indians had "disappeared." By bringing native people's resilience and agency to the attention of the public, scholars have helped establish indigenous movements as legitimate actors worthy of respect and legal protection. In the process, however, theorists and activists who advocate for indigenous rights run the risk of creating other, equally misleading, myths. The widespread discourse of resistance is sometimes accompanied by a generic image of indigenous movements struggling against universal kinds of oppression, fighting to protect the environment, with a common agenda of citizenship and autonomy. This is, of course, inaccurate: not all Indians are "good stewards of the rainforest," nor do they all want the same things. The danger with reductive representations is that they make it impossible to understand what is really happening. By focusing on the commonalities among movements, scholars often overlook critical questions that arise from an examination of the movements' particularities: What role do indigenous struggles play in the broader framework of society as a whole? How do these struggles fit with other social processes of race, class, and political relations? And, more generally, how will these struggles affect the redefinitions of citizenship and democracy in the immediate future?

This chapter seeks to establish conceptual frameworks to allow us to understand the diversity that exists among indigenous movements, their demands, and their strategies. The characteristics of the movements and the struggles in which they are involved are highly specific to the countries and regions in which they act. They reflect the interactions of numerous factors: the demography of the countries or regions in which they act; the history of relations with the state and the assimilation policies the state has implemented; the place indigenousness plays in the imaginary of the nation; and the political system and traditions of the country. This is not to deny that there are common cross-country factors. Ethnic relations in Latin America emerge from a shared history of colonialism and racism. Yet, if we look at other trends that swept across Latin America – agrarian reform, military dictatorships, ISI economic policies – we see that each had a specific development and outcome depending upon the specificities of the country. The struggle for indigenous rights is no different. Ultimately, it is at the level of the nation-state where movements wage their principal struggles, and where the Indian Question will be played out (Urban and Sherzer 1991, Otero 2003).

The essays below all explore the specific factors that shape the trajectory of each country's indigenous movement and the strategies that native peoples have chosen to follow. While organizing and contestation occur at the local, regional, national, and international level, the focus here is on the national level. The authors, who presented their papers at a conference in Cochabamba, Bolivia, in May 2003, were asked to analyze the indigenous social movements in each country and to evaluate the chosen strategies and the results. How do things stand after fifteen years of indigenous organizing? What is now at stake? What are the obstacles, and what does the future promise? By comparing the complex cases of each of the countries in this volume, we hope to be able to trace the irreducible diversity and identify factors influencing the strategies and the outcomes; and examine the patterns that might exist in this diversity. It is impossible to find one factor that explains everything, one dependent variable that can illuminate all the cases. Our subject area is a whole continent with millions of inhabitants and hundreds of years of history. Nevertheless, we believe it is possible to discern certain patterns on the basis of comparative analyses focusing on four critical areas of investigation.

First, which theoretical frameworks should be used to appraise the meanings of the struggles of indigenous groups? While we make use of established concepts through which social science has traditionally viewed these issues, such as the study of ethnicity and social movements, we introduce here conceptual tools that are more sensitive to the specificities of the current situations of Latin America's native peoples. In this context, our proposal of what we call the Indian Question is one of the central contributions of this volume. We consider the Indian Question as a framework of contestation, where the future of indigenous citizenship is at stake. Our definition allows us to make the critical analytical distinction between the issue of the citizenship status of indigenous populations, on the one hand, and the processes involved in the definition of that status, including the struggles of indigenous movements, on the other.

Second, how does the Indian Question arise in different contexts and what is the role of social movements in that process? That is, how does it come to be important politically? Here, what interests us are the conjunctures, the specific historical circumstances under which the debate over the status of indigenous populations gains centrality in the national political agenda. In examining these processes, we do not accept the agency of indigenous movements as given. Whether particular movements are able to assume greater or lesser roles in the politicization of the Indian Question depends on many factors, including the heterogeneity of the groups, the history of incorporation of these groups into the life of the nation, and the interplay between ethnicity and social class.

Third, what is at stake in the contestation over the status of the Indians; what are they actually fighting for? In the initial round of studies, there was a tendency to lump the demands of all the various groups together, depicting a sort of generic indigenous agenda. A closer analysis of the specific actions and practices reveals that different groups are in fact fighting for, and against, different things. Even where international standards, like

Convention 169 of the International Labor Organization (which recommended the recognition of a variety of indigenous rights; see ILO 1989) provide common references, the ways in which those standards are interpreted vary widely from country to country. How are the specificities of these strategies and actions related to other factors, such as the relative majority or minority status of indigenous populations in the country? While we cannot yet offer a systematic response to these questions, we believe the papers organized in this book offer clues as to what is shaping indigenous strategies and the likelihood of their success.

Fourth, what is the relation between neoliberalism and the politicization of indigenous demands? We look at this contextual factor separately because government-implemented neoliberal economic and political programs have been among the most important factors shaping the scenario of conflict in Latin America. Yashar (1998, 1999) has argued that indigenous groups organized in response to the costly changes wrought by neoliberal reforms. Others (Roper *et al.* 2003, Assies *et al.* 2000) suggest that the reforms provided both opportunities and challenges. We take this initial discussion further by showing how indigenous responses to neoliberalism connect their struggles to those of other sectors. The papers in this volume show that the kinds of relations indigenous groups form with other sectors, be it alliance, articulation, or resistance, may determine the nature, the momentum, and even the results of their struggles for indigenous rights. Where indigenous movements are able to gain social and political capital through their responses to neoliberalism, they may be better able to bring their agendas to the national political table.

Defining the Indian Question

The conceptualization of the Indian Question provides a useful framework for comparative analysis, serving as a referent against which we can study the variations this volume's contributors describe in their case studies. By "the Indian Question," we refer to the crucial issue of what kinds of rights indigenous people should be granted as citizens of democratic nation-states. This question of citizenship has emerged as a part of the democratization process that has taken place throughout Latin America. The promise of democratization is that the political, social, and economic marginalization that characterized indigenous relations with the state (and the elite classes that controlled it) would be replaced by a full and robust citizenship. As the question of indigenous citizenship has breached national debates, it has prompted societies to rethink what exactly democracy should mean, and how democracy should deal with difference. Should indigenous citizens have all the same rights and obligations as other citizens, or should they also be granted special rights as the descendents of the original peoples of the Americas? If so, what kinds of special rights should they receive? How should this be accomplished? Can the existing state structures serve to bring these formerly marginalized people into the national community, or will the state have to change? Posing these questions raises several important points which require further consideration.

The Indian Question is a question of nationhood, but not in the sense of irredentism or separatism. Some indigenous groups advocate autonomy, although generally they are referring to regional autonomy within existing nation-states, rather than to break-away nations, or a return to a presumed pre-conquest sovereignty. With very rare exceptions, indigenous groups are instead working to redefine their relation to the nation-states in which they live.

Thus, the Indian Question is irrevocably linked to the national question in two separate but related ways. First, citizenship is a condition of belonging ultimately defined and enforced by the nation-state (Schild 1998: 98). Urban and Sherzer (1991) emphasized in their seminal collection that the state is a decisive factor in the construction of indigenous identities. What indigenous citizenship might mean, and what rights and obligations they should have, will depend upon the way the state constructs ethnicity. From this perspective, there are a variety of possible alternatives. At one extreme, there would be what we could call the "ethnic state," where ethnicity appears as a primordial element around which the state is organized (Lijphart 1977, Horowitz 2001). In such a model, state institutions would reflect power-sharing between ethnic groups. At the other extreme, there is a universalist/egalitarian citizenship model, like those of the advanced capitalist countries, where the state is supposedly "blind to ethnicity" in its organization, while assuring free expression of cultural diversity in practice and protection for minorities. Thus, the particularities of national schemes of citizenship will determine the parameters under which the Indian Question is approached.

Second, the particular way in which the Indian Question will be debated and resolved depends upon specific cultural struggles over the meanings of the legacy of colonialism, the history of ethnic relations in the country, and the place native people play in the national imagination (Andolina 2003; Alvarez, Dagnino, and Escobar 1998). Are they seen as a small and unthreatening group, reminiscent of the glories of the past? A terrifying class of subalterns who might subvert the racial domination that underlies traditional power relations? Backward throwbacks who must be assimilated into the national economy? Or culture-bearers for the rest of the society? Perhaps as a block of organized and vigilant voters? How Indians fit into the image of the nation greatly affects both the way the citizenship debate is raised, and the opposition to its resolution. Hale's work on *ladino* (mestizo) fears about growing Maya pride and power in Guatemala shows how complex these issues are (Hale 2002, see also K. Warren 1998b), an issue that will be discussed in greater depth later.

Proposals of special rights for indigenous peoples challenge two notions that are linked in the Western traditions of the modern nation-state: cultural homogeneity and universal rights. There is no intrinsic contradiction between universal rights and cultural diversity under the universalist/egalitarian citizenship model. Yet the notion of special rights makes many people uncomfortable, because it appears to be a modification of the notion of equal rights for all. For instance, many ask, why should a small group of Indians get control over vast extensions of rich Amazonian land when so many other poor people are landless? Are the non-Indian poor not just as deserving as their Indian neighbors? Proponents of multiculturalism have argued that under limited conditions, such special rights do not violate liberal principles, because they are necessary for marginalized people to exercise their individual rights (Kymlicka 1995, Kymlicka and Norman 1996, I. M. Young 1996). Other analysts criticize state-led multicultural policies, especially those in the United States, as a form of diversity management, suggesting they are ultimately de-politicizing and obscuring racism by promoting limited participation opportunities (see Bennett 1998, Goldberg 1994, Okin 1999). Others, like Parehk (1999) and Povinelli (2002, 1998), suggest that such examples demonstrate the inherent flaws in liberal assumptions in the first place. However these debates are ultimately resolved in each country, they bring to the surface radically different, sometimes disturbing, ways of thinking about the nation and citizenship.

Finally, as scholars of citizenship since Marshall (1949) have acknowledged, there are several sorts of rights which must be gained for the promise of democratization to be fulfilled. Indian peoples may struggle for social and economic rights to help them overcome the poverty in which most of them live. They may struggle for cultural rights to be able to live according to their customs, speak their languages, and share their values with their children. They may want civil rights – personal freedoms like the right to own property and to equal justice before the law. They may want to be protected from violence, and especially from state violence (Caldeira 2000, Caldeira and Holston 1999). They may want political rights in the form of demands for territorial autonomy or full and equal participation in the political process by which the state governs them.

What is at stake in the Indian Question is ultimately the right of indigenous people to have a say in the political, economic, and cultural processes that determine their lives as citizens. It is the right to be a protagonist as well as a subject, the "right to have rights," to be able to define the system to which they belong (Dagnino 1998: 50). It is, ultimately, about how power is controlled and shared in a democracy. As such, these are extremely complex political and cultural struggles that can only be examined on a case-by-case basis.

Nancy Grey Postero and Leon Zamosc

Contexts of Politicization

Earlier studies of indigenous movements have confused indigenous movements' agendas and the movements themselves. In asking how the Indian Question becomes a political question, we want to make clear the distinction between indigenous rights as an *issue* to be fought for, and indigenous movements as *actors* in the struggle. Indigenous actors are always present in some way when the issue arises on the political scene, but they may not be the main protagonists or have control over the way it is framed or decided. We must ask specifically in each case, what is the role of the indigenous movements in raising the Indian Question as a political issue? In some cases, indigenous movements play central roles in establishing the issue on the political agenda, and are engaged in emancipatory projects to empower their own people. In other cases, their role is subordinated to that of other sectors, or subsumed within a hegemonic project which helps the dominant sector accomplish what Gramsci called *aggiornamento* – "updating" its political system to appear modern and liberal, while gaining political support for its policies (Gramsci 1971).

The possibility of retaining control over how the issues are framed depends to a great extent upon the context in which the question arises. Our analysis shows that, empirically, the Indian Question has arisen in three main ways: through direct actions of indigenous movements; as part of the negotiations in the aftermath of armed conflict; and as a factor in the electoral process. Of course, these are not hermetically distinctive contexts. In practice, most indigenous movements have operated in situations which combine elements of each of the situations outlined below.

First, indigenous groups may bring the Indian Question to national attention through their own efforts. In this case, indigenous groups organize their base membership, craft their agendas, and engage in political actions to influence the government and the society. Through the strength of their mobilization, they bring the issues directly to the political stage. As Leon Zamosc' chapter in this volume shows, Ecuador's CONAIE, *Confederación de Nacionalidades Indígenas del Ecuador,* arguably the most successful organization on the continent, stands out for its ability to organize mass demonstrations and roadblocks, which have given them sufficient political power to negotiate directly with the state. CONAIE's skilled leaders have managed a discourse of rights and resistance which, while putting forward an alternative vision of resource management and economic policies, has not been perceived as a threat to democracy. Critical to this has been their ability to bridge differences between Andean and Amazonian groups. They have also shown a notable ability to manage the kinds of representations indigenous groups and issues receive in the national press (Bose, 2004).

8

A number of factors may influence the ability of indigenous movements to control the way the question is framed. Do they have the organizational apparatus necessary to link local organizations to regional and national struggles? Do they have a competent leadership which is able to recognize and take advantage of political opportunities? Can they articulate demands and represent their members in interactions with the state and other sectors? What capacity do they show in mobilizing their membership to action? This is particularly important for those movements that assume a style that might be called *contestatario*, or, confrontational – those groups which use protest and other forms of direct action to achieve their goals. In Ecuador, the disposition to mobilize and the capacity for political action have been instrumental in CONAIE's successes in gaining constitutional recognition for a wide range of indigenous rights. In Bolivia, the initial combativeness of the lowland peoples in the early 1990s faded as the national leadership allied with political parties. In 2003, however, highland Indians were able to mobilize large numbers, and along with other sectors, stage a six-week uprising that ultimately toppled Bolivia's president. In Chile, the Mapuche people have responded to threats to their lands with vehement public demonstrations, and sometimes violent reactions to state policies. In these countries, then, we see a marked contrast with Guatemala, where different sectors of the pan-Maya movement have grown in stature over the last decades without developing an overtly confrontational profile.

This brings us to the second principal context in which the Indian Question has become relevant at the national level: the negotiations around the resolution of armed conflict. Throughout the last few decades, Latin American countries have suffered, as deeply rooted political, economic, and social conflicts resulted in civil wars. As countries emerged from those wars, the state negotiated with the combatants to reach a social equilibrium and peaceful co-existence. These negotiations provided important opportunities for indigenous groups to enter the debates about how the state should be reorganized, and to insert their demands for indigenous rights into the accords. This has occurred in three countries: Guatemala, Mexico, and Colombia. In the 1996 negotiations to bring Guatemala's bitter civil war to an end, Maya leaders played an active role as advisers at the talks. While the guerrilla combatants did not raise indigenous rights as an actual demand, indigenous groups including Rigoberta Menchú, the Maya Nobel Peace Laureate, were able to bring the Indian Question into the international limelight and obtain important concessions as part of the final peace accord. There are differences in the roles indigenous movements can play, however, and Edward Fischer argues that, despite the fact that the public decried the terrible suffering of Indian populations under the military regime, the Guatemalan indigenous movement was not sufficiently organized to consolidate these gains in the political sphere after the peace accords. Their inability to mobilize political pressure from the movement's base communities, or from the rest of Guatemalan society, resulted in the defeat of the proposed indigenous law during the national public referendum of 1999.

Mexico's peace negotiations followed a similar path. The Zapatista army's 1994 uprising brought the plight of Chiapas' native peoples to the international media and "cyber attention" – that is, promotion via the world wide web (Collier and Quaratielo 1994). Initially, the Zapatistas did not identify themselves as an indigenous army, but rather a revolutionary army of the poor with a strong indigenous base. Over time, as the indigenous base became more important in the army's political wing, indigenous issues took on a greater centrality. When, under great pressure from international human rights organizations, the Mexican government negotiated to end the Zapatista war in San Andrés, the issue of indigenous rights was one of the first issues both sides agreed upon. The negotiations were attended by many civil society organizations and were overseen by Bishop Ruiz, a long-time advocate for the Indians of Chiapas. Again, however, political weaknesses impeded the institutionalization of the advances. In the reform approved in 2001 by the Mexican congress, indigenous rights were diluted, diverted, or directly rejected. Although the Zapatistas organized a national march to demand the approval of the San Andrés accords, the pressure was insufficient. As a result, the Indian Question in Mexico continues unresolved.

Colombia's far-reaching indigenous rights legislation also came about within the framework of efforts to end armed conflict. In 1990, the state and various guerilla organizations signed a peace accord, ending one phase of the lengthy civil war. As part of the negotiations, the parties agreed to a constituent assembly to reorganize the state and pacify a divided society. Well-organized indigenous organizations took advantage of this opportunity, and at the assembly in 1991, they negotiated important indigenous rights, including the guarantee of indigenous representation in Colombia's congress. More legislation followed, giving native peoples the right to representation in local elections. Teodor Rathgeber reveals, however, that these legal rights have not been implemented on the ground, despite the efforts of Colombia's active indigenous organization, CRIC (Indigenous Regional Council of Cauca). Indigenous groups in Colombia continue to struggle to maintain their lands, partly because of the continuing conflicts with guerrillas and narco-mafia, but partly because of government-sponsored resource extraction schemes on indigenous lands.

The Indian Question has also been politicized through the framework of the electoral process. As democratization sweeps the continent, indigenous issues have become more and more important in electoral campaigns. Even in the case of elections, however, it is essential to carefully analyze who raises the issue and how. María Elena García and José Antonio Lucero describe how Alejandro Toledo, a neoliberal economist educated in the United States, made the Indian Question an important element of his electoral campaign in Peru's 2001 elections. Claiming an indigenous identity, he showed off his *campesino* father and Quechua-speaking wife, and held rallies wearing ponchos and draped with corn, symbols of his Inca heritage. He held his inauguration at Machu Picchu, symbolizing the return of the fallen Inca. While Peruvian indigenous groups had previously raised the issue of indigenous rights, here a politician directly and indirectly invoked the Indian issue for electoral ends. In Ecuador, the national indigenous organization, CONAIE, has entered the electoral process, forming a new political party, Pachakutik, and gaining important seats in congress, demonstrating how the Indian Question has been innovatively used by indigenous groups themselves to push for indigenous rights. Building on its earlier successes achieved by leading mobilizations both against neoliberal policies and building class alliances, CONAIE has begun a new strategy: direct political challenge. Bolivian indigenous groups have recently begun to follow this model as well as alliances with traditional political parties failed. In 2001, a new party, MAS (*Movimiento al Socialismo*), made up of peasants, indigenous groups, and other popular sectors, formed, gaining 20 percent of parliamentary seats in the 2002 election. A second indigenous party, MIP (*Movimiento Indígena Pachakutik*) won an additional 7 percent (Van Cott 2003). In the 2003 uprising, Indian leaders capitalized on this electoral success to publicly contest neoliberal programs, and push for a constituent assembly to reform the structure of the state.

Clearly, these contexts do not exist in a vacuum; rather, they often operate in tandem. Peru's election came at the end of a bloody civil war in which ethnicity played a major part. The Truth Commission reported that almost 90 percent of the 69,000 victims of the war between the military and the leftist guerrilla group *Sendero Luminoso* were Quechua-speaking Indians. While the ethnic question was not a part of the public political agenda, it was a fundamental part of the trauma Peru would have to resolve in order to move forward. Ecuador's elections would have had very different results had the CONAIE not already been a major protagonist in its own right. As the Indian Question is raised, and indigenous movements gain a foothold in national politics, various responses are also generated. The Guatemalan peace accords may not have resulted in legislative or constitutional changes, but it did set the stage for the dynamization of the pan-Maya movement, which began along mainly cultural and linguistic grounds. As that movement has grown, it has begun to turn from cultural to more overtly political agendas and strategies, as Mayans now control some local governments and some important national ministries.

Attention also need to be drawn to another critical factor that differentiates indigenous organizations and may determine their ability or desire to raise the Indian Question: the interplay between ethnicity and class. Some groups are called "indigenous" because their participants are

Indians, but their objectives may be economic, or class-based, without making any specific ethnic demands or defining themselves as ethnic. Such is the case of many rural peasant or workers' organizations, whose members might be defined as indigenous but whose agendas are strictly limited by class as defined by the old left. The CSUTCB of Bolivia was, for many years, one such organization, advocating on behalf of peasants and rural workers, almost all of whom would be considered Indians. On the other hand, there are also organizations which have explicit indigenous agendas. This is the model for most of the national indigenous federations, such as Ecuador's CONAIE, Bolivia's CIDOB, and the regional and national indigenous organizations in Colombia.

A key issue, then, is the continuing ambiguity between ethnicity and class, which in many cases, appear as two faces of the same coin. The perception that "we are poor because we are Indians" often goes together with a construction of an ethnic identity opposed to modern middle-class *mestizo* identity, so that the counterpart to the former statement becomes "we are Indians because we are poor." In those regions where native people are the majority, some describe them as an "ethnoclass," where social class and ethnicity coincide: Indians are peasants, peasants are Indians (Van den Berghe and Primove 1977, Gurr 1993). This illustrates that what appears as ambiguity to outside observers may not be experienced as such by indigenous peasants. For them, being indigenous and being peasants may simply be two aspects of a lived identity. In cases such as Mexico, Peru, and Bolivia, a further blurring of these categories resulted from the widespread institution of the government- sponsored peasant unions, the corporate model which tied indigenous peasants to the state.

A further complication involves *mestizaje,* that is, the emergence of non-Indian social sectors which results from miscegenation and cultural syncretism. Much excellent work has revealed how notions of race and *mestizaje* have been used in state-building projects to mold national identity (Knight 1990, Smith 1990). Recently, however, as part of "return of the native" trope, scholars have played down the existence of *mestizos* to highlight instead the survival of indigenous peoples, the so-called *país profundo* underlying contemporary societies (Bonfil Batalla 1996, Basadre 1978). While the focus here is on Indian actors, we should recognize that *mestizaje* is still a critical source of the ambiguities surrounding indigenous identity. *Mestizaje* is not a myth, but a social reality. Its polysemous meanings and ideological uses should be seen as subjects of future investigation, rather than obstacles to understanding.

To understand the ethnic positioning of indigenous groups, one must examine the history of ethnic incorporation in the region. This is particularly salient in the highland/lowland distinction which Urban and Sherzer (1991) noted at the beginning of the indigenous studies boom. In all the countries which have distinct ecosystems in the highlands and lowlands, there has been a marked difference between the kinds of indigenous activism that has emerged and the goals of the organizations. Lowland populations, most of whom were nomadic hunter gatherers or small-scale subsistence farmers, are much smaller, tend to be more sparsely concentrated across the lands, and have usually been relatively isolated until recently. In contrast, highland populations are much larger, more concentrated, much more urban, and tend to have much greater integration in national (and international) markets. Lowland groups were less exposed to formal education and have less political experience, as their political organizations have arisen more recently. These are not just the result of geographical location, but reflect the history of indigenous incorporation. European colonizers arrived much earlier in the highland areas, and began the centuries-long process of assimilation and *mestizaje*. The lowlands, on the other hand, were "regions of refuge," where native people managed to maintain their ways of life much longer, fleeing deeper and deeper into the forest as the frontiers were pushed back. As a result, lowland peoples often have a strong notion of the importance of territory. These characterizations do not apply to all such groups, as many Amazonian tribes were forced into Jesuit and Franciscan *reducciones* in the seventeenth century or coerced into servitude in the region's infamous rubber booms (Herrera Sarmiento 2003, Taussig 1987). One notable result is that lowland groups tend to have a more homogenous ethnic identification, since they were not the subjects of such long-term and relentless assimilation policies. In highland areas of Peru, Ecuador, and Bolivia, as well as in the Mesoamerican countries of Mexico and Guatemala, long histories of interaction with colonial and then national states resulted in the erasure of many original identities. Such ethno-transformations blurred differences between original indigenous groups and favored what has been aptly described as a "generic Indian ascription identity" (Muratorio 1991, Zamosc 1994). At the same time, Indians began to identify more with their communities, so that "being Indian" came to mean being a member of a particular local community. Over time, *mestizaje* and modernization further diluted the meanings of indigenousness.

Indigenous subjectivity is formed through a complex process of interpellation into socially constructed ethnic and class categories, and (sometimes) fluid movement between those categories. De la Cadena (2000) has shown how *mestizos* in Cuzco, Peru maintain their indigenous customs while rejecting the inferior status associated with being "indigenous." Herrera Sarmiento (2003) and Jonathan Warren (2001) describe the interesting political and social processes by which people who see themselves as *mestizos* or *caboclos* (of "mixed blood") begin to identify themselves as indigenous. How fluidly these borders can be crossed depends on the particular context of each country and the intellectual histories that underlie notions of race and ethnicity. These categories are extraordinarily dynamic, responding to political, economic, and cultural changes.

Two major engines of change exist in the ambiguous relationship between ethnicity and class in indigenous movements: ethnification of peasant organizations, and class differentiation within indigenous groups. One of the most significant processes occurring across Latin America is the indianization of many peasant organizations. As Gunther Dietz's chapter on Mexico shows in great detail, many of the movements that now appear as indigenous began as peasant organizations, often sponsored by the government. Through time, as a result of changing discourses and new political openings for indigenous groups, these peasant groups have begun to identify as indigenous and to struggle for more clearly defined ethnic goals. This is a gradual process, and its specific shape depends upon the context. Dietz explains how the retrenchment of the state under Mexico's neoliberal administrations made this more and more possible. Similar processes have occurred in both Ecuador and Colombia. In Bolivia, ethnification is taking a somewhat different and, again, more ambiguous turn. The CSUTCB, the national peasant federation, and long one of the most important forces of contestation against the elite-lead state in Bolivia, continues to characterize itself and its agenda as *campesino*, or peasant. It has recently begun to incorporate some indigenous demands into its discourse, and one of the main leaders is Felipe Quispe, known as Mallku, who is pushing a radical form of Aymara nationalism. Similarly, Guatemala's national peasant organization, the CUC, whose members are mostly Indians, had steadfastly remained on the peasant side of the divide, though this is beginning to change as the CUC acknowledges its indigenous membership.

One result of these transitions is a new form of political-ethnic hybridity. María Elena García and José Antonio Lucero describe several forms of indigenous activism that do not fit into previous categories. In one example, they describe highland Indian families organizing to take control over their children's schools, in part because they object to bilingual education, which they fear will further marginalize their children. In another example, a highland community takes over a sulfur mine to create a community business. Most of its members are indigenous, but the project does not characterize itself as such. These examples show that the new indigenous organizing is not necessarily going to be based upon identity politics, but, rather, on a fluid mixture of livelihood and culture. Mixing class and ethnic demands has been a central strategy of Mexico's Zapatista army. It combines indigenous claims with a sort of national class solidarity, claiming to represent all the poor of Mexico who deserve a representative state which does not sell it out to international commerce.

The other process of class ethnicity transition is the class differentiation that is occurring as Indians move into urban areas. Here we refer not only to indigenous elites in the artesanal and entrepreneurial fields, but also to the new, younger generations attending schools and universities, and working for government agencies and NGOs. The urban areas have been important cauldrons of growth for indigenous intellectuals who have infused the movements with ideas, resources, and allies (Assies *et al.* 2000, Zamosc 1994). Notable examples are the Kataristas in Bolivia (Albó 1994), the urban Mapuche activists in Chile (A. Herrera 2003), the Otavaleños of Ecuador (Korovkin 1998), and the pan-Maya movement in Guatemala, which arose in great part from the activities of Maya linguists and cultural intellectuals in the cities (Fischer 2001, Warren 1998a). These intellectuals face the classic problem of incongruous status: educated, receiving salaries, and politically aware, they still face social discrimination. This provides them with strong motives to organize, yet subjects them to the continuing challenge of staying in contact with the residents of the base communities they represent, most of whom remain poor and uneducated.

What is at Stake in Indian Struggles?

If indigenous groups vary so widely across countries in makeup and in mobilizing power, so do the objectives of their organizations. There are, of course, many common issues. A key demand from all groups is the recognition of cultural difference and its corollary, the need for protection of indigenous culture. Indigenous groups have pushed the definitions of both democracy and multiculturalism as they claim citizenship rights in multi-ethnic societies. Exactly how that is to be accomplished, however, is a point of debate. For most indigenous groups, the implementation of bilingual intercultural education policies is a keystone of the new citizenship (Luykx 1999, Garcia forthcoming). There is less clarity, however, when it comes to issues of political autonomy, territorial control, and political participation. While the latter are often presented in the literature as part of a standard menu of indigenous goals, the cases in this volume demonstrate that there is no such thing as a universal set of indigenous demands. Which factors determine whether or not these goals appear on the agenda of indigenous movements?

Given the diversity of context and strategy, it is not possible to give a definitive answer. However, one important clue which has not been considered in the existing studies may be found in the differing demographics of each country. In Guatemala and Bolivia, Indians are the majority of the population. In Peru and Ecuador, they are a substantial minority. In Mexico, Colombia, Brazil, and Chile, however, indigenous groups must be defined as minorities. Does this determine or influence the objectives of indigenous struggles? What can an indigenous population which is a minority sector within a nation-state expect to win when the Indian Question is raised? How does that differ from indigenous populations who are in the majority and could win political power through electoral strategies?

In order to answer these questions, we must first ask where it is that indigenous groups are pushing for political autonomy as the main strategic goal. The notion of autonomy refers to various ideas. It may, for example, mean decision-making at the local level. One result of the neoliberal political decentralization programs that have been implemented across Latin America is increased participation by citizens in local development decisions. In Bolivia and Colombia, some native people have been able to take advantage of these reforms to make local politics more representative of their cultural and economic needs. Autonomy can also mean political autonomy, which guarantees self government for indigenous peoples. This is the type of autonomy referred to here. Such a political-juridical regime would recognize their rights to choose their own authorities, exercise legal responsibilities, legislate their internal life, and administer their own affairs (Díaz Polanco 1997: 95).

While most indigenous groups want some sort of local control, it is those that are clearly in the minority who appear to be fighting for territorial and political autonomy. Autonomy appears as a central goal for most lowland groups, who are small in numbers, such as the native people of the Amazonian basin and the Central American coasts. This is also true for the Mapuche in Chile and the native groups in Mexico and Colombia – clearly numerical minorities in large nation-states. In these cases, what the indigenous peoples want and need is protection and special rights to be able to live in their territories according to their customs. Thus we see the demand for political autonomy paired with demands for access to land and territorial titling. This minority status does not mean that indigenous peoples are invisible or unimportant to the political affairs of the country, however. On the contrary, as Jonathan Warren argues, indigenous peoples who are in the minority can still have a significant effect on the wider population by raising critical questions about racial discrimination in general.

It is notable, however, that neither autonomy nor territory have emerged as the main demands in highland Bolivia or Guatemala, where Indians are estimated to comprise at least half the population. In these cases, Indian movements are articulated more in terms of equality, participation, and multiculturalism. They reflect the aspiration to take part in the political processes of the nation-state as equal citizens. It would seem that Indians have begun to visualize societies in which they can be equal participants, and their demands are beginning to reflect this possibility.

A second pattern in indigenous politics is the growing importance of the indigenous vote. Indigenous groups have begun to form political parties and run for political office. In Ecuador, as Zamosc describes, CONAIE's political party, Pachakutik, opened the way for Indian candidates to win positions of power at local and regional levels, as well as substantial representation in Congress. In 2002, its participation in a winning alliance gave Pachakutik several ministerial positions in the national government. Although this alliance did not last long, it is a sign that indigenous voters, which only make up 15 percent of the electorate, can have a significant effect on Ecuadorian politics (Zamosc 1995). In Bolivia, where the population is almost 60 percent indigenous, the success of Evo Morales and his MAS party in the June 2002 election reflects a population that is beginning to vote according to its ethnic makeup (Van Cott 2003). Certainly, the strong indigenous response to appeals by Toledo and Fujimori in Peru's election marks the emergence of the indigenous vote there. In Guatemala, Maya leaders have begun to seek electoral power, starting at the municipal level, in towns where they are the majority group (Fisher 2001). They also hold several important ministerial positions, as Guatemalan political parties begin to recognize the importance of including Maya personalities in their administrations.

What are we to make of these two current trends? We can speculate that where indigenous people carry significant weight in the population, the Indian Question will be raised not in terms of protection for minority rights, but in terms of political power and participation; that is, what is at stake may be the definition of the nation-state as a truly democratic institution. This, of course, can be construed as a threat by the non-indigenous minorities which have historically controlled the state. It also makes it clear why some governments have suddenly taken an interest in multicultural reforms. Nancy Postero's chapter on Bolivia in this volume demonstrates how states have seen the need to address this emerging sector's demands for participation. State-led multiculturalism is one way to temporarily and partially mollify such demands.

Now, however, large indigenous populations are beginning to avail themselves of the basic democratic instrument: the ballot box. If their goals cannot be accomplished through alliances with dominant classes, negotiations with the state, or constituent assemblies, the electoral path may offer a more direct route to power. This strategy is relevant for Guatemala and Bolivia, and perhaps to some extent for Peru where it is estimated that almost one third of the population is Indian. Of course, success on this path is not automatically guaranteed by sheer demographics. The Ecuadorian case shows that to win elections, indigenous movements must develop effective political organizations that are capable of "bringing out the vote" and firmly establishing the Indian Question as part of the national political agenda. In Bolivia, the MAS has appeared as a new populist party that appeals explicitly to ethnic identity. After the 2003 uprising, in which it was able to convoke massive public response, its electoral fortunes are likely to improve. Its success will depend upon the ability of Indian activists to strengthen their position within the current transitional government and offer a platform acceptable to a large cross-section of the population. While the leaders and participants were largely highland Indians, they raised their demands on behalf of the Bolivian people. Here we begin to see a blending of indigenous ideals with a new populist notion of the nation. If the popular organizations can articulate this new idiom of Bolivian nationalism, they may be able to win a sufficient majority and gain control of the state.

In Latin America, the Indian Question takes a bifurcated form. In the case of small minorities, it is a matter of survival, expressed primarily through demands for territory, autonomy, and special rights which would allow them to maintain their ways of life as indigenous peoples. The resolution of the Indian Question for these minorities does not require a radical transformation of the state institutions, but a series of reforms that recognize the special status of indigenous peoples and define the terms of their relationship with the national state. Where native populations have substantial demographic weight, however, the Indian Question is a matter of equality and participation, which invariably means a reconsideration of the concept of the nation and the model of the state. One such model would be what we have described as the "ethnic state," in which ethnic difference is the basis of power sharing. This would require fundamental changes to political institutions, along the lines of what is known in the ethnic conflict literature as "consociational systems" (Lijphart 1977, Horowitz 2001). While these kinds of systems exist in other parts of the world, they have no precedent in Latin America. Few indigenous voices have propagated consociationism as a realistic option. Bolivian leader Felipe Quispe has sometimes referred to the re-establishment of *Kollasuyo*, the Aymara nation that existed before the Spanish conquest (Gómez and Giordano 2002). Maya intellectual Jesús Gómez has also proposed a power-sharing solution for Guatemala (Gómez 2001). But the evidence to date shows that even in these two nations, Indian goals are articulated predominantly in terms of the universalist / egalitarian model, where all citizens have the same rights.

This calls attention to the disjunction between the existence of formal citizenship rights and the possibility of actually exercising these rights (Holston and Caldeira 1999). While Latin American states may have been modeled on the universalist/egalitarian blueprint, most observers of the region's realities would agree that systematic discrimination denies the social, political, and cultural rights of indigenous populations. Centuries of expropriation and economic exploitation have left a legacy of poverty. As a result, Indians continue to be among the poorest and most marginalized members of their societies, a pattern that is reinforced by the fact that states rarely invest sufficiently in social services and education in the regions where they live. In a similar vein, indigenous people have not been able to effectively exercise their political rights. Because of their marginality, their votes have not, until recently, translated into political power. Indians have rarely held political office, their customary systems of government were ignored or co-opted by the state, and their participation has invariably been channeled through powerful political parties, which never represented their aspirations. Finally, in a truly egalitarian situation, one would expect that the culture of significant indigenous sectors would be a recognized part of national culture. However, what we see instead is that education, government, and public life are dominated by the language and values of the hegemonic Western culture.

While Latin America has seen advances in democratization, institutional reforms are still necessary for achieving effective political, social, and cultural equality. Several countries have recently acknowledged in their constitutions the multicultural nature of their societies. To be more than empty rhetoric, however, such declarations must be accompanied by concrete reforms. Intercultural education must be funded, teachers trained in Indian languages, and new curricula disseminated. Similar reforms may be necessary in terms of the ways in which political representation is structured. In Bolivia, for instance, one result of the 2003 uprising was the promise to hold a constituent assembly to consider reforms of the electoral system. Affirmative action is another area of possible institutional reform: in the Guatemalan peace accord process, for instance, the government agreed to sponsor temporary programs to provide special opportunities for the disadvantaged Maya population.

Institutional changes are necessary to create functioning universal and egalitarian models of the state. Yet legal modifications do not herald the end of racism and discrimination. The struggle for social and cultural equality is waged at the level of practices, in daily interactions and in civil society. Politics and culture are inextricably linked sites of contestation over power. Adequate laws may allow Indians to run for office, but capturing a significant share of power will require a radical change in the imagination of the citizenry as a whole. In other words, the national community must come to see indigenous people and their representatives as natural bearers of the national interest. Such changes must happen on discursive and symbolic levels as well as institutional ones. This will require work at the complex and historically sedimented boundary between "the indigenous Other" and the nation, a boundary reinforced by language, custom, and power-laden practices. While this boundary may never be dissolved, for the universalist/egalitarian model to function, indigenousness must be understood and felt as a natural and rightful aspect of the national character.

The crucial issue, then, is how the goal of full, effective citizenships in the universalist/egalitarian state can be accomplished. The cases of Guatemala and Bolivia demonstrate two very different strategies toward this end: cultural struggle, and popular alliances.

In Guatemala, the pan-Maya movement has focused on culture and language as the starting point for building political power. By demanding state recognition of Maya languages, writing, and religion, Maya leaders and intellectuals have embarked on what they see as *reivindicación*, a claim or vindication of their rights as native Guatemalans. Rather than starting by pushing for political or civil rights, this movement has emphasized cultural rights, and particularly, intercultural education that valorizes Maya history and customs as it teaches native languages. As their identity is becoming accepted and even celebrated (Warren 1998a), the pan-Maya movement is beginning to transform its cultural capital into political power. The increasing presence of Maya activists in local electoral contests and national government positions is a clear expression of this development. How far this cultural project can go, and what it can accomplish remains to be seen. So far, the pan-Maya movement has impacted mostly urban intellectuals, without making significant changes in the lives of the predominantly rural Maya majority.

A different strategy is being pursued by Indian leaders in Bolivia, where, they have played critical roles in popular movements opposing the traditional elite politicians. In the process, they have made alliances with other sectors also negatively impacted by the governments' neoliberal economic policies. In Bolivia the 1990s were marked by the rise of indigenous groups that organized around ethnic identity. Now, however, leaders of those organizations appear to be strategically blurring the lines between ethnicity and class as part of an attempt to articulate a national popular project. Initially, Evo Morales argued that the root cause of Bolivia's current political crisis lay in the centuries-old racial domination of the Indian majority. But now, while continuing to acknowledge the crippling racism of the country, he calls for the creation of *el poder del pueblo*, the power of the people, which can only be built by setting aside the interests of particular groups. For Morales, what is important is the ability to mobilize "the power of all the people, of all the nation" in the struggle against neoliberalism and imperialism (Morales 2003).

The Guatemalan and Bolivian struggles are, then, both political, and profoundly cultural. They represent attempts to redefine the meaning of ethnicity and establish the legitimacy of Indians as the moral backbone of the nation. If "hegemony is hard work" (Comaroff 1991), so is struggling against it, even where indigenous people make up the majority.

Neoliberalism

Finally, one particularly important factor in the historical context in which the Indian Question is being raised and debated needs to be outlined: neoliberalism. Across Latin America, as democratization and political liberalization provided new opportunities for civil society actors to participate in and contest state processes, neoliberal policies have radically altered the economic and social contexts in which those actors are struggling. Neoliberalism, like other trends across the continent, takes varied shapes from country to country, but there are three main ways in which neoliberal reforms have affected indigenous populations: (1) political restructuring, which has changed relations between Indian groups and the state; (2) a new emphasis on resource extraction schemes, which has threatened their lands; and (3) economic restructuring, which has caused drastic economic crises. Indians have responded to these threats in a number of ways. In some cases, they have cooperated with neoliberal governments, taking advantage of the political openings provided by new programs. In other cases, they have simply endured the effects along with everyone else. There have been some situations, however, in which Indian groups have mounted overt opposition to neoliberal reforms. Such struggles against neoliberalism provide indigenous groups with important opportunities to ally with other sectors. Especially where indigenous people are in the majority, these articulations are critical to the ability to gain political power, and then utilize that power to politicize their demands.

One of the most important changes effected by neoliberal governments has been a radical restructuring of the state. A central tenet of neoliberal philosophy is the need to keep the state apparatus as efficient and lean as possible. Consequently, Latin American states, seen as bloated, overly bureaucratic, and often corrupt, were targeted for surgery. State-owned companies were sold in privatization programs, and centralized state bureaucracies were split up in decentralization programs. These reforms also changed the ways rural indigenous groups were related to and integrated into the state. Previous developmental states had institutionalized these relationships through corporatist models, such as peasant unions, which channeled credit, property titles, and recognition from the state (Yashar 1998). In almost all countries in Latin America, agrarian reforms (stretching from the Mexican ejido movement in the 1930s to the populist reforms in Peru in the late 1960s) defined Indians as peasants and established them in a patronage system as essential parts of nation-building and modernization projects. Neoliberal reforms abandoned this corporatist model, and have instead instituted models based on individual citizenship, autonomy, and responsibility (Yashar 1999: 85). Often this new policy also means the end of important material assistance to rural indigenous organizations. In Mexico, as Gunther Dietz's chapter shows, the state has not only withdrawn credit and assistance to farmers, but, by reforming Article 27 of the Constitution, has undermined the basis for collective property titles. Many Indians felt these changes were fundamental betrayals of the basic contract they had with the state.

However, such corporatism was not uniformly present in all areas of Latin America. In Bolivia and Mexico, strong political parties (the MNR and the PRI, respectively) used these same models to tie peasant workers to the parties. In Peru and Ecuador, in contrast, these reforms were carried out by the military, which implemented them weakly and unevenly. Even in countries where the model was strongly implemented, its effect depended upon other factors. Rivera Cusicanqui (1987) points out that the *campesino* unions were accepted more easily in the Quechua areas of Cochabamba, Bolivia, than the Aymara areas of northern La Paz. There, the model did not fit with native cultural or land-holding models, and was seen as an imposition of a colonialist state. Such particularities are crucial when evaluating the effects of the neoliberal retrenchment of the corporatist model.

Yashar has argued that the corporatist models unintentionally created local political and economic autonomy, allowing indigenous groups to practice "an indigenous identity derived from and structured by local practices" (1998: 33). These refuges of indigenous jurisdiction, she claims, where collective property rights and cultural practices were maintained, are now under threat from individualist models and the uncertainty resulting from indebtedness, declining incomes, and loss of land In some places, indigenous groups have contested this change in their efforts to retain collective control over resources, property, and cultural expression.

For many groups, however, these changes have also offered new opportunities, and perhaps, new freedoms. At an institutional level, the retreat of the state from the peasant unions in Mexico resulted in unprecedented local and regional ethnic organizing, with new allies, such as the opposition PRD (*Partido de la Revolución Democrática*) party. As a result, they have emerged from the protection and control of the state, some of these groups have begun to develop a more indigenous identity as they have articulated with other cultural organizations. This is one example of the indianization of peasant organizations. Warren and Jackson (2002) suggest that the retreat of the state has also allowed some indigenous groups to negotiate directly with international companies and NGOs, doing away with the state as middleman (2002: 24). Fischer's 2001 study of Maya farmers in Guatemala highlands makes a similar argument: selling directly to transnational agri-businesses has allowed Maya farmers to maintain their small farms.

Political reforms like decentralization projects, while often flawed, may also offer indigenous groups increased authority and financial control at the local level. Nancy Postero shows how in Bolivia in the 1990s, indigenous organizations allied with the ruling MNR party, which imposed both liberal political reforms, granting indigenous peoples cultural and territorial rights, and neoliberal economic reforms. While they may not have agreed with the overall neoliberal philosophy, indigenous groups cooperated with the political parties controlling the government because they believed they could gain political power and access to resources through the reforms. Especially important was the Law of Popular Participation, which gave indigenous groups the right to participate in local development decisions and elections. Teodor Rathgeber demonstrates much the same in his chapter on Colombia, where decentralization has allowed indigenous groups to elect indigenous officials at the local level. The state benefited from this alliance, because the state-lead multicultural reforms served to palliate public opinion of economic reforms, and to give the state a modern, liberal, and egalitarian image. Both Rathgeber and Postero, however, show how such palliative images crumbled over time as indigenous groups found the political reforms insufficient to lead to economic equality or political power.

There has also been an increased emphasis by states on attracting and facilitating profitable resource extraction schemes. Across the Amazon, forest concessions overlay new indigenous territories and national parks. In Chile, neoliberal economic strategies were preceded by juridical reforms that make the mining on Mapuche lands part of national sovereignty rights (Herrera 2003). Rathgeber's chapter on Colombia and García and Lucero's chapter on Peru also show how mining and oil exploration continue to threaten indigenous lands and livelihoods throughout the region. These threats have been the rallying cry for indigenous organizing: to protect their lands and their livelihoods, indigenous groups across the continent have mounted campaigns of resistance. Chile's Mapuche Indians have mobilized strongly to save their lands from copper mining and hydroelectric dams; these demonstrations have met with violent resistance from the state (Herrera 2003). In Colombia, the U'wa people, determined not to give in to environmental destruction, threatened mass suicide. The U'wa's resistance was aided by national and international allies uniting to fight transnational resource extraction.

Indigenous responses to these threats to their lands and resources are not limited to resistance. Rathgeber describes the many creative alternatives that the CRIC, the Cauca Regional Indigenous Council, have proposed. He suggests that for them, development can only be understood as part of a whole social fabric. This requires social and economic processes distinct from pure market forces, which incorporate social and cultural considerations, and is the basis for the widespread concern about territorial control. The Mapuches of Chile are offering alternatives to stripping natural resources from their lands not only because it threatens their material subsistence, but also because it undermines their ability to maintain their cultural relations with each other and the wider community (Herrera 2003).

Indigenous resistance has been especially successful in responding to the economic and social crises caused by neoliberal restructuring. In Latin America, the 1980s are known as the "lost decade" because, instead of continuing to grow, most national economies slid back to the levels of the mid-1970s. Facing stagflation, many countries were on the verge of defaulting their debts. Against this backdrop, the IMF pressured governments to adopt aggressive reforms (Roper *et al.* 2003, Varas 1995, Bierstecker 1990, Mosley *et al.* 1991). The ensuing neoliberal economic policies sought to privatize state enterprises, fire or "displace" public workers (as in the case of Bolivia's tin miners, see Sambria 2000, Gill

2000), eliminate protections and tariffs, end subsidies for locally produced agricultural products, and drastically reduce social welfare spending (Assies *et al.* 2000: 9). The social costs have been devastating for the poor (Vilas 1996): despite the social emergency funds intended to alleviate the worst suffering (Benería and Mendoza 1995), structural adjustment programs have reduced real wages for urban workers (Portes and Hoffman 2003), and made access to the essential resources – food, cooking oil, medical services – increasingly difficult for all sectors. Indigenous farmers have found their products no longer sell at a profitable price. Thus, as Yashar (1998, 1999) has argued, while democratic reforms have expanded political rights, social rights – that is the right to social welfare – have been dramatically reduced. Though these economic crises hit indigenous sectors particularly hard, the costs were born by all of each nation's poor.

In Ecuador and Bolivia, indigenous organizations have used these conditions as a point of common action to ally with other popular sectors to fight against the neoliberal reforms. In Ecuador, as Leon Zamosc shows, CONAIE, the national indigenous organization, spearheaded national protests against the drastic social costs of economic restructuring, winning many indigenous demands in the process. The CONAIE's most important strategy has been to act on behalf of a multi-sector public, rather than strictly pushing for indigenous demands. By leading successful massive public demonstrations against price raises and dollarization, for instance, measures which harmed all the poor, CONAIE was able to gain sufficient political capital to later win its own indigenous demands. Bolivia's 2003 uprising was initiated by disparate indigenous groups who made claims on behalf of all poor Bolivians against the neoliberal government. The uprising took shape as a protest against the government's proposed plan to see Bolivia's newfound natural gas resources to the United States via a pipeline in Chile. Objections to the plan, viewed by the working class and the poor as yet another neoliberal scheme which would benefit the rich, brought together Indians, the middle class, peasants, and urban poor. Their combined power, and the violence with which the neoliberal state responded, forced Presiden Sánchez de Lozada to resign, giving Indian leaders leverage to make political demands to the new government. Besides a resolution of the gas issue, they include demands for clarity in coca eradication laws, rejection of the ALCA free trade agreement, rejection of harsh national security laws, and demands for better wages. Most important was their demand – which has been granted by the transitional government – for a constituent assembly, through which critical questions about the makeup of the state, and the role of ethnicity, will be rethought.

It is in countries where the indigenous population is most substantial that indigenous leaders have been able to form these strategic alliances with other sectors. Especially in response to the costs of neoliberalism, the ambiguities of class and ethnicity are heightened. By responding to questions of livelihood that they may share with other non-indigenous sectors, indigenous leaders begin to establish themselves as national leaders, responsible for the interests of all the country's citizens. These class alliances, in turn, make it possible for indigenous organizations to raise the Indian Question to a wider and more sympathetic audience, and present indigenous rights as a part of broadly defined set of social and political issues (such as social justice or human rights) that unite the popular sectors.

An Emerging Agenda

This chapter has identified patterns within the diversity in the struggle for indigenous rights in Latin America. We have highlighted several issues that, in our opinion, are central to understanding the demands and strategies of indigenous movements. We have also offered a conceptual framework – the Indian Question – for examining the trajectories of these movements. The effects of their struggles depend upon the particularities of each country, including the history of ethnic relations, the political context, and the modalities of indigenous organization. The relative weight of the Indian population is a major factor influencing the direction of the movements' demands.

The chapters in this volume have furnished invaluable information for discussions on the politicization of the Indian Question. Here, we briefly outline other issues raised by these case studies, for the benefit of future comparative analyses.

First, some of the studies in this volume have foregrounded the inherent ambiguities of the relation between class and ethnicity. Rapid socio-economic changes are further blurring these boundaries in Latin America (Garcia Canclini 2001). Several contributors underline the hybridizing effects of global restructurings, describing indigenous efforts to combine market strategies with "traditional" values. But can we take the notion of hybridity in its literal sense, or might it be more useful to explore its meaning as the interplay of multiple identities? Perhaps more importantly, how is this tension perceived in the lived experience of Indians themselves? In La Paz, for instance, Aymaras make up the bulk of vendors and business-people. How do they negotiate their different identities? Much more work is necessary to tease out the threads of this complicated relationship.

Second, these class–ethnicity ambiguities are often compounded when *mestizaje* and race enter the picture. As we know, *mestizaje* is not just a matter of miscegenation. As people migrate, go to school, and enter the urban labor force, they often assume *mestizo* identities. For some, this is a way to avoid discrimination; for others, it reflects a desire to be part of the "modern" nation (Bonfil Batalla 1996). De la Cadena (2000) has shown, however, that *mestizo* identities do not necessarily preclude indigenous customs or values. How people identify themselves is a complex interplay of social, cultural, political, and psychological factors. In this volume, we have concentrated mostly on the political dimension, noting its complex interconnections with the cultural dimension. We have not been able to focus sufficiently on the importance of discourses of race and ethnicity, and the ways indigenous struggles relate to them. Peter Wade (1997) argues that while most indigenous struggles are framed in terms of ethnicity, we should not ignore the fact that the racism experienced by native people has its roots in colonial discourses of race. Jonathan Warren rightly points out that, in some contexts, indigenous movements can make important contributions by raising issues of race. It is to be hoped that future researchers will be able to shed more light on the relation between race and ethnic politics. When and how are indigenous movements using and re-working notions of race? How are media representations aiding or hindering these debates? As pro-forma neoliberal versions of multiculturalism prove unsatisfying, what part might race and ethnicity play in bottom-up multiculturalist projects? And are these questions debated differently in countries where the Indians are in the majority? How this might be changing as indigenous groups enter the contest for political power is of particular interest. As the Indian Question becomes successfully politicized, will more people begin to identify themselves as indigenous?

We have argued that demographics is a critical factor in shaping the kinds of demands that indigenous groups are making. This volume provided a first, tentative approximation to an issue that requires much more elaboration. How the different demographic configurations interact with other factors necessitates further investigation. For example, our arguments about situations in which Indians are a sizeable part of the population may seem appropriate for Bolivia and Guatemala, but why do some of these arguments also ring true for Ecuador, where Indians are a minority? And why do they not seem to work in the Peruvian case, which does have a substantial Indian population?

Fourth, because our studies were intentionally focused on the national scene, we have not examined other, equally important, levels of analysis. Indigenous struggles and demands often vary substantially from region to region, just as they do from country to country. Several of our case studies mentioned these differences. More research is required, however, to examine how indigenous movements deal with these fractures. Why do some movements, like Ecuador's CONAIE, emerge as a powerful force uniting the various indigenous sectors? Macro-level studies may also neglect the many examples of successful indigenous organizing at the local level, or mistakenly assume that national successes, like constitutional and legal reforms, necessarily have positive effects for local indigenous communities and livelihoods. At the other extreme, it is also important to look beyond the level of the nation to the international frameworks that influence national laws and empower local activists (Brysk 2000). Some of our contributors have begun to combine these levels of analysis, focusing on local community processes as examples of national and international trends. Yet this continues to be one of the most difficult challenges for future research.

Many more issues raised at the Cochabamba meetings remain, including the role of Indian intellectuals, the place of gender in indigenous organizations, the contribution of the movements in proposing alternative models for economic and environmental management, and the possibilities and downsides of indigenous participation in government. While indigenous movements and intellectuals have not yet achieved all their goals, their activism over the last two decades has secured greater participation for their constituencies and inspired other social movements as well. Their protagonism is an encouraging sign of what seems to be a broader development in Latin America: the increasing trend toward a more active civil society.

Note

1   We recognize that there has been a long debate over terms identifying native peoples. Such terms may have profound political implications and, as many authors have pointed out, often reflect colonial and racist legacies (Dean and Levi 2003, Assies *et al.* 2000, Warren and Jackson 2002). There is little standardization of usage, however, and the terms vary from country to country. Moreover, indigenous people themselves use different terms, some preferring the term *indigenous* over *indio,* which may carry negative connotations; others reclaiming *indio* with pride. In some areas, *pueblos originarios,* or original peoples, is used. We did not require the authors in this collection to use particular terms, so there is considerable difference among them. In this chapter, we use the terms *indigenous, native,* and *Indian* interchangeably. The title of the chapter exemplifies this approach.

References

Albó, Xavier. 1991. El Retorno del Indio. *Revista Andina,* 9(2): 299–345.
——. 1994. And from Kataristas to MNRistas? The Surprising and Bold Alliance between Aymaras and Neoliberals in Bolivia. *Indigenous Peoples and Democracy in Latin America.* Donna Lee Van Cott, ed. New York: St. Martin's Press.
Alvarez, Sonia, Evelina Dagnino, and Arturo Escobar, eds. 1998. *Cultures of Politics, Politics of Culture.* Boulder: Westview Press.
Andolina, Robert. 2003. The Sovereign and its Shadow: Constituent Assembly and the Indigenous Movement in Ecuador. *Journal of Latin American Studies,* 35: 721.
Assies, Willem *et al.,* eds, 2000. *The Challenge of Diversity, Indigenous Peoples and Reform of the State in Latin America.* Amsterdam: Thela Thesis.

Basadre, Jose. 1978. *Apertura: Textos sobre temas de historia, educación, cultura, y política, escritos entre 1924 y 1977*, Patricio Ricketts, ed. Lima: Ediciones Taller.

Benería, Lourdes and B. Mendoza. 1995. Structural Adjustment and Social Emergency Funds: The Cases of Honduras, Mexico, and Nicaragua. *The European Journal of Development*, 7 (1): 53–76.

Bennett, David. 1998. *Multicultural States, Rethinking Difference and Identity*. London: Routledge.

Bierstecker, Thomas. 1990. Reducing the Role of the State in the Economy: A Conceptual Exploration of IMF and World Bank Prescriptions. *International Studies Quarterly*, 34(4) 1990: 477–92.

Bonfil Batalla, Guillermo. 1996. *México Profundo: Reclaiming a Civilization*, translated by Philip Dennis. Austin: University of Texas Press.

Bose, Michael. 2004. *The Indigenous Movement in the Ecuadorian Press*. Unpublished Master's Thesis, Center for Iberian and Latin American Studies, University of California, San Diego.

Brysk, Alison. 2000. *From Tribal Village to Global Village, Indian Rights and International Relations in Latin America*. Stanford, CA: Stanford University Press.

———. 1994. Acting Globally: Indian Rights and International Politics in Latin America. *Indigenous Peoples and Democracy in Latin America*, Donna Lee Van Cott, ed. New York: St. Martin's Press.

Caldeira, Teresa P. R. 2000. *City of Walls, Crime, Segregation, and Citizenship in São Paulo*. Berkeley: University of California Press.

Caldeira, Teresa P. R. and James Holston. 1999. Democracy and Violence in Brazil. *Society for Comparative Study of Society and History*, 1999: 691–729.

Collier, George and Quaratielo, Elizabeth Lowery. 1994. *Basta! Land and the Zapatista Rebellion in Chiapas*. Oakland: Institute for Food and Development Policy.

Comaroff, Jean and Comaroff, John. 1991. *Of Revelation and Revolution: Christianity, Colonialism, and Consciousness in South Africa*. Chicago: University of Chicago Press.

Dagnino, Evelina. 1998. Culture, Citizenship, and Democracy. *Cultures of Politics, Politics of Culture*, Alvarez, Sonia, Evelina Dagnino, and Arturo Escobar, eds. Boulder: Westview Press.

de la Cadena, Marisol. 2000. *Indigenous Mestizos, The Politics of Race and Culture in Cuzco, Peru, 1919–1991*. Durham, NC: Duke University Press.

Díaz Polanco, Héctor. 1997. *Indigenous Peoples in Latin America, The Quest for Self-Determination*. Boulder, CO: Westview Press.

Dean, Bartholomew and Jerome M. Levi. 2003. *At the Risk of Being Heard: Identity, Indigenous Rights, and Postcolonial States*. Ann Arbor: University of Michigan Press.

Fischer, Edward. 2001. *Cultural Logics and Global Economies, Maya Identity in Thought and Practice*. Austin: University of Texas Press.

García, María Elena. Forthcoming. *Making Indigenous Citizens: Identities, Education, and Multicultural Development in Peru*. Stanford: Stanford University Press.

Gill, Lesley. 2000. *Teetering on the Rim, Global Restructuring, Daily Life, and the Armed Retreat of the Bolivian State*. New York: Colombia University Press.

Goldberg, David Theo. 1994. *Multiculturalism: A Critical Reader*. Oxford: Blackwell.

Gómez, Luis and Al Giordano. 2002. El Mallku Speaks: Indigenous Autonomy and Coca, The Narco News Interview with Felipe Quispe. Online <http://narconews.com/felipe1eng.html>.

Gómez, Jesús. 2001. Que Nazca la Nación! *Siglo XXI, Guatemala*. Online <http://www.geocities.com/tayacan_2000/aportes/aportes.html>

Gramsci, Antonio. 1971. *Selections from the Prison Notebooks*. Q. Hoare and G. N. Smith, eds. New York: International Publishers.

Gurr, Ted Robert. 1993. *Minorities at Risk*. Washington, D.C.: United States Institute of Peace Press.

Hale, Charles. 2002. Does Multiculturalism Menace? Governance, Cultural Rights, and the Politics of Identity in Guatemala. *Journal of Latin American Studies*, 34: 485–524.

——. 1994. Between Che Guevarra and the Pachamama: Mestizos, Indians, and Identity Politics in the Anti-Quincentenary Campaign. *Critique of Anthropology*, 14(1): 9–39.

Herrera, Alejandro. 2003. Public Policies and the Mapuche Movement in Chile. Paper presented at the international seminar, Movimientos Indígenas y Estado en América Latina, Cochabamba, Bolivia, May 2003.

Herrera Sarmiento, Enrique. 2003. La Nueva Legislación Agraria Boliviana y la Construcción de lo "Tacana" en el Norte Amazónico. Paper presented at the international seminar, Movimientos Indígenas y Estado en América Latina, Cochabamba, Bolivia, May 2003.

Horowitz, D. L. 2001. *Ethnic Groups in Conflict*. Berkeley: University of California Press.

ILO – International Labor Organization. 1989. Convention (No. 169) concerning indigenous and tribal peoples in independent countries. *ILO Official Bulletin*, 72 (2).

Knight, Alan. 1990. Racism, Revolution, and Indigenismo: Mexico, 1910–1940. *The Idea of Race in Latin America, 1870–1940*, Richard Graham, ed. Austin: University of Texas Press.

Korovkin, Tanya. 1998. Commodity Production and Ethnic Culture: Otavalo, Northern Ecuador. *Economic Development and Cultural Change*, 47(1).

Kymlicka, Will. 1995. *Multicultural Citizenship*. Oxford: Oxford University Press.

Kymlicka, Will, and Norman, Wayne. 1996. Return of the Citizen: A Survey of Recent Work on Citizenship Theory. *Theorizing Citizenship*, Ronald Beiner, ed. Albany: State University of New York.

Lijphart, A. 1977. *Democracy in Plural Societies*. New Haven: Yale University Press.

Luykx, Aurolyn. 1999. *The Citizen Factory: Schooling and Cultural Production in Bolivia*. Albany: State University of New York Press.

Marshall, T. H. 1949. *Citizenship and Social Class, in Class, Citizenship, and Social Development*. Garden City, NY: Anchor Books.

Mason, Phillip. 1970. *Patterns of Dominance*. Oxford: Oxford University Press.

Morales, Evo. 2003. Bolivia, el Poder del Pueblo. Speech delivered at a conference entitled En Defensa de la Humanidad (In Defense of Humanity), October 24,

2003, Mexico City. Translated by Bruce Campbell. Online <http://www.amer-icas.org>.

Morales, Mario. 1998. *La Articulación de las Diferencias o el Síndrome de Maximón.* Guatemala: Facultad Latinoamericano de Ciencias Sociales (FLACSO).

Mosley, Samuel *et al.* 1991. *Aid and Power: The World Bank and Policy-Based Lending.* London: Routledge.

Muratorio, Blanca. 1991. *The Life and Times of Grandfather Alonso, Culture and History in the Upper Amazon.* New Brunswick, NJ : Rutgers University Press.

Okin, Susan Moller. 1999. *Is Multiculturalism Bad for Women?* Princeton: Princeton University Press.

Otero, Gerardo. 2003. The "Indian Question" in Latin America, Class, State, and Ethnic Identity Construction. *Latin American Research Review*, 38 (1): 248–67.

Parekh, Bhikhu. 1999. A Varied Moral World. *Is Multiculturalism Bad for Women?* Susan Moller Okin, ed. Princeton: Princeton University Press.

Portes, Alejandro and Kelly Hoffman. 2003. Latin American Class Structures: Their Composition and Change During the Neoliberal Era. *Latin America Research Review*, 38, (1): 41–82.

Povinelli, Elizabeth A. 2002. *The Cunning of Recognition.* Durham, NC: Duke University Press.

——. 1998. The State of Shame: Australian Multiculturalism and the Crisis of Indigenous Citizenship. *Critical Inquiry*, 24: 575.

Rivera Cusicanqui, Silvia. 1987. *Oppressed but Not Defeated, Peasant Struggles among the Aymara and Qhechwa in Bolivia, 1900–1980* (English translation). Geneva, Switzerland: United Nations Research Institute for Social Development.

Roper, J. Montgomery *et al.* 2003. Introduction to Special Issue on Indigenous Transformational Movements in Contemporary Latin America. *Latin American Perspectives*, 30(1).

Sanabria, Harry. 2000. Resistance and the Arts of Domination, Miners and the Bolivian State. *Latin American Perspectives*, 27 (1): 56–81.

Schild, Verónica. 1998. New Subjects of Rights? Women's Movements and the Construction of Citizenship in the "New Democracies." *Cultures of Politics, Politics of Culture*, Alvarez, Sonia, Evelina Dagnino, and Arturo Escobar, eds. Boulder, CO: Westview Press.

Smith, Carol. 1990. *Guatemalan Indians and the State: 1540 to 1988.* Austin: University of Texas Press.

Stephen, Lynn. 2002. *Zapata Lives! Histories and Cultural Politics in Southern Mexico.* Berkeley: University of California Press.

Taussig, Michael. 1987. *Shamanism, Colonialism, and the Wild Man, A Study in Terror and Healing.* Chicago: University of Chicago Press.

Urban, Greg, and Joel Sherzer. 1991. *Nation-States and Indians in Latin America.* Austin: University of Texas Press.

Van Cott, Donna Lee. 2003. From Exclusion to Inclusion: Bolivia's 2002 Elections. *Journal of Latin American Studies*, 35: 751.

——. 2000. *The Friendly Liquidation of the Past, The Politics of Diversity in Latin America.* Pittsburgh: University of Pittsburgh Press.

———. 1994 *Indigenous Peoples and Democracy in Latin America*. New York: St. Martin's Press.

Van der Berghe, Pierre L. 1970. *Race and Ethnicity*. New York: Basic Books.

Van der Berghe, Pierre, and George Primove. 1977. *Inequality in the Peruvian Andes: Class and Ethnicity in Cuzco*. Columbia, MO: University of Missouri Press.

Varas, Augusto. 1995. Latin America. Barbara Stallings ed. *Global Change, Regional Response*. Cambridge: Cambridge University Press.

Varese, Stefano. 1996. Parroquialismo y Globalización, las Etnicidades Indígenas ante el Tercer Milenio. *Pueblos Indios, Soberania, y Globalismo*. Quito, Ecuador: Ediciones Abya-Yala.

Vilas, Carlos, 1996. Neoliberal Social Policy: Managing Poverty (Somehow). *NACLA Report on the Americas*, May/June 1996: 16–25.

Wade, Peter. 1991. *Race and Ethnicity in Latin America*. London: Pluto Press.

Warren, Jonathan. 2001. *Racial Revolutions, Antiracism and Indian Resurgence in Brazil*. Durham: Duke University Press.

Warren, Kay. 1998a. *Indigenous Movements and Their Critics, Pan-Maya Activism in Guatemala*. Princeton: Princeton University Press.

———. 1998b. Indigenous Movements in Guatemala. *Cultures of Politics, Politics of Culture*, Alvarez, Sonia, Evelina Dagnino, and Arturo Escobar, eds. Boulder: Westview Press.

Warren, Kay, and Jean Jackson, eds. 2002. *Indigenous Movements, Self-Representation, and the State in Latin America*. Austin: University of Texas Press.

Yashar, Deborah. 1999. Democracy, Indigenous Movements, and the Postliberal Challenge in Latin America. *World Politics*, 52: 76–104.

———. 1998. Contesting Citizenship: Indigenous Movements and Democracy in Latin America. *Comparative Politics*, 1998: 23–42.

Young, Crawford. 1976. *The Politics of Cultural Pluralism*. Madison: University of Wisconsin Press.

Young, Iris Marion. 1996. Polity and Group Difference: A Critique of the Ideal of Universal Citizenship. *Theorizing Citizenship*, Ronald Beiner, ed. Albany: State University of New York.

Zamosc, Leon. 1994. Agrarian Protest and the Indian Movement in the Ecuadorian Highlands. *Latin American Research Review*, 29(3).

———. 1995. *Estadística de las Áreas de Predominio Étnico de la Sierra Ecuatoriana: Población Rural, Indicadores Cantonales y Organizaciones de Base*. Quito: Abya-Yala.

From Indigenismo to Zapatismo

The Struggle for a Multi-ethnic Mexican Society

Gunther Dietz

Over the past decades, and particularly since the mid-eighties, an "ethnic revival" (Smith 1981) has been recorded in Mexico as in almost every other part of the world. Newly emerging or re-emerging "ethnic groups" or "units" (Elwert 1989) challenge national institutions by claiming political and territorial autonomy while demanding more than just linguistic and cultural privileges granted to indigenous peoples by nation-state governments. Now, in Mexico as well as in other Latin American countries (Urban and Sherzer 1994, Santana 1995), the privatization of indigenous land and the rapid monetarization of their subsistence-oriented economy threaten the territorial and social foundations of native groups.

Responding to these tendencies, new supra-local ethnic organizations have emerged over the last twenty years, and indigenous organizations and movements[1] have arisen on the local, regional and national level. Mexico is an important site for study not only because of the overwhelming presence indigenous movements have acquired there during the last two decades, but also because of the current political transition from authoritarian rule to representative democracy (Cornelius 1996). This offers important insights into the contribution of ethnic movements to democratization and political participation.

This chapter analyzes the evolution of indigenous movements in twentieth-century Mexico and their struggles for recognition of indigenous rights. After framing indigenous claims within the history of state-society relations and Mexican nationalism, I analyze and compare the two basic frameworks within which indigenous groups have raised demands since the Mexican Revolution: the *agrarista* (agrarianist) tradition of state-dominated land reform and its impact on rural corporatism and peasant social organization, and the *indigenista* (indigenist) tradition of implementing particular development and integration policies for ethnically-identified regions and communities.

The central focus of this chapter contrasts the contents and organizational forms achieved by the main indigenous actors who have emerged since the 1970s in response to the failure of both *indigenismo* and *agrarismo* to resolve the "Indian Question" in Mexico. Both state-sponsored and independent, class-based and ethnically defined organizations are compared in the course of their struggles *vis-à-vis* the nation-state and *mestizo* society. Since the 1990s, in the course of the neoliberal retreat of the state from development and integration polices, state-society as well as minority-majority relations are being redefined by new ethnic actors, of whom the Zapatista National Liberation Army (EZLN) is only the most visible. The process through which these innovative coalitions of communities and alliances of highly heterogeneous social actors appeared, first in the regional and then in the national arena, are illustrated with examples from different Mexican regions.

Finally, the EZLN phenomenon and the zapatista movement are analyzed as platforms of articulation and of convergence of old and new indigenous claims. This case study shows how contemporary struggles for territorial autonomy, decentralization, and the democratization of Mexican society are redefining the meanings of community, belonging, participation, and citizenship.

The National Historical Framework of Indigenous Mobilization

In Mexico, the persistence of ethnically differentiated populations represents the continuity of contradictory processes of colonization and resistance, whose origins date back to the beginnings of European expansion in the Americas. Throughout these processes, autochthonous social structures and institutions were reduced to a local level of organization, through their forced inclusion into a bipolar system of *castas* (racial categories).[2] The logic of this system distinguished between "us" and "them," between Europeans and "Indians," between the rural and locally confined *república de indios* (republic of the Indians), on the one hand, and the urban and increasingly cosmopolitan *república de españoles* (republic of the Spaniards), on the other hand. Willingly or not, the establishment of the colonial caste system and the simultaneous forced re-settlement of entire populations transformed the *comunidad indígena* (indigenous community) into the central identity marker of its inhabitants (Bennholdt-Thomsen 1976, Varese 2001), while all supra-local entities were reduced to "broken memories" (Florescano 1999), which were precariously retained as weak regional ethnic traditions.

Liberalism and the Dissolution of the Indigenous Community

Throughout the colonial period, the segregational bipolar system was maintained despite increasing economic and infrastructural integration of the subsystems of *haciendas* (large land holdings), mining industries, and other extractive exploitations (Gibson 1964, Lockhart 1992). This colonial system was not challenged by the new *criollo* (American-born Spaniards) elites who consolidated political power throughout the independence wars. Instead, in the nineteenth century, the nascent Mexican nation-state further threatened the position of the indigenous community via three policy axes: administrative "modernization," privatization of collective land tenure, and agricultural industrialization.[3]

In order to gain minimal local political control, the *criollo* elite deepened administrative reforms already initiated by the late Bourbon regime. Nearly all *mestizo* villages situated in indigenous regions become *cabeceras*, or head towns of the new municipal governments, while the indigenous communities were classified as *tenencias* (possessions), which depend directly on their respective municipal governments. As a result of this politics of "municipalization" and "re-municipalization," which in different Mexican regions were expanded and continuously updated during the nineteenth and twentieth centuries, the colonial *mestizo* enclaves emerged as a main pillar of the nation-state's presence in the countryside. Consequently, the bipolar colonial system was reinforced by the structural asymmetry established by the *cabecera-tenencia* dichotomy (Hoffmann 1989, Aguirre Beltrán 1991 [1953]).

As the empowerment of the *mestizo* enclaves did not succeed altogether in dissolving indigenous communal identities and forms of organization – still shaped by the customary principles – the urban elite, strongly influenced by political as well as economic liberalism, tried to impose the nation-state's sovereignty and "positive law" upon the outstanding "remnants" of colonial corporatism: the corporate land held by the Catholic Church as well as by indigenous communities.[4] The privatization of collective land tenure was officially promoted by the *Leyes de Colonización* (Laws of Colonization, 1824), which dispossessed the indigenous communities of their so-called *tierras baldías* (empty lands), and by *the Ley de Desamortización* (Law of Entailment, 1856), which directly dissolved the corporate nature of the community by canceling its legal basis.[5] In reaction to the political and judicial resistance exhibited by the communities against these step-by-step privatizations, these so-called "extinguished communities" were no longer legally able to fight against the parceling and privatization process. Passive resistance became the only way of obstructing these processes.

In its effort to combine privatization and industrialization, the Porfirio Díaz administration expanded the abilities of outside companies to demarcate and acquire indigenous lands beginning in 1876. The new *Leyes de Colonización* (1875 and 1883) allowed private companies to demarcate and sell all parcels of land which lacked formal, individual ownership. Thus, the only way in which communities could legally defend their land was by demarcating and distributing the collective land among the *comuneros* (members of indigenous communities) themselves. This legal process not only produced conflict inside the indigenous communities, but it was also very expensive. Consequently, by the end of the century most indigenous communities had lost the largest and most productive parts of their formerly collectively-owned lands and remained highly indebted to external agencies and/or companies.

The Mexican Revolution and the Ideology of Mestizaje

It was precisely in these indigenous regions where participation in the Mexican Revolution was highest. Local indigenous actors engaged in the armed struggle either to re-gain communal land from *mestizo* outsiders and from community neighbors who succeeded in monopolizing individual land tenure, or from neighboring communities, which claimed the land because of overlapping and conflicting demarcation procedures. In contrast to impoverished *mestizo* day-laborers, who actively participated in the Revolution in order to have access to land for the first time, in most of the indigenous regions, the Mexican Revolution is characterized more by its restorative than its revolutionary nature (Tutino 1986). Due to this basic aim of defending and reestablishing the "sovereignty" of the indigenous community against external intruders, the officially proclaimed agrarian revolution often was limited to local rebellions.[6]

With regards to the degree of communal decomposition suffered inside indigenous regions during the nineteenth century, two kinds of actors can be distinguished (Knight 1998): uprooted communal peasants and landless day-laborers who fought for a state-led redistribution of land, and the still locally integrated indigenous *comuneros* who struggled for formal recognition of their communities and the restitution of their former collective property. As a consequence, two models of agrarian reform emerged.[7] First was the state-dominated model of top-down *dotación* (land grant), in which the nation-state concedes the usufruct of land to a particular group of landless peasants or former day-laborers. Second was the communalist model of bottom-up *restitución* (restitution), in which the community is acknowledged as a "free confederation of agrarian communities" and the basic entity of the post-revolutionary state.

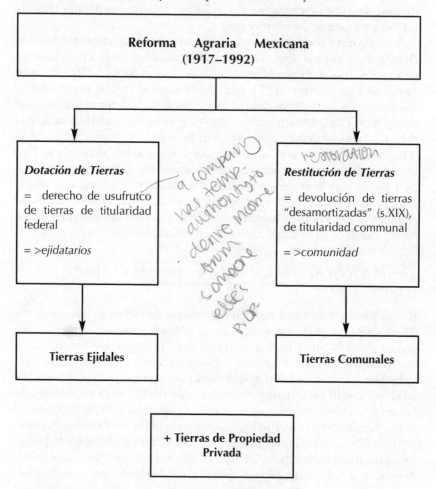

Reforma Agraria Mexicana (1917–1992)

Dotación de Tierras

= derecho de usufrutco de tierras de titularidad federal

= >ejidatarios

Restitución de Tierras

= devolución de tierras "desamortizadas" (s.XIX), de titularidad communal

= >comunidad

Tierras Ejidales

Tierras Comunales

+ Tierras de Propiedad Privada

Figure 1.1 The Mexican Agrarian Reform (Dietz 1999:156)

The military defeat of the Zapata's army during the Mexican Revolution symbolized the formal victory of the state-led model of agrarian reform over the community-based model. As indigenous communities continued struggling for recognition within a post-revolutionary framework, the agrarian reform process was accompanied by a campaign of "ideological penetration" (Corbett and Whiteford 1986) by the nation-state in the communities. Under the influence of the *Ateneo de la Juventud* (the Atheneum of Youth), a pre-revolutionary group of urban intellectuals engaged in re-defining the "national project," the exclusive and Eurocentric *criollo* nationalism of the postcolonial elites (Anderson 1988) was substituted by an integrationist nationalist discourse, according to which the emerging Mexican nation would be a merger of pre-colonial indigenous, colonial European, and *criollo* elements. The resulting *mestizo*, who until then had only been perceived as the illegitimate result of the forbidden crossing of boundaries between the segregated *república de españoles* and *república de indios*, was no longer seen as a "biological bastard," but as a new "cosmic race" (Vasconcelos 1997 [1925]), the seed and symbol of the new, post-revolutionary nation.

This ideological turn, which was already prepared by nineteenth-century precedents,[8] was made official through institutional processes undertaken in the 1920s. In 1921, General Obregón chose José Vasconcelos, one of the central figures of the Ateneo movement and main theorist of the *mestizaje* ideology, to be founding minister of the *Secretaría de Educación Pública* (SEP – Secretary of Public Education), the emblematic Ministry of Education conceived by Vasconcelos as an avant-garde institution that would bring the revolution to the countryside. In political terms, the project of national *mestizaje* implied specific measures for "integrating" into the *mestizo* nation-state those groups which did not. identify as *mestizos*, i.e. the indigenous populations of Mexico (Maihold 1986). Ideological *mestizo*filia (Basave Benítez 1992) was thus turned into integrationist politics.

It is in this domain of integrationist post-revolutionary politics in which Mexican indigenous struggles must be situated. An analysis of the emergence and evolution of indigenous dissidence in rural Mexico during this century allows for an evaluation of its national impact. Two factors have been decisive for the step-by-step emancipation of Mexican indigenous struggles from their post-revolutionary institutional tutelage: the crisis of agrarian corporatism and of the governing state-party, and the failure of *indigenismo* to homogenize and integrate the Mexican indigenous populations.

Agrarismo *and the Limits of Rural Corporatism*

Since the end of the armed conflict and until the late 1960s, the model conceived by president Lázaro Cárdenas (1934–1940) of a "corporate state" had successfully accomplished its dual function: to institutionally tie up the vast majority of Mexicans as a rural and urban "base" for the state-party, and to open up channels to articulate the claims and necessities of this base and to absorb the sporadic expressions of its opposition and dissent.

This corporatist model was expanded toward indigenous regions as well. In this case, however, the post-revolutionary state did not succeed in creating a closely-knit network of powerful and loyal regional *caciques* (local "chiefs") This failure was due to the persistence of corporate communal structures of local politics, and the omnipresence of Lázaro Cárdenas who acted as personal mediator between the *mestizo* state and the indigenous communities in land reform and other procedures (Friedrich 1981, Becker 1987).

In those indigenous regions which opposed state-run agrarian reform, Cárdenas and Vasconcelos started ambitious educational campaigns that sent *maestros agraristas* (agrarian teachers) out to educate the "stubborn peasants" and convince them of the merits of institutionalized revolution (Gledhill 1991, Vaughan 1997). Although public schools were finally accepted in most communities, local resistance was mainly directed against agrarista teachers as representatives of the state-dominated agrarian reform project. Resisting the agrarian reform project, communities still claimed the alternative "utopia" of community-controlled land tenure in which "the subject of the land is neither a ward of the state nor an individualist entrepreneur, but a member of a rural collectivity with significant autonomy in the administration of its lands" (Nugent and Alonso 1994: 246).

This position contrasted sharply with the regime's interpretation, codified in Article 27 of the Mexican Constitution, which acknowledged the nation-state's original ownership of all lands, which it could transfer by way of *dotación* or *restitución* to any given community (Warman 1984). Cárdenas and the *agraristas* generally favored the *dotación ejidal* (granting of communal lands) alternative, as it created the new administrative entity, the *ejido*, which offered opportunities for intervention in local affairs through the selection of loyal beneficiaries as *ejidatarios* (members/owners of communal lands) and through mediation of the decisive broker figure of the *comisariado ejidal* (ejido commissioner).

Any procedure of agrarian reform affecting indigenous communities was thus perceived by the local population as a negotiation process between the nation-state and the community. By actively participating in this negotiation, indigenous communities started integrating into the national project – they participated asymmetrically, but independently. Agrarian reform was perceived as a social contract, a bilaterally binding agreement between the state and the community. This post-revolutionary social contract was often identified with and embodied by the figure of Lázaro Cárdenas (Spenser and Levinson 1999: 245).[9]

The post-revolutionary state thus succeeded in institutionalizing agrarian reform for state formation purposes by integrating the peasant population into the vertical state-party structure: the *Confederación Nacional Campesina* (CNC – National Peasant Federation), the "peasant sector" of the PRI, soon obtained a monopoly in negotiating *ejido* concessions with state agencies. Already under the Cárdenas presidency, all communities that struggled for land distribution had to integrate into a

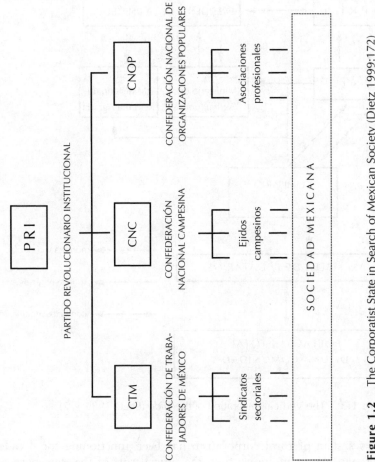

Figure 1.2 The Corporatist State in Search of Mexican Society (Dietz 1999:172)

local *Liga Agraria* (Agrarian League) which was a member of the CNC (Reitmeier 1990). Once the land was distributed, the *comisariado ejidal* would form the last link in the chain of state-society intermediation (Huizer 1982, Warman 1984). These local brokers acted as "hinges" between state and party interests on the one hand, and local demands and needs, on the other.

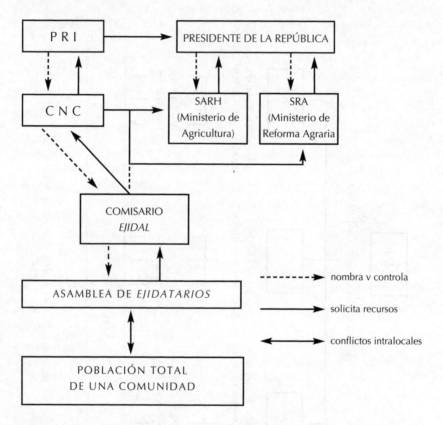

Figure 1.3   The Vertical Integration of the *Ejido* (Dietz 1999:177)

This system of rural corporatism has been functioning for decades under two main conditions: first, the official role of the state party in deepening the process of agrarian reform throughout the *ejido*; and second, the political will of state agencies to promote rural development initiatives aimed at small-holder *ejidatarios* (Piñar Alvarez 2002). Since the neoliberal turn at the beginning of the 1980s, neither condition is being fulfilled. Nevertheless, the corporatist agrarian regime came into crisis even before this due to two different actors who were never successfully integrated into the vertical scheme of corporate control. First were the landless day-laborers who never received any land, and, second, indigenous communities which resisted the *dotación* option of agrarian reform.

In the first case, despite Cárdenas's efforts to abolish large estates and redistribute former hacienda land among its former *jornaleros*, in many Mexican regions agrarian reform was never implemented for political reasons. For example, if a large estate was owned by members of the "revolutionary family" of former generals of the Mexican Revolution or by members of the victorious faction of the post-revolutionary civil war, neither *devolución* nor *restitución* were ways of gaining title to the disputed land. In those cases, the landless peasants were encouraged to occupy newly exploitable – and often economically unattractive – land as *colonos* (settlers). Since the 1970s, both the landless laborers and the marginalized *colonos* have contributed to rural dissidence (Canabal Cristiani 1983, Astorga Lira 1988).

The second source of rural dissidence is tied directly to contemporary Mexican indigenous movements. Those communities which after decades of negotiations and contentious mobilizations finally succeeded in resisting state-led agrarian reform through *restitución* were frequently marginalized by rural development agencies, since their local representatives often resisted integration into the CNC hierarchies (Aguado López 1989, Dietz 1999). The local authorities maintained the control of local politics even after the agrarian certification procedure ended. Then, new institutions headed by officials called the *representante de bienes comunales* (communal land representative) were integrated into the pre-existing system of customary, rotating posts and responsibilities, called *cargos*.[10] Accordingly, the indigenous communities which maintain communal control of their land distinguish themselves from the *ejido* communities by their lesser degree of political integration into the corporatist system of governance. Their frequent marginalization by public development agencies constituted a major point of departure for innovative independent mobilizations at the margins of the corporatist system.

The Legacy of Indigenismo

As a response to the limited integration of indigenous groups into national *mestizo* society, the post-revolutionary state developed a second set of integration policies specifically targeted at the indigenous communities: *indigenismo*. All development projects implemented since the thirties in the indigenous regions of Mexico were part of this approach. The strategy, aimed at "mexicanizing the indian" (Cárdenas 1978 [1940]), aimed to integrate the indigenous population socially, culturally, and ethnically into Mexican society by means of "planned acculturation," and to "modernize" the local and regional indigenous economy through the forced opening toward the market economy.

These policies, inspired by the principle of "integration through accul-turation," were applied by governmental agencies such as the *Instituto Nacional Indigenista* (INI – National Indigenist Institute) and the Ministry of Education, SEP.[11] The INI coordinated socio-cultural as well as economic policies. Its programs were elaborated outside of indigenous regions, with headquarters in Mexico City, and were then implemented through local projects carried out by trained bilingual "indigenous promoters." The emphasis of these projects lay in educational programs and economic development schemes (Dietz 1995, 1999). With regard to *mestizaje*-inspired educational politics, indigenismo experimented with pioneer literacy and bilingual education projects beginning in 1939 that for the first time viewed indigenous language – with the gradual substi-tution of Spanish – as a "key" for the hispanization of indigenous children in primary education. Economic measures were aimed at overcoming the supposed "under-development" of indigenous agriculture and crafts by means of industrializing the peasant mode of production. Peasants were inserted in cooperatives supervised by urban *mestizo* "experts" who taught industrial methods and production techniques. Access to credit and subsidies was conditioned for decades by compulsory participation in these cooperatives. Simultaneously, the indigenous regions were opened to the outside world through the development of roads and communica-tion infrastructure, which encouraged the establishment of agro-industrial and timber-producing enterprises.

In the vast majority of indigenous regions, indigenismo failed on both respects. Instead of promoting *mestizaje* through free access to educa-tion, the educational policies profoundly divided the local population into a small minority that actually succeeded in getting a secondary or high school education in the provincial cities located outside indigenous regions, and the majority of the regional population who either barely finished or abandoned primary school. Thus, a limited number of indigenous peasants were individually "acculturated" and emigrated to the large urban sprawls, while most of the indigenous population acquired only the basic skills necessary for dealing with *mestizo* society. Access to these skills, however, did not influence their ethnic identity (Dietz 1999). On the other hand, indigenismo also failed in its attempt to "open" communities and "proletarize" indigenous peasant units. Without exception, each of the "co-operatives" and production-schools established in the regions collapsed as a result of the local population's unwillingness to participate.

Despite these obvious and often criticized failures,[12] indigenismo unin-tentionally provided an important platform for the emergence of new ethnic actors and for the articulation of indigenous struggles. Since the beginning of indigenismo, the nation-state perceived the need for a specif-ically trained group of "culture promoters" and bilingual teachers who came from the regions and who would be in charge of carrying out the different literacy campaigns. These "promoters" of national mestizo culture, for example the bilingual teachers, were to fulfill a double task: teaching children within the formal school system, and carrying out diverse out-of-school activities in the areas of adult education and community development (Aguirre Beltrán 1992 [1973]).

By the 1970s, however, the failure of indigenous teachers in accomplishing both tasks became evident. In the school context, the allegedly bilingual character of primary education frequently turned out to be fictitious. The indigenous language was hardly ever really taught or used at school. The reason for this failure had to do with the shortcomings of the bilingual teachers who viewed the indigenous language as a temporary tool for achieving final hispanization (Ros Romero 1981). These teachers also failed in their community development responsibilities, since they were actively resisted by the local populations and particularly by the traditional village authorities, who perceived them as intruders sent by the indigenismo agencies (Dietz 1999).

The Stakes in the Classic Struggles for Indigenous Rights

Two different forms of indigenous organization prevailed in nearly every indigenous region until the 1980s. On the one hand, the bilingual teachers and other indigenous civil servants who gained positions inside the institutions of indigenismo created their own pressure groups such as the *Consejo Nacional de Pueblos Indígenas* (CNPI – National Council of Indigenous Peoples) and the *Alianza Nacional de Profesionales Indígenas Bilingües* (ANPIBAC – National Alliance of Bilingual Indigenous Professionals). Although these lobbying groups of emerging indigenous intellectuals achieved considerable influence inside the government's educational and cultural institutions, their representation within their own communities of origin remained limited (Mejía Piñeros and Sarmiento Silva 1991). In addition to these lobbying associations, regional and national peasant organizations were formed in response to the promise of agrarian reform and later to the gradual retreat of the state from rural areas. Forged around leaders of urban origin, these peasant organizations specialized in channeling claims for agrarian reform and agricultural development (Reitmeier 1990). Despite their often revolutionary ambitions, however, these organizations depended heavily on the benevolence of governmental institutions in their day-to-day operations. Until recently, the struggle for indigenous rights in Mexico has still reflected this sharp division between peasant movements holding onto the old promises of the Mexican Revolution, on the one hand, and ethnic movements struggling for recognition and participation inside cultural and educational indigenismo institutions, on the other.

Toward an "Indigenous Intelligentsia"?

In order to increase grassroots participation in their projects and to prevent failures such as those mentioned above, beginning in the 1970s, indigenist institutions started to complement their economic, infrastructural, and educational activities with the creation and/or promotion of indigenous organizations. For example, state and party institutions promoted and oversaw the formation of a *Consejo Supremo* (Supreme Council) for each ethnic group in Mexico. Similar to the sectoral pillar of the CNC inside the PRI, these Supreme Councils were designed to articulate local indigenous interests inside party and state institutions through loyal and reliable intermediaries.[13] These councils were promoted at the first meeting of independent indigenous organizations in 1974 in San Cristóbal de las Casas, Chiapas, and again one year later at the "First National Congress of Indigenous Peoples" in Pátzcuaro, sponsored by INI and other state institutions. As a result of this second congress, the *Consejo Nacional de Pueblos Indígenas* (CNPI – National Council of Indigenous Peoples) was created to represent the diverse Supreme Councils of indigenous groups. From its founding in 1975 onward, the CNPI has struggled with the problem of a lack of local representation. Beginning at the Pátzcuaro congress, a division occurred among indigenous delegates between those directly appointed by local authorities and those sent as institutionally-loyal INI and SEP representatives. Consequently, the CNPI subsisted for decades at the margins of local organizational processes.

The formation of the already mentioned ANPIBAC, the *Alianza Nacional de Profesionales Indígenas Bilingües*, was a second attempt to create indigenous organizations which were at the same time both locally rooted and loyal to state and party hierarchies. From its foundation in the late 1970s, ANPIBAC was designed as a lobbying organization for bilingual indigenous teachers used as culture brokers in the indigenismo projects. In its negotiations with the Ministry of Education, ANPIBAC evolved into a sort of trade union for the emerging indigenous intelligentsia employed at higher levels of the INI and SEP agencies. By skillfully counseling and advising government institutions in their attempt to avoid the frequent failures of their educational projects, ANPIBAC was officially acknowledged beginning in the 1980s as an "expert organization" directly collaborating with the educational authorities in improving bilingual education.[14]

Bilingual and Bicultural Indigenous Education

As an official reaction to the many failures and to the increasing criticism expressed by communities as well as teachers who felt dissatisfied with their role as agents of acculturation, in 1979 the SEP re-organized its activities in indigenous regions and updated its teacher-training and primary school curricula. An intimate and fruitful collaboration emerged as a result between the Ministry and ANPIBAC. The product of this convergence of interests was an alternative program of bilingual and bicultural education which sought to abolish the use of bilingualism to hispanicize the children and develop instead a genuinely bicultural curriculum (Gabriel Hernández 1981: 179). Given that this process of "biculturalizing" all those who were taught in the primary schools required the active and permanent participation of highly prepared and culturally hybrid actors, the Ministry was forced to open its internal hierarchies to an increasing number of teachers and academics of indigenous origin beginning in the 1980s (Guzmán Gómez 1990).

Although the bicultural education program proposed by ANPIBAC was rightly considered to be a crucial achievement of the indigenous intellectuals working inside the SEP, in reality it exhibited the same shortcomings of its monocultural *mestizo* predecessor: the superficial and inadequate training of its bilingual teachers, a lack of teaching materials and infrastructural support, a clientelistic method of allocating teachers to regions and communities according to the interests of the monopolistic and party-loyal Mexican teachers' trade union, and the resulting controversy over the role of the bilingual teachers inside the community (Dietz 1999).

In this context, the indigenous teacher was reduced to "a transmitter of some basic knowledge of national education, a handbook technician of the indigenous language and a manager of material services for the community" (Calvo Pontón and Donnadieu Aguado 1992: 172). Overburdened with multiple roles of educational, cultural, and economic intermediation (Vargas 1994), many of the bilingual teachers additionally perceived a profound conflict of loyalty between the indigenismo institutions and their local beneficiaries (Varese 1987: 189).

The Limits of Trade Unionism

As representatives of the nascent indigenous intelligentsia, both ANPIBAC and the CNPI ultimately failed to carry out their objectives. In order to counter their lack of local representation, both organizations were gradually forced to project the interests, demands, and initiatives issued by their communities to the national level. Thus semi-official indigenous organizations were forced from below to emancipate themselves from their institutional patronage, becoming the voice for indigenous communities. In 1981, the CNPI split into two factions when its president overtly and officially criticized the José López Portillo government's visible shift toward cost-effectiveness as the main criterion for agricultural development policy. As a reaction to this criticism, López

Gunther Dietz

Portillo immediately sacked the whole CNPI executive and forced its new leadership to integrate directly into the CNC structure. Although dissidents created an alternative and independent organization, the *Coordinadora Nacional de Pueblos Indios* (the National Council of Indian Peoples), this organization also lacked real grassroots representation (Sarmiento Silva 1985).

ANPIBAC, on the other hand, was excluded from institutional participation precisely when their leaders started engaging in non-educational activities in their communities of origin. Through its participation in struggles over the control of communal land, ANPIBAC diversified its agenda, until then limited to educational and cultural demands (Hernández Hernández 1988). Again, as in the case of the CNPI, this new dynamic ended up dividing the organization into two groups. On one side were the teachers and educational planners who remained loyal to the regime and who limited their activities to the sphere of educational and cultural programs. Although the members of this group lost their local links to their own communities, they gained privileged access into new institutional spaces as part of the urban intelligentsia within the SEP and INI hierarchies. On the other side were the teachers who remained in their communities and participated in local political activities, effectively renouncing any possibility of upward mobility within the institutional hierarchy. While some of these teachers limited their non-school activities to their local arena, others maintained the remnants of their ANPIBAC contacts to create an informal network of teachers working in different regions. In order to exchange experiences of grassroots mobilization and participation between different regions, they created the journal *Etnias* (Ethnicities), produced and distributed among bilingual teachers mainly from Oaxaca, Chiapas, Michoacán, Veracruz, and Guerrero.

The evolution of both organizational frameworks illustrates a further failure of indigenismo in its attempt to integrate the nascent indigenous elites into the corporate apparatus of the state-party. Today, those parts of the semi-official organizations which have survived the periodic waves of factionalist division lack any representation and thus can no longer control or mediate any of the contemporary struggles of the indigenous peoples of Mexico. Throughout the 1990s, they have been substituted by organizations which have opted for open dissidence and which have collaborated in the slow erosion of the corporatist heritage of the CNC and PRI institutions.

Indigenous Participation in Independent Peasant Organizations

Beginning with the first "neoliberal" administrations of the late 1970s and early 1980s, indigenous dissidents began to express their demands through organizations and movements which emphasized their common peasant condition as opposed to their distinctively ethnic identities. The main advantage of these newly emerging organizations resided in their structural and programmatic flexibility, in contrast to the rigid, single-issue orientation and external dependence of ANPIBAC and the CNPI. This allowed them to adapt easily to the structure of the indigenous community.

The struggle for recognition of communal land tenure through the *restitución* variant of agrarian reform evolved completely outside corporatist hierarchies. As the communal claims-making process took years and even decades, several communities united and went together to their state capital or to Mexico City in order to force the *Secretaría de Reforma Agraria* (the Secretary of Agrarian Reform) to carry out its promise. However, because this process was politically dangerous and judicially complicated, local authorities began seeking support starting in the late 1970s from the generation of urban dissidents, the "survivors of Tlatelolco" (the 1968 army massacre of the student movement), who began emigrating from Mexico City to the countryside. The organizations of these urban dissidents, in particular the Trotskyist *Línea Proletaria* (Proletarian Line) and the Maoist-inspired *Línea de Masas* (Line of the Masses), started searching for a non-urban "revolutionary subject" among the Mexican peasantry (Harvey 1990). The subsequent encounter between indigenous communities and their new "external advisers" generated new alliances such as the *Unión de Comuneros Emiliano Zapata* (UCEZ – Emilio Zapata Union of Communities), founded in 1979 in Michoacán among Purhépecha and Ñahñu communities, and the *Organización Campesina Emiliano Zapata* (OCEZ – Emilio Zapata Peasant Organization) active since 1982 in Chiapas among different ethnic groups.[15] Although the ideological content of these new organizations is openly revolutionary and socialist in orientation, their actual activities have focused on the old Zapatista promise of community-based agrarian reform.

As the nation-state is the primary target of indigenous peasant claims for agrarian reform, the regional peasant organizations quickly created national representations (Canabal Cristiani 1983). Two national frameworks for independent peasant organizations appeared at the end of the 1970s and beginning of the 1980s. On the one hand, the mainly indigenous communities struggling for the restitution of their lands participated as communities in the *Coordinadora Nacional Plan de Ayala* (CNPA – Plan of Ayala National Council), created in 1979 to struggle for fulfillment of the original version of the agrarian reform as presented by Emiliano Zapata in the 1911 Ayala manifesto (Flores Lúa, Paré, and Sarmiento Silva 1988). On the other hand, those peasants who completely lacked any land tended to participate in the *Central Independiente de Obreros Agrícolas y Campesinos* (CIOAC – Independent Federation of Agricultural Workers and Peasants), which specialized in political and legal representation of laborer and *colono* claims-making (Harvey 1990;

cf. above). Both organizations work closely together as they often share the same legal advisers in Mexico City and the same ideological orientations.

The main weakness of both organizations, and of the other independent Mexican peasant movements of the 1970s and 1980s, resulted from their overwhelming emphasis on agrarian reform and on legal-political issues. The communities only participated in the movement until they obtained the claimed land titles, returning to their daily business as family-run peasant production units once this was achieved. This localist attitude was in sharp contrast with the revolutionary program adhered to by their external advisers.

The Struggle Over Control of Peasant Production

The shift toward emphasis on production perceivable since the 1980s among Mexican peasant movements resulted both from external governmental policy changes and from reactions to the structural weakness of the peasant organizations mentioned above. Under the administration of López Portillo, and still under the CNC umbrella, *ejidatario* peasants were officially encouraged to form producers' alliances in order to jointly acquire resources and market products as means of increasing peasant productivity (Otero 1990, Martínez Borrego 1991). Agricultural productivity came to dominate the official rural development policies implemented by subsequent administrations starting in the late 1970s through the last PRI presidency of Ernesto Zedillo (Piñar Alvarez 2002). The priviledged forms of organization became the *Uniones de Ejidos* (Unions of Ejidos) and *Asociaciones Rurales de Interés Colectivo* (ARIC – Rural Associations of Collective Interest), local or regional groupings of family-based peasant production units, which now received support and legal recognition.[16]

In practice, however, these organizations are only accessible to the so-called *campesinado medio* (middle-class peasantry, García 1991), peasant groups specializing in externally marketable products as opposed to subsistence crops. A wide range of analysts, politicians, and "external advisers" of peasant organizations encouraged traditional indigenous peasants to turn to this new kind of "modern production" as a means of increasing income (Marion Singer 1989, Salazar Peralta 1994). A major reasoning behind this push was that in order to maintain their continuity and political independence, the peasant organizations had to strive for economic autonomy as well. They had to fight not only for access to communally owned land, but also for control over the entire process of production. By this logic, cooperatives and collective production units should substitute the peasant household as the basic unit of production, distribution, and marketing of agricultural, cattle, timber, and craft products (Cruz Hernández & Zuvire Lucas 1991). This profound re-structuring of local economies was strongly resisted by indigenous peasant households, since it implied an indirect "proletarization" of their workforce which seemed rather similar to the original and long-abandoned *indigenismo* projects of "modernizing" indigenous economic activities (Dietz 1999). However, in those regions where certain marketable products such as coffee and timber had created nearly monocultural situations, sectoral organizations of producers emerged. In 1982, they formed the *Unión de Organizaciones Regionales Campesinas Autónomas* (UNORCA – Union of Regional Autonomous Peasant Organizations), a national association representing their particular entrepreneurial interests in contrast to the agrarista interest of the older independent peasant organizations.[17]

This new generation of peasant organizations distinguished itself from its predecessors not only by the wider scope of their demands – access to public credit schemes for their peasant enterprises, state support for entering external markets, limitations on private (coyote) monopolies of intermediation etc. – but also by their attitude toward government agencies. These producer organizations targeted the state institutions as an increasingly professionalized lobby and not as an intrinsic enemy. Direct negotiation and collaboration, particularly with the Salinas de Gortari administration, turned UNORCA and other producer associations into officially acknowledged partners. As a consequence, inside these new organizations there is a widespread fear of being "co-opted" by the state-party regime's attempt to legitimize its neoliberal policies (Harvey 1993). As in the case of the ANPIBAC and CNPI lobbying organizations, these political alliances with the state-party resulted in internal polarization, dividing and paralyzing these producer organizations in face of the debate over neoliberal privatizations of the Mexican countryside (see below).

Between Community and Nation-State: New Sites of Struggle

At the end of the 1980s and particularly during the 1990s, both the indigenous teachers' unions and the peasant organizations faced an existential crisis. The Mexican nation-state had officially recognized the failure of indigenismo to ethnically homogenize the rural indigenous population, and declared its neoliberal retreat from former agrarian reform and agricultural development policies. Consequently, both indigenous and peasant movements lost their institutional counterpart and thus their legitimacy with regard to local constituencies. Gradually, new community, regional, and national actors appeared to substitute for these classic organizations of rural Mexico.

From "Indians" and "Peasants" to "Citizens"

In response to the retreat of state agencies and the attempts to privatize communal and ejidal land tenure, in different indigenous regions of Mexico communities began to form political coalitions. More often than not, these coalitions included groups different ethnic origins. These "alliances of convenience" of mono-ethnic or pluri-ethnic composition did not develop into large and centrally structured organizations, but continued to consider the community as its basic unit and the community's sovereignty as its principal claim. The recognition of customary laws and practices would later lead to the struggle for territorial autonomy on the local and regional levels.

A profound rupture occurred during the administration of Carlos Salinas de Gortari (1988–94). In order to mitigate the political consequences of both the regime's obvious fraud in the 1988 presidential elections and to at least partially relieve the consequences of the new government's de-regulation and privatization policies, all existing indigenismo and development programs were substituted by direct assistance. The PRONASOL and PROCAMPO (*Programa de Apoyos Directos al Campo* – Program for Direct Aid to the Countryside) programs, which consisted of public funds raised through the privatization of state-owned enterprises, started distributing public resources in cash and in kind beginning in the early 1990s. The strategic importance of these funds had to do with their distribution mechanisms. Parallel to the existing corporatist structures and channels, the money was distributed through so-called *comités de solidaridad* (solidarity committees) newly created local groups of peasants who declared themselves loyal not merely to the old state-party – against which the new neoliberal technocratic elite fights – but also to the president. Thus, highly personalized neo-corporatist channels were promoted which marginalized not only old party-structures, but also the customary *cargos* of indigenous communities.[18]

The second consequence of the 1988 election schism is reflected in the appearance and consolidation first of a socio-political movement and then of a political party which, for the first time since the end of the Mexican Revolution, represented a real political alternative. Although the *neocardenistas*, led by Cuauhtemoc Cárdenas, the son of the mythic president of agrarian reform, were the direct victims of the 1988 election fraud, they succeeded in creating a new party which echoed many of the claims made by the dissident indigenous and peasant organizations of the 1980s. The *Partido de la Revolución Democrática* (PRD – Party of the Democratic Revolution) promoted alliances with independent producer associations and with the emerging community coalitions, which opened new spaces for political participation at municipal, state, and national levels. Nevertheless, the PRD quickly began to reproduce corporatist practices similar to those of its PRI and CNC antagonists. Controlled from above, party-faithful peasant organizations such as the *Central Campesina Cardenista* (CCC – Cardenista Peasants Federation) and the *Unión Campesina Democrática* (UCD – Democratic Peasant Union) threatened to close again the new spaces conquered by the independent organizations and movements.[19]

Although these old corporatist practices limited the impact and presence of the new organizations, in the long run the most important consequence of the 1988 events was the confluence of highly heterogeneous social and political actors. Since then, peasant activists and their external advisors, members of non-governmental organizations (NGOs), human rights campaigners, faith-based grassroots movements such as the ecclesiastic base communities and political party representatives, as well as dissident indigenous teacher unions jointly perceived the necessity of ending state-party monopoly by following and closely monitoring election processes on the municipal, state, and national levels.[20] Beginning with the municipal elections of 1989, the resulting *Convergencia de Organismos Civiles por la Democracia* (Convergence of Civil Society Organizations for Democracy) succeeded in publicly demonstrating and denouncing the practice of governmental election rigging (Calderón Alzati and Cazés 1996).

In 1993, an even larger coalition of observer associations, NGOs, and citizen organizations, the *Alianza Cívica* (Civil Alliance) promoted campaigns of "civic education" in order to make voters aware of their constitutional rights. These campaigns proved highly efficient above all in those indigenous regions which traditionally had been subject to fraudulent practices and, since 1988, to violent clashes between local PRI and PRD committee members (Calderón Mólgora 1994, Viqueira and Sonnleitner 2000). The knowledge of specific and enforceable human rights, formally recognized in the 1917 Constitution, was converted into a means of empowerment by the entire local rural population, be they *mestizo* or indigenous, and a common process of *cuidadanización* (citizenship-making) mitigated long-standing tensions between those identifying with indigenist cultural promoters and those struggling for collective land tenure. Nevertheless, as will be shown below, in the indigenous regions *ciudadanización* became quickly ethnicized, and "ethnic citizenship" (de la Peña 1998) based on human rights became an integral part of the predominant struggle to re-conquer the community as a political entity (Kearney 1994: 61).

The Ethnization and Communalization of Indigenous Claims-Making

Despite this process of *ciudadanización*, which is perceivable in different indigenous regions of Mexico, it is ethnicity and not formal, individually defined citizenship that is the main issue at stake in current indigenous struggles. This is due to the coincidence at the beginning of the 1990s of three factors which together accelerated the "ethnic revival" in the indigenous regions of Mexico.

First, the local population's interest and participation in elections was not significant. Despite the re-integrated teachers' insistence on the importance of expressing dissidence through polls, an increasing number of their *comunero* neighbors were deeply concerned about the resulting internal polarization of the community. Following the spread of violence after the 1991 municipal elections, the indigenous population massively abandoned party politics as a channel of participation. Second, the dissident bilingual teachers and indigenous intellectuals actively participated in the controversial debate which arose over the multiethnic composition of Mexico and its indigenous peoples' right to claim ethnic and cultural difference. Highly aware of their public national impact, these intellectuals painstakingly elaborated a new ethnic discourse aimed at overcoming the traditionally localist and parochial limits of the indigenous identity horizon. Third, the decision taken by the Salinas de Gortari administration to modify the Mexican Constitution's historic Article 27, thereby canceling the agrarian reform process and promoting the individualization and privatization of communal land tenure, led external affairs representatives of indigenous villages to organize massive regional assemblies of communities keen on defending their communal land tenure.

The different local indigenous and peasant actors of the former movements all shared the feeling that they had been abused and exploited as easily mobilizable forces by the national urban and *mestizo* actors. Indigenous teachers and union leaders came to occupy lower ranks in the new opposition party structure, local authorities and *comuneros* were only addressed in election campaigns, and the few indigenous representatives who succeeded in attaining higher-level positions often lost their connection to their former constituencies. This process of disenchantment coincided with the governmental retreat from indigenismo and development policies, and old intermediaries disappeared without being substituted by new ones. Even for members of the indigenous intelligentsia, possible career options outside the indigenous regions were cancelled or limited. Neoliberal reforms widened the gap which had historically persisted between the state and the community. As a result, most of the mediators between the *mestizo* nation-state and the indigenous community were forced to chose between two mutually incompatible alternatives. They could rescue their career opportunities in far away urban centers, thus losing their traditional links and obligations in the community; or they could re-integrate into communal life at the expense of abandoning their external institutional loyalties.

The national and continental debates surrounding the Quincentennial of the "Columbus discovery"[21] temporarily postponed this decision for these mediators. The debates went beyond academic circles to encompass political issues of national importance. The question at stake was the identity and self-definition of Latin American nation-states, and their relation to the original peoples inhabiting their territories (Díaz Gómez 1992, Ce-Acatl 1992). For the first time since the externally enforced rupture of ANPIBAC and CNPI, a common platform emerged between indigenous intellectuals who remained loyal to the regime and worked in urban indigenist institutions, and returned indigenous dissidents who reintegrated into their communities (Baudot 1992, Sarmiento Silva 2001).

Although ephemeral, the resulting *Consejo Mexicano 500 Años de Resistencia Indígena* (The Mexican Council for 500 Years of Indigenous Resistance) succeeded in re-establishing a dialogue between pro-governmental and oppositional indigenous representatives. The common ground for their re-encounter was shared ethnicity. The re-indianización of the claims and struggles of semi-official as well as independent organizations encompassed both educational and cultural demands (promoted by the urban indigenous intelligentsia) and agrarian and political demands (promoted by independent indigenous-peasant leaders and local authorities). Diplomatically and skillfully postponing the debate over the priority of cultural-linguistic vs. communal-agrarian identity markers of Indian-ness, both factions agreed on the necessity of re-conquering political and legal spaces to define concrete expressions of indigenous ethnicity (Dietz 1999).

They immediately focused on the legal framework of the Mexican nation-state. As a result of their efforts, the Salinas de Gortari government was forced to include in Article 4 an official re-definition of Mexico as a nation "of pluri-cultural composition, which is originally sustained by its indigenous peoples" (*Poder Ejecutivo Federal* 1990: viii). This constitutional recognition forced the Mexican state to "respect the traditional rights and customs," but it did not specify what these rights were and how they would be enforced (ALAI 1990). Despite these legal shortcomings, the constitutional reform was a major success of the new indigenous platforms created during the Quincentennial debate, recognizing collective rights for the first time and introducing the criterion of "ethnic difference" as a source of rights (*Consejo Guerrerense 500 Años de Resistencia Indígena* 1993: 7).

Community and Communalism

Following the Quincentennial, however, confluences between officialist and dissident indigenous leaders fell off markedly. Given the general retreat of the state, the new indigenous intellectual elite lost its slowly conquered spheres of influence inside governmental indigenismo and its educational and cultural programs. As the indigenismo approach itself was increasingly marginalized in the face of neoliberal Mexican policies, a growing number of bilingual teachers, "culture promoters," civil servants, and trade unionists began to desert the *mestizo* project of the nation-state. Throughout the 1980s a new group of indigenous dissidents thus emerged, renouncing their loyalty to the official national project and consciously reintegrating into their communities of origin. They thus began a move away from an ethnicized discourse of re-indianization, and instead focused on customary local institutions such as the communal assembly and the cargo system of community service as new targets of political engagement (*Coalición de Pueblos Serranos Zapotecos y Chinantecos* 1994: 1).

Instead of introducing externally conceived structures such as political parties, unions, production co-operatives, or peasant organizations into their communities, the returned indigenous teachers, union, and party representatives struggled to recover their often lost status as *comuneros* by fulfilling their local *cargo* responsibilities. Many of the "returned intellectuals" concentrated on writing down customary law and fixing common procedures in *estatutos comunales* (communal statutes, Márquez Joaquín 1988). By reintegrating *cargos,* their main task was to avoid or diminish the internal divisions created by political parties or other institutional factionalism.

An example from a Triqui community in Oaxaca (San Andrés Chicahuaxtla 1994: 1–2) as well as other case studies of Purhépecha communities in Michoacán (Dietz 1999) illustrate that despite the tensions created by the intrusion of external agents of development into the indigenous community during the former indigenismo programs and their PRONASOL successors, the communal structure of indigenous peasants' daily life had been maintained. The nuclear family still constitutes the main unit of production, while the village community remains the main unit that shapes its inhabitants' principal economic, social, religious, and political activities. Following one's social status as a member of the community, acquired by birth or by marriage, the individual not only gains access to communal lands, but also becomes an integral part of the social and political life of the community.

According to customary law, the totality of the *comuneros* determines the village's political life. The communal assembly, in which traditionally only married males enjoy the right to speak and/or to vote, distributes the *cargos,* the local posts and offices. Nowadays, these ranks and posts, which frequently imply important amounts of personal spending, comprise both the surviving *cargos* of the civil-religious hierarchy intimately associated with the cult of the local patron saint, and the new administrative offices introduced in the course of the twentieth century by the nation-state, but re-appropriated by the local cargo logic.

The communal assembly, the local authorities designated by the assembly, and the "council of elders" (an institution of consultation and arbitration formed by senior villagers who already have passed through each rank in the cargo hierarchy) were all rediscovered, revitalized, and re-functionalized by the formerly "lost generation" of indigenous intellectuals who deserted from indigenismo and party politics. Thus, many teachers and civil servants once again started to participate in communal assemblies and hold local *cargos,* hoping to strengthen their communities against external political and institutional agents.

The activities carried out by this newly "re-communalized" indigenous intelligentsia took two different forms. In some villages, young teachers succeeded in occupying the main *cargos,* while elder peasant *comuneros* withdrew to the council of elders; the subsequent divergences and tensions between both groups were handled by the communal assembly, where the older generation still enjoyed considerable reputation and influence. In other cases, however, these initial confrontations resulted in an inter-generational division of work: while the traditional authorities, who were often recognized by their local neighbors as "natural leaders," maintained control over intra-local, domestic affairs, the younger teachers, civil servants, and students were invited to draw on their experiences in dealing with governmental institutions and bureaucratic administrations by dedicating themselves to the village's external relations. Thus, new informal *cargos* emerged to complement the traditional ones without necessarily defying their customary status inside the community.

Once the division of work between internal and external cargos was settled, the holders of the new and the old ranks and offices tended to collaborate intimately in their common goal to strengthen the community and regain its independence from outside agents. In order to achieve this goal, some fundamental traditions of local life were recovered in many villages: the *faena* or *tequio,* compulsory collective work employed especially in public works; the redistribution of economic surplus through financing of communal fiestas; and resurgence of the customary principle of equal participation of the different *barrios*[22] in any community affair.

These attempts to regain and revitalize ancient traditions have been complemented by the introduction of new elements of urban or *mestizo* origin. For example, a few years ago the teachers – many of whom are women or unmarried young men, thus lacking the comunero status – started struggling to enlarge the very concept of the comunero. In many indigenous communities they have succeeded in extending the rights and duties of political participation to the female and unmarried population of the village.

Another internal transformation initiated by the younger teachers affected the prevalent decision-making mechanism of the communal assembly. The customary principle of consensus, which in many villages successfully avoided intra-local polarizations along minority and majority votes and mitigated confrontations between "winners" and "losers," had the disadvantage of turning the assembly sessions into lengthy, tedious and unattractive events. Consequently, the teachers carried through an internal reform, according to which all minor issues are to be decided by the principle of voting and majority decisions, nearly always taken by acclamation. Nevertheless, all communal assemblies keep the principle of consensus for those decisions which affect central aspects of community life and whose enforcement – for example, against reluctant external agents – also requires participation of the whole village.

The (Re-)Appropriation of Community Development

Throughout the 1980s and 1990s, several indigenous communities abandoned their passive role as mere recipients of externally conceived development projects. As resistance against governmental measures which only benefited a tiny minority of the local population and against external intermediaries was growing in many communities, the local authorities felt it necessary to define their communities' real priorities, specifying their own project proposals including elaborate details on how to carry out and finance them. In order to cope with such a bureaucratic endeavor, the communal assemblies as well as local authorities once again turned to the younger returnees. Thus, in many communities the indigenous intelligentsia was entrusted with the task of writing down the development priorities fixed in the local assembly. As these project proposals specified not only the requested external resources, but also the resources contributed by the community itself through collective *faenas* or *tequios*, the assembly and the elected authorities had to approve the entire project draft before submitting them to external development agencies. As a result of this cyclical process, the community started to participate intimately and permanently in the global procedure of developing a self-managed project. The success or failure of these self-managed projects depended on the tense and often difficult collaboration between the communal cargos, the council of elders, the young teachers and/or agronomists. All these different local actors recognized that the development of their own projects was much more laborious than simply "waiting for the expert from the capital." Nevertheless, a variety of different arts, forestry, educational, and cultural projects in several communities and regions[23] have shown that the community's intimate participation in a project's elaboration will decisively increase its dedication to the project.

Despite these first steps toward recovering control over communal development initiatives, two major problems cannot be solved by this new type of self-directed local development. First, the community lacks formal recognition as a legal entity needed to start, plan, execute or evaluate any communal project. Even those communities that de facto act autonomously cannot officially negotiate their project policies with government or NGO agencies. Second, the recent success of communal development projects threatens to envigorate localist and isolationist tendencies, subduing the pan-indigenous identities claimed at the national and even continental level.

Agrarian Counter-reform as a Cancellation of the Social Contract

The structural handicaps of community-centered political action became immediately evident during the governmental initiative to reform Article 27 of the Mexican Constitution (Moguel 1992, Piñar Alvarez 2002). Allowing the division, marketing, and privatization of both communal and ejidal lands, this agrarian "counter-reform" was perceived in nearly all indigenous regions as a unilateral cancellation of the original *contrat social* signed between the communities and the nation-state in the aftermath of the Mexican Revolution. As the counter-reform promotes and encourages the commercialization of collective land tenure, the territorial basis of the indigenous community was threatened (Stanford 1994). This radical shift in state-community relations was countered by local and regional responses, in which coalitions of communities declared the sovereignty, autonomy, and historical rights of the indigenous community and rejected the changes to Article 27 (Nación Purhépecha 1991: 3).

In this environment of generalized concern, anxiety, and upheaval, the re-integrated indigenist culture brokers and intellectuals suddenly gained vital importance as external liaison cargos among communities in a given region as well as in relation to non-indigenous actors. Information campaigns were organized with former peasant advisers and leaders, workshops were held with the support of rural development NGOs, and press conferences were organized with human rights lawyers and activists. These massive mobilizations were initiated by, but not limited to, the indigenous communities. As the privatization of land tenure was implemented by the Salinas de Gortari administration in conjunction with the abrupt liberalization of all agricultural markets – as part of the preparatory measures for Mexico's integration into the North American Free Trade Association (NAFTA) – even the well-integrated *campesinado medio* was direclty affected by the resulting drop in commodity prices and competition with cheap imports coming from highly subsidized US agriculture (Salazar Peralta 1994, Foley 1995). Consequently, and parallel to the communities' movement against privatization, a movement of bankrupt producers appeared in formerly flourishing agricultural regions of central, western and northern Mexico (Concheiro Bórquez 1993, UNORCA 1993). Even though the socio-economic positions as well as the identities of these heterogeneous ethnic and political actors were completely diverse and often distanced considerably from one another, most of them sought fulfillment of the "Revolution's promises." Thus, the mythic figure of Emiliano Zapata re-appeared at the turn of the century.

Zapatismo and the Indigenous Issue

The broad range of movements reacting to the unilateral neoliberal cancellation of the heritage of the Mexican Revolution is illustrated by the processes of civil society organization unleashed by the armed uprising carried out in southern Mexico in 1994 by one of the new community-based indigenous organizations, the *Ejército Zapatista de Liberación Nacional* (Zapatista Army of National Liberation). *El México profundo* (deep Mexico), the indigenous, rural Mexico, in and through which the ancient Mesoamerican civilization persists (Bonfil Batalla 1987), suddenly returned to the national and even international political scene.

On the symbolically chosen date of January 1, 1994, the start of Mexico's integration into NAFTA, the previously unknown EZLN occupied four district towns in Chiapas, declared war on the federal government and demanded "liberty, democracy and justice" for all Mexicans. Although the administration of Carlos Salinas de Gortari, fearing a capital flight of foreign investments and a subsequent failure of its outward-oriented economic modernization project, insisted on the Central American origin and locally confined characteristics of the "EZLN phenomenon," it soon proved to be a phenomenon that was entirely Mexican in nature. The neoliberal economic policies driving the uprising affected all of rural Mexico (Burbach & Rosset 1994). Furthermore, the zapatista claims targeted the country as a whole, not only the Chiapas highlands or the Selva Lacandona (the Lacandon Jungle). In its internal structure and discourse, the new armed movement reflected its rooting in a broad range of peasant and indigenous movements (Benjamin 1996, Legorreta Díaz 1998). Accordingly, they were quickly picked up and adopted by organizations and movements from other rural and urban regions as well (Nash 1997).

The new zapatista uprising culminated rural Mexico's coming of age and its emancipation from traditional state and party paternalism. In the contemporary national and international context, the subsequent clash between *el México transnacional* (transnational Mexico), an increasingly liberalized and globalized economy and politics on the one hand, and the re-appearance of *el México profundo*, a rising, mostly ethnically defined social mobilization on the other hand (Zermeño 1994), has created a dynamic which is focused on the struggle over the control of rural Mexico's natural and cultural resources. Thus, the question of local and regional sovereignty and autonomy has become central to the country's political agenda, constituting a turning point in the history of indigenous movements in Mexico.

The "EZLN Phenomenon"

The claims made by the EZLN since its public appearance in 1994 have been dual in nature. On the one hand, they are concerned with the most basic infrastructure necessary to cover the land, housing, health, and education needs of a particular zone of the Selva Lacandona, a region of recent colonization by Tzeltal, Tzotzil, Mam, Tojolabal, and Chol peasants who are landless or who had been expelled from their land in the Chiapas highlands (Ce-Acatl 1994). On the other hand, the political demands issued by the zapatistas are limited to the fulfillment and respect for the Mexican Constitution of 1917, a rather defensive claim, which nevertheless would be revolutionary in its de facto consequences for democratization of rural Mexico as a whole (Dietz 1994).

Thus, the defense of *México profundo* converges with formal democratization of the political and legal system in EZLN's agenda. In their demands, the heritage of classical indigenous and peasant movements is combined with the main features of the new citizens' and NGO movements of the 1990s (Rubio 1994). The EZLN spokespersons always emphasize that their own demands are only part of a broader range of citizenship claims, which should be taken up and refueled by other rural as well as urban movements. This pluralist approach, which is the most strikingly innovative feature of the zapatistas as compared to other, "classic" Central American guerrilla movements, culminated in a *Convención Nacional Democrática* (CND – National Democratic Convention), a massively attended assembly of social movements invited to the Lacandon forest in August 1994 (CND 1994).

Both the CND and the establishment in December 1994 of an alternative "Transition Governor in Rebellion" for the state of Chiapas – promoted by the EZLN, human rights NGOs, faith-based liberation theology groups – definitively challenged the notion of "historical avantgarde," a defining feature of the Cuban and Central American guerrillas of the second half of the twentieth century (Dietrich 1994, Esteva 1994a, 1994b). Programmatic plurality thus corresponded with a plurality of internal forms of organization and action (EZLN 1994: 149).

The basic difference with classical guerrillas and the most outstanding commonality with other new ethno-regional indigenous movements lies in the EZLN's organizational structure. Apart from the classic military distinction between trained professional soldiers and the civil population, the EZLN is comprised of a peasant militia which effectively functions as *bases zapatistas de apoyo* (zapatista bases of support) thus allowing for close co-ordination between its military and political branch.[24] The civil and political branch, which has been in charge of all political decisions and negotiations with government representatives sent to the conflict zone since January 1994, is structured according to the pluri-ethnic composition of the Lacandon region. The communal assembly forms the basic organizational unit, which sends delegates to the assembly of all communities of the same ethnic group, which in turn sends representatives to the regional assembly. The highest level political unit, the *Comité Clandestino Revolucionario Indígena* (Clandestine Revolutionary Indigenous Committee), consists of one representative from each of the ethnic groups participating in the zapatista movement.

EZLN

Ejército Zapatista de Liberación Nacional

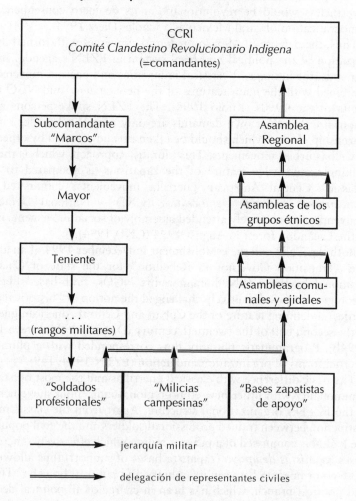

Figure 1.4   The Internal Structure of the EZLN (Dietz 1999:403)

This dual structure reflects the origins of the EZLN as a training and co-ordination group created by different communal self-defense units against external intruders threatening the communal and ejidal lands. Particularly threatening were the *guardias blancas* (white guards), the paramilitary groups maintained by the landlords of cattle and coffee estates, whose expansionist tendencies were stimulated by the government's land privatization policy. The common resistance against these forces has grown since the 1980s in the form of village defense units and small and isolated guerrilla groups. Re-functionalized as military training units, the EZLN abandoned their original avant-garde approach, and external members of the nascent EZLN such as Subcomandante Marcos were integrated and subordinated to the already existing informal political structures of the indigenous communities.[25]

The Widespread Emergence of Ethno-Regional Movements

The political structure of the EZLN has evolved simultaneously with and parallel to the new indigenous movements appearing since 1991 in other regions of Mexico. In several regions the defensive, reactive nature of the communities' responses to official privatization efforts have been transformed into innovative, pro-active mechanisms. The communities have undertaken a similar process of regionalization in order to overcome their habitual political isolation (Dietz 1999). The starting point for the emergence of a more permanent regional convergence of the communities' interests has been formed once again by the local indigenous intellectuals, commissioned by their respective local assemblies to represent their communities and their projects to external agents. Together with some experienced local authorities, these returnees have built up an informal network of relations which have led to the establishment of a "coalition" of the different communities' shared interests. During the periodic assemblies held at the regional level, the local authorities and their external affairs representatives join the nascent network, exchange their main problems and claims, and discuss possible solutions.

These regional assemblies proceed in a ritualized and diplomatic if often tense manner. Above all in Michoacán, Oaxaca, and Veracruz, ancient conflicts persist over the boundaries of communal lands. Consequently, during the regional sessions the generation of younger teachers have tried to stress the region's common features and downplay local particularities, whereas the older cargos tend to highlight their localism and their differences from neighboring communities. As a compromise, in this first phase of the regional network the assemblies have limited themselves to formulation of shared concerns and claims *vis-à-vis* government bureaucracies, development agencies, and NGOs. These regional assemblies are retrospectively interpreted as the founding moment of an entirely new type of ethno-regional organization. *Ireta P'orhecha / Nación Purhépecha* (Purhépecha Nation) in Michoacán, the *Consejo de Pueblos Nahuas del Alto Balsas* (Council of The Nahua Peoples of Alto Basos) in Guerrero and the Oaxacan organizations *Asamblea de Autoridades Mixes* (Assembly of Mixes Leaders) and *Movimiento de Unificación de la Lucha Triqui* (Unification Movement of the Triqui Struggle) are examples of this new type of organization, which rises from an informal coalition of communities that declare themselves sovereign before a nation-state which defies the customary essence of the community's self-definition.

As communal sovereignty remains unassailable by regional organizations, they are still considered to be merely inter-communal alliances, which are not allowed to create centralized agencies beyond the regional assembly of local representatives and its ad hoc commissions of delegations appointed by the assembly. The rotating and decentralized organization avoids the consolidation of internal hierarchies which would be easily co-optable and/or repressible by government institutions. Moreover, the permanent rotation of ranks and assembly locations strives to promote and strengthen a comprehensive ethnic identity that overcomes the limitations of communal identities.

The regional organizations suffer from the same central problem as its member communities: they lack an officially recognized legal status. Accordingly, their range of activities is limited to two different spheres. On the one hand, the regional coalition continues to function as a catalyst for local claims. The assemblies held in different communities bring together a variety of demands – i.e. the enlargement of a primary school, the drilling of a well for drinking water, the extension of electricity, or the recognition of communal boundaries – and present them on a common platform to the institutions concerned with each of the respective demands. The obvious advantage of this procedure is the collective capacity of an entire region, and not only a single community, to counter governmental and bureaucratic negligence or unwillingness to solve local problems which have worsened in the era of neoliberal retreat. In order to put pressure on the responsible agencies, the regional assembly's measures include massive "visits" to the institution's headquarters, press conferences and rallies in the respective state capital or in Mexico City, and the blockading of vital roads surrounding the indigenous region. It is due to this explicitly political practice that the younger bilingual teachers have succeeded in taking up the mentioned *ciudadanización* process, merging it with ethno-regional demands, and thus stimulating a switch in attitude among their neighbors from submissively asking the government for help to actively claiming rights they have as Mexican citizens *vis-à-vis* "their" nation-state. The formerly "poor indians" are thus becoming self-conscious citizens struggling for their legitimate demands.

In addition to jointly requesting governmental development initiatives, in the last few years a new terrain for collective action has emerged. As the majority of agencies have retreated from rural development, the regional coalitions have been forced by their member communities to expand their range of actions to include the elaboration of projects and the search for financial support. The communal assemblies and authorities prefer to pass on these new tasks to the regional assembly and its specialized commissions in order to take advantage of the professional and technical know-how existing in the respective region as a whole and not only in their own community. Thus, the regional organizations are being transformed into new and influential agents of development, carrying out such projects as the establishment of supralocal craft training and trading centers, the creation of bilingual and bicultural secondary schools for agro-forestry, and the promotion and recovery of family-based subsistence agriculture.[26]

The Struggle for Territorial Autonomy

Although their economic and social impacts have been limited so far, these pioneering regional projects, which are jointly self-managed by representatives of different indigenous communities, are very important politically. Given that organizations no longer confine themselves to the articulation of specific demands directed toward the state, and begin implementing their own development projects as coalitions of communities, the respective state governments tried to counteract this potentially new concentration of power. However, since their potential to recover their protagonist role in rural development is limited by the prevailing neoliberal strategy, the state and federal administrations were finally forced, after massive mobilizations carried out throughout 1993 and 1994, to recognize the regional indigenous organizations as legitimate (if informal) representatives of the local population.

Regional coalitions are still striving for official legal recognition by state agencies, which would not only entitle them to obtain governmental as well as non-governmental financial support for their projects, but also would imply access to channels of participation inside the remaining state-dominated and indigenist institutions. In the long run, this process of consolidation is likely to result in the establishment of a new, intermediate level of regional administration between municipal government and the state level. This regional council of self-administration formed by all indigenous communities of a particular area, however, requires constitutional reform, since the political project of autonomy aims to explic- itly legalize two already existing actors: community and regional organization.

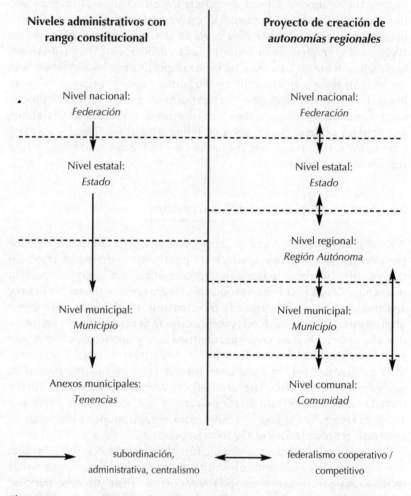

**LA *COMUNIDAD INDÍGENA*
EN LA JERARQUÍA ADMINISTRATIVA MEXICANA**

**Niveles administrativos con
rango constitucional**

**Proyecto de creación de
*autonomías regionales***

Nivel nacional:
Federación

Nivel nacional:
Federación

Nivel estatal:
Estado

Nivel estatal:
Estado

Nivel regional:
Región Autónoma

Nivel municipal:
Municipio

Nivel municipal:
Municipio

Anexos municipales:
Tenencias

Nivel comunal:
Comunidad

→ subordinación,
administrativa, centralismo

↔ federalismo cooperativo /
competitivo

Figure 1.5   Community and Autonomy Inside the Mexican State (Dietz 1999: 406)

Zapatismo as National Confluence of Ethno-Regional Movements

Although these regional coalitions have emerged since 1992 in different indigenous areas of Mexico, the debate on regional territorial autonomy and constitutional reforms was definitely boosted by the appearance of the EZLN in 1994 and by the subsequent process of negotiations over the legal reforms necessary to recognize, protect and develop indigenous rights (CNI 1994: 1). While the programmatic proposals of the 1992 anti-Quincentennial campaign had been formulated without the involvement of local and regional indigenous movements, the 1994 negotiations between the EZLN and the government prompted a swift process of national convergence, bringing together the ethno-regional coalitions of communities that had been formed in the previous years. Immediately after the armed uprising in Chiapas, a *Consejo Estatal de Organizaciones Indígenas y Campesinas de Chiapas* (CEOIC – State Council of Indigenous and Peasant Organizations of Chiapas) was created under the auspices of the *Frente Independiente de Pueblos Indios* (FIPI – Independent Front of Indigenous Peoples), an umbrella organization which had been leading the above-mentioned struggle for reforming Article 4 of the Mexican Constitution.[27]

Both the FIPI and the newly created *Asamblea Nacional Indígena Plural por la Autonomía* (ANIPA – National Assembly of Indigenous Pluralities for Autonomy) started elaborating a detailed proposal for amending the Mexican Constitution in order to legalize the autonomous entities of indigenous self-government, which were already being created above all in the zapatista-controlled region of Chiapas.[28] Nevertheless, the main obstacle to these national initiatives still stems from their 1992 origins. They are promoted in Mexico City by dissident indigenous intellectuals and scholars who are well integrated into the national political arena, most of them belonging to the PRD opposition party, but who lack direct contact to the new regional movements.

This obstacle was overcome during the EZLN–government negotiations in San Andrés Sacam Ch'en, convened by the new president Ernesto Zedillo (1994–2000) and for which the zapatista negotiators successfully summoned the entire spectrum of new indigenous organizations, intellectuals, and scholars as part of their negotiation team. In order to prepare for the subsequent rounds of these negotiations centered on the recognition of indigenous rights, the first *Convención Nacional Indígena* (CNI – National Indigenous Convention) was held in Tlapa, in the mountains of Guerrero, in December 1994 (CNI 1994). Since then, three large National Indigenous Congresses have been held in different regions, thus transforming the CNI into the most representative forum of indigenous organizations currently in Mexico.

Toward the Recognition of Indigenous Rights

According to the ethno-regional organizations represented at the CNI, regional autonomy would not mean territorial segregation, but rather a redefinition of the Mexican nation-state and its relationship with indigenous communities (CNI 1994: 3). In several local and regional assemblies, local authorities warned the external affairs representatives that autonomy begins at the communal level and that the future regionalization of local autonomy must not relieve the nation-state of its development obligations in the indigenous regions (Dietz 1999).

Since the first CNI and the *Diálogos* (Dialogues) of Sacam Ch'en in 1995, two positions emerged among indigenous movements regarding the question of autonomy. On the one hand, local authorities, urban social movement activists and even some INI representatives at the San Andrés negotiations favored a model of territorial autonomy that recognizes the community as the basic unit of political organization and the legalization and recognition of indigenous customary law.[29] While some urban activists aimed to extend the notion of community to their local struggles for recovering control of barrios such as Tepito in Mexico City, most advocates of communal autonomy limited their claims to indigenous regions, justifying these claims on the basis of International Labor Office Convention 169 on "Indigenous and Tribal Peoples in Independent Countries," signed by the Mexican government in 1990, which ensures territorial rights to indigenous populations (OIT 1992). As customary law is only practiced locally, they argued that regional-level autonomy would create a legal and political vacuum which could easily be exploited by external actors such as political parties.

On the other hand, many activists of the new ethno-regional coalitions, as well as a few professional indigenous politicians and deputies, prefer a broader reform which would introduce communal and regional autonomy into Mexico's current federal structure (cf. figure 1.5). In their view, limiting the territorial dimension of indigenous self-government to the local sphere would only serve to extend the colonial heritage (Consejo Guerrerense 500 Años de Resistencia Indígena *et al.* 1994: 3–4). Thus, they advocated that the ethno-regional coalition of communities should evolve toward a regional council of self-government that would be competent in administrative, political, and cultural terms and which would allocate and supervise any resources invested in a given indigenous region.

These regions would not be defined through strictly ethnic criteria, since it is clear that in Mexico there is no region inhabited solely by indigenous populations. Therefore, the ANIPA assembly promotes a definition and delimitation of *regiones autónomas pluriétnicas* which would encompass *mestizo* municipalities as well (ANIPA 1995). These regions would be part of a broader structure of political and administrative decentralization.[30] As said before, this view invokes ILO Convention 169 as its international legal basis; together with the Draft Declaration of the Rights of Indigenous Peoples, which is being elaborated and negotiated through the Geneva-based United Nations Working Group on Indigenous Peoples, and asserts indigenous peoples' right to territorial integrity (Softestad 1993, Concha Malo 1995).

This divergence in the definition of autonomy and its levels and territorial extension – local vs. regional – as well as its "sovereign" subject – the community vs. the indigenous people or ethnic group[31] – was frequently used by government representatives to block the negotiation process lasting from 1994 to 1996 and culminating in the official signature of the San Andrés Peace Accords on February 16, 1996 (Ce-Acatl 1995, 1996; CDHMAPJ 2000). The main obstacle to successfully implementing the San Andrés accords did not arise from the participating indigenous actors, who were flexible enough to reach a series of agreements with the *Comisión Parlamentaria de Concordia y Pacificación* (COCOPA – the Parliamentary Commission of Concordance and Pacification), the multi-party parliamentary commission which was officially commissioned by the Zedillo administration to negotiate the details of the pending agreements related to "indigenous rights and culture." These agreements, presented in a proposal in 1996 to include both options of autonomy, were accepted by the EZLN and by the indigenous organizations, but were rejected by the Zedillo government (Pérez Ruiz 2001).

As a consequence of this official blockade strategy, during the course of which some reforms were unilaterally introduced in several state constitutions through 2000, the EZLN rejected any further negotiations with the Zedillo government, which then tried to modify the Mexican Constitution without seeking consent from the indigenous organizations. This strategy was interrupted by the defeat suffered by the PRI in the 2000 presidential elections. The current president Vicente Fox, who for the first time is not from the PRI but from the conservative and pro-business *Partido de Acción Nacional*, (PAN – National Action Party), succeeded in imposing a constitutional reform and an indigenous law, both of which remain far short of the San Andrés accords and the COCOPA proposal. The territorial rights guaranteed by ILO 169 are not translated into legal standards and procedures, and the indigenous community is not recognized as a legal entity of public law but only as an entity of "public interest" (FIDH 2002). In response, the EZLN together with a wide range of regional indigenous organizations staged a massive "March of Indigenous Dignity," which expressed the ever widening gap between the state and the indigenous communities (Gabbert 2001). During the Third National Indigenous Congress held in the Purhépecha community of Nurío, Michoacán, in March 2001, the common struggle for legal recognition was jointly asserted (CNI 2002).

Conclusion

In their struggle to de-colonize local and regional politics and regain territorial, cultural, and political self-determination, the new indigenous actors exhibit three key features of what may be called the contemporary re-shaping of the "phenomenology" of modernity:

1   the process of re-ethnicization of identities, a process which is not confined to revivalist movements invoking a pre-colonial past, but which includes contemporary phenomena of "ethnogenesis" (Roosens 1989);
2   a parallel process of unlocking once relatively self-confined traditional cultures in light of market globalization. These contemporary "hybrid cultures" are not victimizable as simple epi-phenomena of a globalized economy, but constitute vital resources for emerging new social actors (García Canclini 1989a, 2000; Kearney 1996); and
3   a common tendency to create, devolve and/or conquer new intermediate social and political spaces, increasingly articulated on a regional level (Díaz-Polanco 1992).

The confluence of these key features of the contemporary face of modernization means that the Mexican and Latin American indigenous movements represent the complexities of the intermixing of ethnogenesis, cultural hybridity, and regionalism (Dietz 1999). The transition from local to regional and national activities and mobilizations currently taking place illustrates an important turning-point in the history of Mexican indigenous struggles, leaving behind the historical isolation of the indigenous community. The rooting in specific local problems, on the one hand, and the expansion toward national organizations associated with zapatismo, on the other hand, will in the long run force any Mexican government to recognize the individual and collective rights of their indigenous citizens. The transition from particular claims – be they educational, linguistic and cultural, or agrarian and economic in orientation – to the general re-negotiation of the *contrat social* between the community and the nation-state has proved decisive to overcoming old divisions between ethnic and peasant priorities, generating not only a completely new political agenda, but also an innovative political actor.

New ethno-regional organizations, ranging from *Nación Purhépecha* and the *Consejo Guerrerense 500 Años de Resistencia Indígena* to the EZLN itself, are achieving the integration of both "tradition" and "modernity," and of communalist and regionalist cultural revivalism and nationally and even internationally experienced cultural hybridity. By reducing ancient inter-communal conflicts over boundaries and consciously promoting an ethno-regional identity beyond local particularities, the regional organization manages to integrate the rural population. Moreover, the community coalition's political activities, particularly its insistence on the nation-state's accountability and responsibility toward its indigenous citizens and its struggle to establish regional councils of self-government, succeeds in strengthening indigenous participation in national affairs as Mexican citizens. Hence, it is paradoxically an independent and overtly dissident indigenous movement that achieves what indigenismo had been expected to achieve during the last century of exogenously imposed "development": an equal participation and integration of the indigenous communities and their inhabitants not only into the nation-state – now reluctantly redefining itself as a pluricultural hybrid – but also into multi-ethnic Mexican society.

Notes

This chapter presents the results of ethnographic research carried out in the Western Mexican state of Michoacán (cf. Dietz 1999), which is contrasted with indigenous movements from other Mexican states such as Chiapas, Oaxaca, Veracruz and Guerrero.

1 The term "indigenous movements" refers to any organization which is shaped by a majority of indigenous leaders, members and/or followers; thus, according to its respective programmatic emphasis, some indigenous movements define themselves as agrarian organizations (as part of peasant movements), while others present their activities and struggles in ethnocultural terms (as *Nahua, Purhépecha* etc. movements).
2 Cf. Maihold (1986), Vasconcelos and Carballo (1989), Esteva-Fabregat (1995) and Wade (1997); the Spanish peninsular roots of this dichotomy are analyzed by Stallaert (1998).
3 A comparative study of the changing and conflictive relations between nation-states and communities in the nineteenth century is provided by Reina (1997).
4 These processes are detailed in Lomnitz-Adler (1995), Mallon (1995), Fowler (1996) and Guardino (1996).
5 Cf. Mendieta y Núñez (1946), Tutino (1986) and Rugeley (2002).
6 Details on the local actors and their role in the Revolution are provided by Tutino (1986), Taylor (1993) and Joseph and Nugent (1994), whereas P. H. Smith (1981) analyzes the formation and regeneration of national political elites in Mexico.
7 Warman (1985) and Knight (1986, 1997); see figure 1.1, chapter 2, present volume.
8 *Mestizaje* as a project of "anti-imperialist" national identity was first expressed in 1892 during the *IV Centenario* of the Colón discoveries; from this date on, the official hispanism of the "Day of the Race" starts being redefined and re-appropriated by a still weak national actor, the "integrantes de la raza cósmica que luchan contra el materialismo del Norte" (Rodríguez 1994: 161).
9 Cf. Becker (1995), Lomnitz-Aler (1995) and Mallon (1995). As illustrated by Adler-Lomnitz and Lomnitz Adler (1994), the symbolic importance of the negotiated and ritualized character of the relations between the Mexican state and the indigenous communities is even maintained in the presidential election campaigns of the neoliberal era.
10 For details on the systems of *cargos* and their often diverging

anthropological interpretations, cf. Carrasco (1961, 1990), Chance and Taylor (1985), Korsbaek (1992) and the monographic volume edited by Korsbaek & Topete (2000).

11   A general appraisal of Mexican *indigenismo*, its continuities and discontinuities is offered in Dietz (1995).

12   For illustrative case studies, cf. Köhler (1975), Strug (1975), Friedlander (1977), Medina (1983), Bonfil Batalla (1988) and Dietz (1995).

13   For the following, cf. CNPI (1980), Barre (1982, 1983), López Velasco (1989) and Garduño Cervantes (1993).

14   For details on this organization, cf. ANPIBAC (1979), Hernández Hernández and Gabriel (1979), CNPI and ANPIBAC (1982) and Barre (1983).

15   General aspects of these peasant movements are analyzed by Reitmeier (1990) and Bartra (1985), while details on the UCEZ are presented by Zepeda Patterson (1984), UCEZ (1984) and Zárate Hernández (1991, 1992) and on the OCEZ are offered by Marion Singer (1987) and Harvey (1990, 1998).

16   Fernández and Rello (1990) analyze in detail the legal implications of these new modalities of peasant organization.

17   For details on UNORCA, cf. Marion Singer (1989), Hernández (1992) and Concheiro Bórquez (1993), and for the sectoral organizations cf. García (1991), Alatorre *et al.* (1992), Valencia (1994) and Varese (1994).

18   Cf. Canabal Cristiani (1991), Cornelius, Craig, and Fox (1994), Fox and Aranda (1996) and Piñar Alvarez (1999, 2002).

19   Cf. Harvey (1990), Cornelius (1996) and Dietz (1999).

20   For details, cf. Bartra (1992), Durand Ponte (1994), Amnistía Internacional (1995), Ramírez Casillas (1995).

21   The international political and scholarly debate on the Quincentenary is presented and analyzed by Summerhill and Williams (2000).

22   These *barrios* are intralocal residence units into which the community is divided and whose members share a common, sublocal identity and – apart from the local patron saint – worship an own *barrio* saint; for ethnographic examples, cf. Dietz (1999).

23   For the Purhépecha region of Michoacán, these self-managed projects of community development are analyzed by Dietz (1999),

24   Cf. figure 1.4; the subordination of the military under the political structure is symbollically expressed in the terms used for each of its highest ranks: *subcomandante* for the military one and *comandante* for the political and civil one.

25   Summarized from Collier (1994), EZLN (1994, 1995, 1997), Rovira (1994), Tello Díaz (1995), Castells, Yazawa, and Kiselyova (1996), Dietz (1999), Le Bot (1997), Legorreta Díaz (1998), Nugent (1998), Gabbert (1999) and Gómez (2002).

26   These projects from the Purhépecha region are detailed in Dietz (1999).

27   Cf. CEOIC (1994), Dietz (1994), Harvey (1994, 1998), Moguel (1994), Ruiz Hernández (1994) and ANIPA (1995).

28   Cf. ANIPA (1995), Díaz-Polanco (1995), López y Rivas (1995), Burguete Cal y Mayor (1999a) and Ruiz Hernández (1999).

29   Cf. Esteva (1994a, 1994b), López Bárcenas (1994) and Dietz (1999); the notion of indigenous customary law is analyzed and discussed by Stavenhagen (1988), Gómez (1993) and López Bárcenas (2002).

30   The close relation between proceses of decentralization and new regional

indigenous autonomy movements is illustrated by Burguete Cal y Mayor (1999b) and by Cornelius, Eisenstadt, and Hindley (1999), who offer regional case studies from Oaxaca, Guerrero and Chiapas.

31 Stavenhagen (1999) provides details on the different definitions and concepts of autonomy.

References

Adler-Lomnitz, Larissa and Claudio Lomnitz Adler. 1994. Estado y Etnicidad: Rito y Negociación en la Campaña Presidencial de 1988. *Ibero-Amerikanisches Archiv* 20 (1–2): 53–81.

Aguado López, Eduardo. 1989. *El conflicto social en el campo mexicano, 1976–1982: la lucha por el espacio de reproducción.* Toluca: Colegio Mexiquense.

Aguirre Beltrán, Gonzalo. 1991 [1953]. *Formas de gobierno indígena.* México: FCE.

——. 1992 [1973]. *Teoría y práctica de la educación indígena.* México: FCE.

ALAI. 1990. Por una reforma integral: entrevista a Mayolo Olivera, coordinador de organización del Frente Independiente de Pueblos Indios de México (FIPI). ALAI 132: 22–4.

Alatorre, Gerardo *et al.* 1992. *La empresa social forestal: tercer taller de análisis de experiencias forestales.* México: ERA.

Amnistía Internacional. 1995. *Violaciones de los derechos humanos en México: el reto de los noventa.* London – Madrid: Amnistía Internacional.

Anderson, Benedict. 1988. Afterword. *Ethnicities and Nations: Processes of Interethnic Relations in Latin America, Southeast Asia, and the Pacific,* R. Guidieri, F. Pellizzi, and S. J. Tambiah eds. Houston: Rothko Chapel.

ANIPA. 1995. *Proyecto de iniciativa para la creación de las regiones autónomas.* México: Asamblea Nacional Indígena Plural por la Autonomía.

ANPIBAC. 1979. *I Seminario Nacional de Educación Bilingüe-Bicultural: fundamentos, instrumentos de investigación y agenda de trabajo.* México: Aries.

Astorga Lira, Enrique. 1988. Jornaleros agrícolas y sus organizaciones: notas para buscar un camino. *Las Sociedades Rurales hoy,* J. Zepeda Patterson, ed. Zamora: Colegio de Michoacán.

Barre, Marie-Chantal. 1982. Indigenisme et organisations indiennes au Mexique. *Amérique Latine* 10: 21–8.

——. 1983. *Ideologías indigenistas y movimientos indios.* México: Siglo XXI.

Bartra, Armando. 1985. *Los herederos de Zapata: movimientos campesinos posrevolucionarios en México, 1920–1980.* México: Era.

——. 1992. La ardua construcción del ciudadano (notas sobre el movimiento cívico y la lucha gremial). *Autonomía y nuevos sujetos sociales en el desarrollo rural,* J. Moguel, C. Botey, and L. Hernández, eds. México: Siglo XXI.

Basave Benítez, Agustín. 1992. *México mestizo: análisis del nacionalismo mexicano en torno a la mestizofilia de Andrés Molina Enríquez.* México: FCE.

Baudot, Georges. 1992. Chronologie pour l'émergence d'une organisation amérindienne, politique et culturelle, au Mexique. *Caravelle* 59: 7–17.

Becker, Marjorie. 1987. El cardenismo y la búsqueda de una ideología campesina. *Relaciones* 29: 5–22.

——. 1995. *Setting the Virgin on Fire: Lázaro Cárdenas, Michoacán peasants, and the Redemption of the Mexican revolution.* Berkeley: University of California Press.

Benjamin, Thomas. 1996. *Rich Land, a Poor People: Politics and Society in Modern Chiapas*. Albuquerque: University of New Mexico Press.

Bennholdt-Thomsen, Verónica. 1976. *Zur Bestimmung des Indio: Die soziale, ökonomische und kulturelle Stellung der Indios in Mexiko*. Berlin: Gebr.-Mann-Verlag.

Bonfil Batalla, Guillermo.1987. *México profundo: una civilización negada*. México: CIESAS – SEP.

——. 1988. ¿Problemas conyugales?: una hipótesis sobre las relaciones del estado y la antropología social en México. *Boletín de Antropología Americana* 17: 51–61.

Burbach, Roger and Peter Rosset. 1994. *Chiapas and the Crisis of Mexican Agriculture*. Oakland: Institute for Food and Development Policy.

Burguete Cal and Araceli Mayor. 1999a. Empoderamiento indígena: tendencias autonómicas en la región Altos de Chiapas. *México: experiencias de autonomía indígena*, A. Burguete Cal and Mayor, eds. Copenhague: IWGIA.

——.1999b *México: experiencias de autonomía indígena*. Copenhague: IWGIA.

Calderón Alzati, Enrique and Daniel Cazés. 1996. *Las elecciones presidenciales de 1994*. México: La Jornada – UNAM.

Calderón Mólgora, Marco Antonio. 1994. *Violencia política y elecciones municipales en Michoacán*. Zamora – México: Colegio de Michoacán – Instituto Mora.

Calvo Pontón, Beatriz and Laura Donnadieu Aguado. 1992. *Una educación ¿indígena, bilingüe y bicultural?: Capacitación diferencial de los maestros mazahuas*. México: CIESAS.

Canabal Cristiani, Beatriz. 1983. El movimiento campesino en Sonora (1970–1976). *Revista Mexicana de Ciencias Políticas y Sociales*, 29 (113–14): 67–98.

——. 1991. Las organizaciones campesinas y la política del nuevo gobierno. *Cuadernos Agrarios N.E.* 1: 11–22.

Cárdenas, Lázaro. 1978 [1940]. Discurso del Presidente de la República en el Primer Congreso Indigenista Interamericano, Pátzcuaro, Mich., 14 de abril de 1940. *Palabras y documentos públicos de Lázaro Cárdenas 1928–1974*, vol. I: 402–5. México: Siglo XXI.

Carrasco, Pedro. 1961. The Civil-Religious Hierarchy in Mesoamerican Communities: Pre-hispanic background and colonial development. *American Anthropologist* 63: 483–97.

——.1990. Sobre el origen histórico de la jerarquía político-ceremonial de las comunidades indígenas. *Historia, antropología, política: homenaje a Angel Palerm I*, M. Suárez , ed. México: Alianza Mexicana – UIA.

Castells, Manuel, Shujiro Yazawa, and Emma Kiselyova. 1996. Insurgents Against the Global Order: a comparative analysis of the Zapatists in Mexico, the American Militia and Japan's Aum Shinrikyo. *Berkeley Journal of Sociology*, 40: 21–60.

CDHMAPJ. 2000. *Derecho de los pueblos indígenas: experiencias, documentos y metodologías*. México: Centro de Derechos Humanos Miguel Agustín Pro Juárez, A.C.

Ce-Acatl. 1992. Crónica de un telar multicolor. *Ce-Acatl* 36/37: 3–19.

——. 1994. Los Compromisos para la Paz: resumen de las negociaciones entre los delegados del Ejército Zapatista de Liberación Nacional, el Comisionado para la Paz y la Reconciliación Manuel Camacho Solís y el mediador Samuel Ruiz. *Ce-Acatl* 59: 11–16.

——. 1995. Derechos y Cultura Indígena resultados de la primera fase de la mesa del Diálogo de San Andrés. *Ce-Acatl* 73: 1–48.

——.1996. Diálogo de Sacam Ch'en – Mesa de Trabajo 1: Derechos y Cultura Indígena, Fase Segunda. *Ce-Acatl* 74/75: 1–116.

CEOIC. 1994. Paz, dignidad y desarrollo para nuestros pueblos. *Ce-Acatl* 59: 8–9.

Chance, John K. and William B. Taylor. 1985. "Cofradías" and "Cargos": an historical perspective on the Mesoamerican civil-religious hierarchy. *American Ethnologist* 12 (1): 1–26.

CND. 1994. *Convención Nacional Democrática: Resolutivos*. México: CND.

CNI. 1994. *Convención Nacional Indígena: Declaración de la Montaña de Guerrero*. (Ms.). Tlapa.

——.2002. Tercer Congreso Nacional Indígena: Declaración de Nurío, Michoacán. *Boletín AIPIN Región Centro Occidente* (Julio 2002): 6–7.

CNPI. 1980. *I Congreso Nacional de Pueblos Indígenas, Pátzcuaro, Michoacán, 1975: Conclusiones*. México: CNPI.

CNPI and ANPIBAC. 1982. Política educativa y cultural de los grupos étnicos de México. *Anuario Indigenista* 42: 125–55.

Coalición de Pueblos Serranos Zapotecos y Chinantecos. 1994. *Autonomía y autodeterminación: pasado y futuro de y para nuestros pueblos*. Oaxaca.

Collier, George. 1994. *Basta! Land and the Zapatista Rebellion in Chiapas*. San Francisco: Food First.

Concha Malo, Miguel. 1995. Los derechos de los pueblos indígenas en la Organización de las Naciones Unidas. *Diversidad étnica y conflicto en América Latina: organizaciones indígenas y políticas estatales, vol. 1*, R. Barceló, M. A. Portal, and M. J. Sánchez, eds. México: Plaza Valdés – UNAM-IIS.

Concheiro Bórquez, Luciano. 1993. *Perspectivas de la Unión Nacional de Organizaciones Regionales Campesinas Autónomas (UNORCA) ante los cambios actuales del mundo rural mexicano*. México: UAM-Xochimilco.

Consejo Guerrerense 500 Años de Resistencia Indígena. 1993. *Congreso Estatal de Pueblos Indígenas – resolutivos preliminares*. Chilpancingo.

Consejo Guerrerense 500 Años de Resistencia Indígena *et al*. 1994. *La autonomía como nueva relación entre los pueblos indios y la sociedad nacional*. México.

Corbett, Jack and Scott Whiteford. 1986. La penetración del Estado y el desarrollo en Mesoamérica, 1950–1980. *La herencia de la conquista – treinta años después*, C. Kendall, J. Hawkins, and L. Bossen, eds. México: FCE.

Cornelius, Wayne A. 1996. *Mexican Politics in Transition: the Breakdown of a One-Party-Dominant regime*. San Diego: UCSD – Center for US–Mexican Studies.

Cornelius, Wayne, Ann Craig, and Jonathan Fox. 1994. Mexico's National Solidarity Program: an Overview. *Transforming State-Society Relations in Mexico: the National Solidarity Strategy*, W. Cornelius, A. Craig and J. Fox, eds. San Diego: UCSD – Center for US–Mexican Studies.

Cornelius, Wayne A., Todd A. Eisenstadt, and Jane Hindley. 1999. *Subnational Politics and Democratization in Mexico*. San Diego: UCSD – Center for US–Mexican Studies.

Cruz Hernández, Isabel and Martín Zuvire Lucas. 1991.Uniones de crédito agropecuarias: una red que viene de lejos. *Los nuevos sujetos del desarrollo rural*, A. Bartra *et al*. eds. México: ADN.

de la Peña, Guillermo. 1998. Etnicidad, ciudadanía y cambio agrario: apuntes comparativos sobre tres países latinoamericanos. *Las disputas por el México rural: transformaciones de prácticas, identidades y proyectos, vol. 2,* S. Zendejas and P. de Vries, eds. Zamora: Colegio de Michoacán.

Díaz Gómez, Floriberto. 1992. Las celebraciones de los 500 años. *Caravelle 59*: 33–7.

Díaz-Polanco, Héctor. 1992. *Autonomía regional: la autodeterminación de los pueblos indios.* México: Siglo XXI – UNAM.

——. 1995. La rebelión de los indios zapatista y la autonomía. *Chiapas Insurgente: 5 ensayos sobre la realidad mexicana,* N. Chomsky *et al.* eds. Tafalla: Txalaparta.

Dietrich, Wolfgang. 1994. Die wütende Erde Mexikos. *¡Ya Basta! – Der Aufstand der Zapatistas,* Topitas ed. Hamburg: VLA.

Dietz, Gunther. 1994. Neozapatismo and Ethnic Movements in Chiapas, Mexico: background information on the armed uprising of the EZLN. *Mexicon 16* (2): 27–30.

——. 1995. *Teoría y práctica del Indigenismo: el caso del fomento a la alfarería en Michoacán, México.* Quito – México: Abya-Yala – Instituto Indigenista Interamericano.

——.1999. *"La comunidad purhépecha es nuestra fuerza": etnicidad, cultura y región en un movimiento indígena en México.* Quito: Abya-Yala.

Durand Ponte, Víctor Manuel. 1994. El movimiento por el respeto de los derechos humanos y la transición política. *La construcción de la democracia en México: movimientos sociales y ciudadanía,* V.M. Durand Ponte *et al.,* eds. México: Siglo XXI.

Elwert, Georg. 1989. Nationalismus, Ethnizität und Nativismus: über Wir-Gruppenprozesse. *Ethnizität im Wandel,* P. Waldmann and G. Elwert, eds. Saarbrücken – Fort Lauderdale: Breitenbach.

Esteva, Gustavo. 1994a. Basta! *¡Ya Basta! – Der Aufstand der Zapatistas,* Topitas, ed. Hamburg: VLA.

——. 1994b. *Crónica del fin de una era: el secreto del EZLN.* México: Posada.

Esteva-Fabregat, Claudio. 1995. *Mestizaje in Ibero-America.* Tucson: University of Arizona Press.

——. 1991. Pronunciamiento del Primer Encuentro Nacional de Prensa India. *Etnias,* 2 (9): 30.

EZLN. 1994. *Chiapas – la palabra de los armados de verdad y fuego: entrevistas, cartas y comunicados del EZLN.* Barcelona: Serbal.

——. 1995. *Documentos y comunicados,* 2. México: Era.

——. 1997. *Documentos y comunicados,* 3. México: Era.

Fernández, María Teresa and Fernando Rello. 1990. Las uniones de ejidos y otras organizaciones regionales en México. *Las organizaciones de productores rurales en México,* F. Rello, ed. México: UNAM – Facultad de Economía.

FIDH. 2002. *Informe México: los pueblos indígenas en México.* Paris: Federación Internacional de los Derechos Humanos.

Flores Lúa, Graciela, Luisa Paré, and Sergio Sarmiento Silva. 1988. *Las voces del campo: movimiento campesino y política agraria, 1976–1984.* México: Siglo XXI.

Florescano, Enrique.1999. *Memoria indígena.* México: Taurus.

Foley, Michael D. 1995. Privatizing the Countryside: the Mexican Peasant Movement and Neoliberal reform. *Latin American Perspectives,* 22(1): 59–76.

Fowler, Hill. 1996. Introduction: The "Forgotten Century" – Mexico, 1810–1910. *Bulletin of Latin American Research,* 15 (1): 1–6.

Fox, Jonathan and Josefina Aranda. 1996. *Decentralization and Rural Development in Mexico: Community Participation in Oaxaca's Municipal Funds Program.* San Diego: UCSD – Center for US–Mexican Studies.

Friedlander, Judith. 1977. *Ser indio en Hueyapan: un estudio de identidad obligada en el México contemporáneo.* México: FCE.

Friedrich, Paul. 1981. *Rebelión agraria en una aldea mexicana.* México: CEHAM – FCE.

Gabbert, Wolfgang. 1999. Violence and Social Change in Highland Maya Communities, Chiapas, Mexico. *Ibero-Amerikanisches Archiv,* 25 (3–4): 351–74.

——. 2001. *"Das Vergessen bedeutet die Niederlage!": Der Marsch der Zapatisten nach Mexiko-Stadt.* Hamburg: Institut für Iberoamerika-Kunde.

Gabriel Hernández, Franco. 1981. De la educación indígena tradicional a la educación indígena bilingüe bicultural. *Utopía y revolución: el pensamiento político contemporáneo de los indios en América Latina,* G. Bonfil Batalla, ed. México: Nueva Imagen.

García, Emilio. 1991. Estrategia modernizante y perfil del movimiento campesino en el último cuarto del siglo XX. *Cuadernos Agrarios, N.E.* 1: 23–38.

García Canclini, Néstor. 1989a. *Culturas híbridas: estrategias para entrar y salir de la modernidad.* México: CNCA – Grijalbo.

——. 2000. *La globalización imaginada.* Barcelona: Paidós.

Garduño Cervantes, Julio. 1993. El movimiento indígena en el Estado de México. *Movimientos indígenas contemporáneos en México,* A. Warman and A. Argueta, eds. México: UNAM – Miguel Angel Porrúa.

Gibson, Charles. 1964. *The Aztecs under Spanish Rule: a History of the Indians of the Valley of Mexico, 1519–1819.* Stanford: Stanford University Press.

Gledhill, John. 1991. *Casi Nada: a Study of Agrarian Reform in the Homeland of Cardenismo.* Albany: SUNY – Institute of Meso-American Studies.

Gómez, Magdalena. 1993. Hacia una definición del espacio de lo consuetudinario en el medio indígena y de sus posibilidades de ejercicio en el marco de la nueva legalidad. *Nueva Antropología,* 13 (44): 9–15.

Gómez, Águeda. 2002. Aproximación al análisis de la experiencia de movilización política indígena zapatista. *Cuadernos Americanos,* 92: 80–100.

Guardino, Peter F. 1996. *Peasant, Politics, and the Formation of Mexico's National State, 1800–1857.* Stanford: Stanford University Press.

Guzmán Gómez, Alba. 1990. *Voces indígenas: educación bilingüe bicultural en México.* México: CNCA – INI.

Harvey, Neil. 1990. *The New Agrarian Movement in Mexico, 1979–1990.* London: University of London – Institute of Latin American Studies.

——. 1993. The Limits of Concertation in Rural Mexico. *Mexico: Dilemmas of Transition,* N. Harvey, ed. London: British Academic Press – University of London – Institute of Latin American Studies.

——. 1994. Las organizaciones sociales ante el conflicto armado de Chiapas. *El Cotidiano,* 61: 21–5.

——. 1998. Lucha agraria y reafirmación del poder político en Chiapas. *Las disputas por el México rural: transformaciones de prácticas, identidades y proyectos, vol. 2,* S. Zendejas and P. de Vries, eds. Zamora: Colegio de Michoacán.

Hernández, Luis. 1992. La UNORCA: doce tesis sobre el nuevo liderazgo campesino en México. *Autonomía y nuevos sujetos sociales en el desarrollo rural*, J. Moguel, C. Botey, and L. Hernández, eds. México: Siglo XXI.

Hernández Hernández, Natalio. 1988. Las organizaciones indígenas: ¿autonomía o dependencia? *INI 40 Años*, INI ed. México: INI.

Hernández Hernández, Natalio and Franco Gabriel. 1979. La ANPIBAC y su política de participación. *Indianidad y descolonización en América Latina: documentos de la Segunda Reunión de Barbados*. México: Nueva Imagen.

Hoffmann, Odile. 1989. La part des communautés rurales dans la conformation municipale au Mexique. *Pouvoir local, régionalismes, décentralisation: enjeux territoriaux et territorialité en Amérique Latine*, J. Revel-Mouroz, ed. Paris: IHEAL.

Huizer, Gerrit. 1982. *La lucha campesina en México*. México: Centro Nacional de Investigaciones Agrarias.

Joseph, Gilbert M. and Daniel Nugent. 1994. Popular Culture and State Formation in Revolutionary Mexico. *Everyday Forms of State Formation: Revolution and the Negotiation of Rule in Modern Mexico*, G. M. Joseph and D. Nugent, eds. Durham: Duke University Press.

Kearney, Michael. 1994. Desde el indigenismo a los derechos humanos: etnicidad y política más allá de la mixteca. *Nueva Antropología*, 14 (46): 49–68.

——. 1996. *Reconceptualizing the Peasantry: Anthropology in Global Perspective*. Boulder: Westview.

Knight, Alan. 1986. *The Mexican Revolution. (vols 1–2)*. Cambridge: Cambridge University Press.

——. 1997. The Ideology of the Mexican Revolution, 1910–1940. *Estudios Interdisciplinarios de América Latina*, 8 (1): 77–109.

——. 1998. El campo mexicano en el siglo XX: la dialéctica entre desarrollo y debate. *Las disputas por el México rural: transformaciones de prácticas, identidades y proyectos, vol. 2*, S. Zendejas and P. de Vries, eds. Zamora: Colegio de Michoacán.

Köhler, Ulrich. 1975. *Cambio cultural dirigido en los Altos de Chiapas: un estudio sobre la antropología social aplicada*. México: SEP – INI.

Korsbaek, Leif. 1992. *El sistema de cargos en la antropología chiapaneca: de la antropología tradicional a la moderna*. Tuxtla Gutiérrez: Instituto Chiapaneco de Cultura.

Korsbaek, Leif and Hilario Topete. 2000. *Sistema de cargos (Cuicuilco 7,19)*. México: ENAH.

Le Bot, Yvon. 1997. *Subcomandante Marcos: el sueño zapatista*. México: Plaza y Janés – ENAH.

Legorreta Díaz, Carmen. 1998. *Religión, política y guerrilla en las Cañadas de la Selva Lacandona*. México: Cal y Arena.

Lockhart, James. 1992. *The Nahuas After the Conquest: a Social and Cultural History of the Indians of Central Mexico, Sixteenth through Eighteenth Centuries*. Stanford: Stanford University Press.

Lomnitz Adler, Claudio. 1995. *Las salidas del laberinto: cultura e ieología en el espacio nacional mexicano*. México: Joaquín Mortiz.

López Bárcenas, Francisco. 1994. Los derechos indígenas en México y el Convenio 169 de la OIT. *Ojarasca* 33–4: 43–6.

——. 2002. *Legislación y derechos indígenas en México*. México – Oaxaca: Ce-Acatl – COAPI – Ediciones Casa Vieja.

López Velasco, Vicente Paulino. 1989. *Y surgió la unión . . . : génesis y desarrollo del Consejo Nacional de Pueblos Indígenas.* México: SRA – CEHAM.

López y Rivas, Gilberto. 1995. *Nación y pueblos indios en el neoliberalismo.* México: Plaza y Valdés – UIA.

Maihold, Günther. 1986. *Identitätssuche in Lateinamerika: das indigenistische Denken in Mexiko.* Saarbrücken – Fort Lauderdale: Breitenbach.

Mallon, Florencia E. 1995. *Peasant and Nation: the Making of Postcolonial Mexico and Peru.* Berkeley: University of California Press.

Marion Singer, Marie-Odile. 1987. Pueblos de Chiapas: una democracia a la defensiva. *Revista Mexicana de Sociología,* 49 (4): 37–73.

——. 1989. *Las organizaciones campesinas autónomas: un reto a la producción.* México: INAH.

Márquez Joaquín, Pedro. 1988. Normas para el desarrollo comunitario. *México Indígena,* 4 (25): 38–40.

Martínez Borrego, Estela. 1991. *Organización de productores y movimiento campesino.* México: Siglo XXI – UNAM-IIS.

Medina, Andrés. 1983. Los grupos étnicos y los sistemas tradicionales de poder en México. *Nueva Antropología,* 20: 5–29.

Mejía Piñeros, María Consuelo and Sergio Sarmiento Silva. 1991. *La lucha indígena: un reto a la ortodoxia.* México: Siglo XXI.

Mendieta y Núñez, Lucio. 1946. *El problema agrario en México.* México: Porrúa.

Moguel, Julio. 1992. Reforma constitucional y luchas agrarias en el marco de la transición salinista. *Autonomía y nuevos sujetos sociales en el desarrollo rural,* J. Moguel, C. Botey, and L. Hernández, eds. México: Siglo XXI.

——. 1994. El CEOIC – el otro poder en la guerra de Chiapas. *La Jornada del Campo,* 22.2.94: 1–3.

Nación Purhépecha. 1991. *Decreto de la Nación Purhépecha.* Paracho.

Nash, June. 1997. The Fiesta of the Word: the Zapatista Uprising and Radical Democracy in Mexico. *American Anthropologist,* 99 (2): 261–74.

Nugent, Daniel. 1998. El discurso de los intelectuales como un foco de las disputas por el México rural: reflexiones sobre la antigüedad de identidades postcoloniales en México. *Las disputas por el México rural: transformaciones de prácticas, identidades y proyectos, vol. 2,* S. Zendejas and P. de Vries, eds. Zamora: Colegio de Michoacán.

Nugent, Daniel and Ana María Alonso. 1994. Multiple Selective Traditions in Agrarian Reform and Agrarian Struggle: Popular culture and State formation in the Ejido of Namiquipa, Chihuahua. *Everyday Forms of State Formation: Revolution and the Negotiation of Rule in Modern Mexico,* G. M. Joseph and D. Nugent, eds. Durham: Duke University Press.

OIT. 1992. *Convenio No. 169 sobre Pueblos Indígenas y Tribales en Países Independientes 1989.* Lima: OIT – Oficina Regional para América Latina y el Caribe.

Otero, Gerardo. 1990. El nuevo movimiento agrario: autogestión y producción democrática. *Revista Mexicana de Sociología,* 52 (2): 93–124.

Pérez Ruiz, Maya Lorena. 2001. Los acuerdos de San Andrés en su contexto político y militar. *Boletín CEAS,* 5: 11–16.

Piñar Alvarez, Angeles. 1999. *Campesinos im Neoliberalismus: ländliche Entwicklung und Kreditpolitik in Mexiko.* Hamburg: Wayasbah.

——. 2002. *¿El sistema financiero al servicio del desarrollo rural sustentable? Las* *unidades de producción rural ante las políticas financieras de desarrollo y medio ambiente en la región purhépecha de Michoacán, México.* Quito: Abya-Yala.

Poder Ejecutivo Federal. 1990. *Iniciativa de decreto que adiciona el artículo 4o. de la Constitución Política de los Estados Unidos Mexicanos para el reconocimiento de los derechos culturales de los pueblos indígenas.* México: INI.

Ramírez Casillas, Manuel. 1995. Perfil de los derechos humanos de los indígenas en México durante 1992. *Diversidad étnica y conflicto en América Latina: organizaciones indígenas y políticas estatales, vol. 1,* R. Barceló, M. A. Portal, and M. J. Sánchez, eds. México: Plaza y Valdés – UNAM-IIS.

Reitmeier, Gabriele. 1990. *Unabhängige Campesinobewegungen in Mexiko 1920–1988: Entstehungsbedingungen, Handlungsspielräume und Einflußmöglichkeiten nicht-staatlicher Campesino-Organisationen im nach- und postrevolutionären Mexiko.* Saarbrücken – Fort Lauderdale: Breitenbach.

Reina, Leticia. 1997. *La reindianizaión de América Latina, siglo XIX.* México: Siglo XXI – CIESAS.

Rodríguez, Miguel. 1994. El 12 de octubre: entre el IV y el V Centenario. *Cultura e identidad nacional,* R. Blancarte, ed. México: CNCA – FCE.

Roosens, Eugeen E. 1989. *Creating Ethnicity: the Process of Ethnogenesis.* Newbury Park: SAGE.

Ros Romero, María del Consuelo. 1981. *Bilingüismo y educación: un estudio en Michoacán.* México: INI.

Rovira, Guiomar. 1994. *¡Zapata vive! La rebelión indígena de Chiapas contada por sus protagonistas.* Barcelona: Virus.

Rubio, Blanca. 1994. El EZLN: lo viejo y lo nuevo. *La Jornada del Campo,* 22.2.94: 6–7.

Rugeley, Ferry. 2002. Indians Meet the State, Regions Meet the Center: Nineteenth-Century Mexico Revisited. *Latin American Research Review,* 37 (1): 245–58.

Ruiz Hernández, Margarito. 1994. El Frente Independiente de Pueblos Indios. *Revista Mexicana de Sociología,* 56 (2): 117–32.

——. 1999. La Asamblea Nacional Indígena Plural por la autonomía (ANIPA): proceso de construcción de una propuesta legislativa autonómica nacional. *México: experiencias de autonomía indígena,* A. Burguete Cal y Mayor, ed. Copenhague: IWGIA.

Salazar Peralta, Ana María. 1994. Panorama histórico social de la caficultura chiapaneca: crónica de una crisis anunciada. Paper presented at the 48th Congreso Internacional de Americanistas, Stockholm & Uppsala 4–9/7/94.

San Andrés Chicahuaxtla. 1994. *El Estatuto Comunal de la comunidad triqui de San Andrés Chicahuaxtla.* San Andrés Chicahuaxtla.

Santana, Roberto. 1995. *¿Ciudadanos en la etnicidad? Los indios en la política o la política de los indios.* Quito: Abya-Yala.

Sarmiento Silva, Sergio. 1985. El Consejo Nacional de Pueblos Indígenas y la política indigenista. *Revista Mexicana de Sociología,* 47 (3): 197–215.

——. 2001. El movimiento indio mexicano y la reforma del Estado. *Cuadernos del Sur,* 7 (16): 65–96.

Smith, Anthony D. 1981. *The Ethnic Revival.* Cambridge: Cambridge University Press.

Smith, Peter H. 1981. *Los laberintos del poder: el reclutamiento de las élites políticas en México, 1900–1971.* México: Colegio de México.

Softestad, Lars T. 1993. Indigene Völker und die Vereinten Nationen. *500 Jahre danach: Zur heutigen Lage der indigenen Völker beider Amerika*, P. R. Gerber, ed. Zürich: Völkerkundemuseum & Ethnologisches Seminar der Universität Zürich.

Spenser, Daniela and Bradley A. Levinson. 1999. Linking State and Society in Discourse and Action: Political and Cultural Studies of the Cárdenas era in Mexico. *Latin American Research Review*, 34 (2): 227–45.

Stallaert, Christiane. 1998. *Etnogénesis y etnicidad en España: una aproximación histórico-antropológica al casticismo*. Barcelona: Proyecto A.

Stanford, Lois. 1994. The Privatization of Mexico's Ejidal Sector: Examining Local Impacts, Strategies, and Ideologies. *Urban Anthropology*, 23 (2–3): 97–119.

Stavenhagen, Rodolfo. 1988. *Derecho indígena y derechos humanos en América Latina*. México: Colegio de México – IIDH.

——. 1999. Hacia el derecho de autonomía en México. *México: experiencias de autonomía indígena*, A. Burguete Cal y Mayor, ed. Copenhague: IWGIA.

Strug, David Lawrence. 1975. *An Evaluation of a Program of Applied Anthropology in Michoacán, Mexico*. (Ph.D. thesis). New York: Columbia University.

Summerhill, Stephen J. and John Alexander Williams. 2000. *Sinking Columbus: Contested History, Cultural Politics and Mythmaking during the Quincentenary*. Gainesville: University Press of Florida.

Taylor, William B. 1993. Patterns and Variety in Mexican Village Uprisings. *The Indian in Latin American History: Resistance, Resilience, and Acculturation*, J. E. Kicza, ed. Washington: Scholarly Resources Inc.

Tello Díaz, Carlos.1995. *La rebelión de las Cañadas*. México: Cal y Arena.

Tutino, John. 1986. *From Insurrection to Revolution in Mexico: Social Bases of Agrarian Violence, 1750–1940*. Princeton: Princeton University Press.

UCEZ. 1984. Unión de Comuneros "Emiliano Zapata" de Michoacán: V aniversario, octubre 1979–1984 – Encuentro Tierra y Libertad, 5–7 de octubre de 1984. *Textual – Análisis del Medio Rural*, 15–16: 156–62.

UNORCA.1993. La sociedad rural como reserva del futuro. *La Jornada*, 4.11.93: 20.

Urban, Greg and Joel Sherzer. 1994. Introduction: Indians, Nation-States, and Culture. *Nation-States and Indians in Latin America*, Greg Urban and Joel Sherzer, eds. Austin: University of Texas Press.

Valencia, Guadalupe. 1994. La Unidad de Producción Forestal de Pueblos Mancomunados: la constitución de un sujeto social. *Revista Mexicana de Sociología*, 56 (2): 133–46.

Varese, Stefano. 1987. La cultura como recurso: el desafío de la educación indígena en el marco de un desarrollo nacional autónomo. *Educación en poblaciones indígenas: políticas y estrategias en América Latina*, M. Zúñiga, J. Ansion, and L. Cueva, eds. Santiago de Chile: UNESCO – OREALC.

——. 1994. Subalternos ilegítimos: notas sobre la economía política del movimiento indígena en México. *Cuadernos del Sur*, 3 (6–7): 47–67.

——. 2001. The Territorial Roots of Latin American Indigenous Peoples' Movement for Sovereignty. *International Social Science Review*, 2 (2): 201–17.

Vargas, María Eugenia. 1994. *Educación e ideología – constitución de una categoría de intermediarios en la comunicación interétnica: el caso de los maestros bilingües tarascos (1964–1982)*. México: CIESAS.

Gunther Dietz

Vasconcelos, José. 1997 [1925]. *The Cosmic Race*. Baltimore: Johns Hopkins Press.

Vasconcelos, José and A. L. Carballo. 1989. *Antología del pensamiento político, social y económico de América Latina*. Madrid: Ediciones Cultura Hispánica.

Vaughan, Mary Kay. 1997. *Cultural Politics in Revolution: Teachers, Peasants, and Schools in Mexico, 1930–1940*. Tucson: University of Arizona Press.

Viqueira, Juan Pedro and Willibald Sonnleitner. 2000. *Democracia en tierras indígenas: las elecciones en los altos de Chiapas, 1991–1998*. México: El Colegio de México.

Wade, Peter. 1997. *Race and Ethnicity in Latin America*. London: Pluto.

Warman, Arturo. 1984. La lucha social en el campo de México: un esfuerzo de periodización. *Historia política de los campesinos latinoamericanos, vol. 1*, P. González Casanova, ed. México: Siglo XXI.

——. 1985. *Ensayos sobre el campesinado en México*. México: Nueva Imagen.

Zárate Hernández, José Eduardo. 1991. Notas para la interpretación del movimiento étnico en Michoacán. *El estudio de los movimientos sociales: teoría y método*, V.G. Muro and M. Canto Chac, ed. Zamora: Colegio de Michoacán.

——. 1992. Faccionalismo y movimiento indígena: la UCEZ entre los otomíes de Zitácuaro, Michoacán. *Intermediación social y procesos políticos en Michoacán*, J. Tapia Santamaría, ed. Zamora: Colegio de Michoacán.

Zepeda Patterson, Jorge. 1984. No es lo mismo agrio que agrario ni comuneros que comunistas (la UCEZ en Michoacán). *Estudios Políticos N.E.*, 3 (2): 63–87.

Zermeño, Sergio.1994. Estado y sociedad en el neoliberalismo dependiente. *Revista Mexicana de Sociología*, 56 (4): 109–32.

Beyond Victimization

Maya Movements in Post-War Guatemala

Edward Fischer

The Maya of Guatemala have long been victimized. Witness the brutalities of Spanish conquest, the impositions of colonial rule, the institutionalized discrimination of authoritarian and democratic governments alike, violences both extraordinary and quotidian. For those of a certain age and political sympathy, Guatemala is best remembered for the civil war of the 1970s and early 1980s (of almost unimaginable proportions in its intensity and brutal excesses), which made the country a poster child for human rights causes. While Marxist rebel forces blockaded roads, blew up bridges, and assassinated (*"justificaron"*) plantation owners and minor politicians, the US-supported Guatemalan army kidnapped and tortured thousands of suspects, massacred untold numbers of civilians, and razed hundreds of villages, burning houses and fields, scattering and killing the populations. Exactly how many were killed we will never know–tens of thousands at least. The UN-supported Historical Clarification Commission, set up after 1996 Peace Accords, found that over 90 percent of the 42,000 human rights violations they documented were attributable to the Guatemalan military. The overwhelming majority of these victims were Maya Indians, leading the commission to conclude that the Guatemalan military intentionally targeted Maya populations and thus, like the German Gestapo, was guilty of "acts of genocide."[1]

La violencia (the violence) permeated everyday life in the Guatemala of the early 1980s; it became routinized and internalized, normalized in a

macabre fashion. And the effects linger on. Similar to Germany's relationship to the Holocaust, *la violencia* defines Guatemala today through a
multitude of complex, contradictory, and fluid personal and collective
memories: memories of killings (pregnant women, defenseless children,
and elderly males mercilessly murdered, often in gruesome ways); the
everyday terror of counter-insurgency militarization (not only check-
points and roadblocks but neighborhood informants and strategic
kidnappings); an atmosphere in which one never knew whom to trust and
thus never spoke freely (fostering even more suspicion and social isolation).

People are still reluctant to talk openly about the violence (or *la
situación* as it is often called), and with good reason: death threats, kidnappings, and assassinations of human rights activists, clergy, and social
scientists continue, though not at the horrendous rates of the early 1980s.

November 1999, Nashville, Tennessee. I took Pablo, who is up visiting from
Tecpán, out to the Pancake Pantry for breakfast. Sharp, funny, and intense,
Pablo is a charismatic speaker; I could listen to him talk for hours. Today
our conversation followed a familiar path: catching up on the news of family
and friends, discussing our work, and, as always, winding up with our latest
critiques of Guatemalan politics and society. At one point, talk turned to
the lingering effects of the violence and Pablo's own experiences in the early
1980s. At this point – in what he later described as an unconscious, reflexive
gesture – Pablo lowered his voice and leaned in close across the table, peri-
odically glancing around to see who was seated nearby. He told me a story
– one that I had heard several times before, but that never failed to move
me – of friends and relatives being kidnapped, tortured, and killed, of death
threats he received, and of his years of internal exile. In Pablo's town the
violence had largely died down over 15 years ago, peace accords ending the
war were signed three years ago, and a United Nations commission is in the
process of collecting and publishing first hand accounts of massacres. Yet,
so ingrained was his suspicion of speaking openly and freely, that Pablo,
not normally a man to mince words, instinctively resorted to a hushed
conspiratorial tone. As the Germans discovered after 1989, a wall in the
mind can be more insidious than a material barrier.

Yet, conditions are changing. In the three years following that conversation with Pablo, my friends in Tecpán Guatemala, the Kaqchikel Maya
town of 9,000 where I have conducted much of my fieldwork as a cultural
anthropologist, have had a dramatic shift in their attitude toward
discussing their experiences during the violence. Sitting around kitchen
hearths, drinking sweet instant coffee, people I have known for years are
for the first time telling me stories about the violence to which they had
only alluded before. These same friends are also suddenly much more
open about criticizing the government, they are working in local political
campaigns, they are even once again starting agricultural and artisan
cooperatives.

A similar shift is occurring in the national political arena as well. In December of 1996, peace accords were signed between the Guatemalan government and the *Unidad Revolucionaria Nacional Guatemalteca* (URNG, the National Revolutionary Unity of Guatemala), an umbrella organization of revolutionary groups. These accords formally ended a war between the Guatemalan army and Marxist revolutionaries that some date back to 1960 but that more accurately started in 1978.[2]

A number of book chapters, conferences, and United Nations working groups have commenced the study of what is called "post-war" Guatemala. No one is quite clear on just when this period started. The violence reached its apogee in 1981–2, and it tapered off rather dramatically throughout the late 1980s. By all accounts it was a feeble guerrilla front that signed peace accords with the Guatemalan government in 1996. But by that time, organized crime and freelance crime (drugs, robberies, kidnappings) had in the minds of many people overtaken political violence as an overriding fear.

Regardless of when, or even if, the violence ended, by almost any "objective" measure, the Maya population has been its primary victim. The Maya are victims of historical oppression and a system that continues to systematically disadvantage them. Yet, there is a real danger in this rhetoric of victimhood. It becomes too easy to reduce the Maya to nothing more than victims, to mere reactants to larger forces. This may be necessary for political activism, but it obscures the complex realities we strive for in social analysis. As recent events remind us, the Maya–inasmuch as we may speak about them as a group – are much more than victims–they are also active protagonists in their futures.

Guatemala's genocide sought not only to stamp out the supposed communist threat (reason enough to secure US funding of the war) but to obliterate the ground in which it presumably flourished, traditional Maya communities. Yet, out of the ashes of this destruction has emerged a vibrant social movement working to revitalize Maya cultural forms, to promote Maya ethnic pride, and to create new spaces for Maya peoples in Guatemalan political, economic, and social networks.

July 1994, Tecpán Guatemala. Today I went to go visit Don Domingo, the Maya day-keeper and traditionalist priest who lives in that big two-story house just off of the plaza. Domingo is not a "typical" Tecpaneco in many ways. He owns two trucks and makes his living primarily by hauling produce for farmers, an income meagerly augmented by the donations he accepts for performing ceremonies. In discussing the resurgence in Maya culture after the violence of the early 1980s, Domingo explains how this too is part of a larger cosmological cycle:

Let's consider all that has happened with the people here in [19]81 and [19]80. How many thousands of people died? Thousands, not hundreds, died. They were buried just anywhere as if they were animals. The blood of these people went to the earth and was consummated before God, right? This blood is their spirit, right? Thus our people have now won – and we remember how it was before. We already paid and gave alms. I bought my land, and I am going to buy another house . . . it is much better now.

For Don Domingo, the paradigm of cyclic regeneration provides not only a framework for situating the almost unthinkable atrocities of the violence but also act as a justification and mandate for future action. Such internally logical paradigms underwrite Maya cultural creativity and have given rise to the particular form of indigenous identity politics found in Guatemala.

In the early days of the movement (the mid to late 1980s), pan-Mayanist groups were careful to keep their focus on "non-political" issues, especially linguistic conservation and folkloric cultural revival. In the context of "post-war" Guatemala, this was an incredibly effective strategy, allowing Mayanist leaders to step out of the line of fire (both literal and figurative) between the extreme left and the extreme right (see Stoll 1993). Pan-Mayanists offered a third way alternative that sought nonviolent, culturally-based solutions to Guatemala's ills, and their message fell on receptive ears both among Maya peoples and among international donor organizations. After growing steadily in the late 1980s, the number of Maya non-governmental organizations in Guatemala skyrocketed during the 1990s. At the turn of the century there are hundreds of Maya NGOs, with concerns ranging from language conservation to indigenous religions to politics to economics. These groups benefited from a turn in international attention during the 1990s to issues of indigenous peoples and their rights. In 1992, in the midst of celebrations for the Colombian Quincentenary, Rigoberta Menchú, a Maya woman from Guatemala, was awarded the Nobel Peace Prize for her efforts to bring attention to the plight of Maya peoples in Guatemala during the violence (and also, certainly, to serve as a symbol for all oppressed Native Americans). The United Nations declared the 1990s the Decade of Indigenous Peoples. And funding bodies–mainly the United Nations, the European Union, Scandinavian countries, and the United States–began to target their assistance toward indigenous populations.

In this context, pan-Maya groups have both benefited from and been belittled by their victimization at the hands of others. Here I refer not only to their "actual" victimization – of conquest, colonialism, the violence of the 1980s–but also to their "virtual" victimization – the representational and symbolic violence done to them by the application of categories of victimhood and the models of victimization. These models, while championing the rights of the oppressed, very often give little voice to the very same oppressed, who are seen as victims of larger structural forces that must be righted. Such representation, sympathetic as it may be, is a sort of pornography of poverty, allowing readers a vicarious experience of sadism or masochism, a removed outlet for sublimated fears and desires.

It plays to our hidden and overt presuppositions of superiority – "at least we aren't like that"– even when spoken in the idiom of multicultural pluralism. This "at least" is a an insidious phrase, negating radical alternatives and radical empathy while seducing the speaker with its subtle self-righteousness.

While Maya leaders and groups have been able to capitalize on their symbolic and actual victimization (gaining currency in the UN and other international organizations), the diverse practice of their lived experiences belies the confining, oppositionally defined category of victimhood. They have been victims, certainly, but they are so much more than *just* victims: men and women, adolescents and elderly, urban and rural–individuals defined by unique conjunctures of almost infinite social, cultural, and economic vectors–people living their lives as best they see fit, balancing self-interests with social obligations. Attempting to capture such complexity while trying to avoid further symbolic violence toward Maya peoples, we must proceed beyond the language of victimization. We must not forget the horrors of the violence and we should not turn a blind eye to exploitation and injustice (as we may variably define them), but pan-Maya activism points us also toward the power of subaltern agency and intentionality and to the historically particular convergences of diverse interests that can produce radical social change without intending to be revolutionary.

Background: The Indian Problem in Guatemala

Since the earliest days of colonization, Guatemala's rulers have grappled with the so-called Indian problem. Put simply, the Indian "problem," from the perspective of non-Indian (or, *ladino*) privileged classes, is that there are so many of them (Maya make up about half of the Guatemalan population) and that they represent the antithesis of what a cosmopolitan society should be (backward and brutish, farmers and craftsmen). During the colonial and early independence period of Guatemalan history, conservative factions promoted a policy of social and geographic separation that well suited the interest of many Maya communities. The Conservatives recognized inherent differences between the Indian and Spanish populations, and in trying to avoid mutual corruption their policies insulated – in theory if not always in practice – *pueblos indios* (Indian peoples) from Spanish exploitation. In contrast, Liberal politicians argued that such separation thwarted the development of an educated, ethnically homogenous population that would ensure political stability and economic prosperity. John Browning (1996) cites an illustrative early nineteenth-century speech in which the secretary of Guatemala's liberal *Sociedad Económica* (Economic Society) envisions a booming economic future based on cultural assimilation of the Indian population. He predicted an initial boom in the manufacture and sale of Spanish clothes and shoes to the Indians, as they abandoned their native dress for more modern attire, followed by another economic expansion as Indians began to buy European-style furniture for their houses, and so on, ad infinitum.

Today, the debate over ethnic separation or integration continues. A significant sector of Guatemala's *ladino* intellectual and political elite carry the liberal banner of integration. The most outspoken proponent of this view is Mario Roberto Morales, a literary scholar and fiery editorialist. Conjuring up the Mexican doctrine of *mestizaje* and José Vasconcelos' 1925 notion of "*la raza cósmica*" (the cosmic race), Morales calls on ladino and Maya Guatemalans alike to take pride in their hybrid past, to embrace their *mestizaje*: "el mestizaje es el elemento central que dinamiza nuestras relaciones interétnicas y expresa nuestras identidades" (mestizaje is the the central element which makes our inter-ethnic relations dynamic and expresses our identities) (2000). He writes that there is not only a ladino hegemony, but a Maya hegemony as well, both of which imply racial and cultural purity.

Mario Roberto Morales, writing in the 10 June 2000 edition of Siglo XXI. In as much as our cultural differences articulate in infinite ways – varying according to the social class, gender, and ethnicity of the individual – to emphasize differences rather than their articulations implies the adoption of multiculturalist (separatist) criteria even as our position at the center of such articulation implies the adoption of inter-culturalist (relational) criteria . . . the polarities of Indian-ladino or Maya-*mestizo* meld into an infinity of *mestizo* identities in which the cultural emphasis sometimes tends to the ladino side and sometimes to the Indian side, depending on the existential circumstances, social class, gender, and ethnicity of the individual. So too vary the modalities of discrimination . . . we have yet to come to terms with our existence as inter-ethnic and inter-cultural subjects. Ladinos, assuming with pride their indigenous culture, and Indians, assuming without guilt their ladino culture, and both admitting that they are culturally *mestizo* and that the differences give meaning to their particular mestizo-ness.

For pan-Mayanists, Morales represents a dangerous trend–using the rhetorical tools of postmodernism and multiculturalism to undermine the ideological bases of ethnic activism. They point out that such textual flourishes ignore the all too real material conditions, the structural violences that Maya people suffer in disproportionate numbers. In 2000, Inter-American Development Bank reported that 80 percent of the Guatemalan population lived in poverty, and that over 60 percent lived in extreme poverty (on less than the $2 a day estimated to buy a basket of basic necessities). Tellingly, poverty rates between ethnic groups vary substantially. Whereas 66 percent of the ladino population live in poverty (45% in extreme poverty), over 92 percent of the Maya population live in poverty and 81 percent in extreme poverty. Literacy rates, infant mortality rates, access to electricity and potable water–by virtual all measures of social development the Maya population is much worse off than the ladino population. The majority of Maya households in Guatemala live from subsistence farming, and they are hurt most by the country's highly unequal distribution of land. Based on the last (1979) agricultural census, 2.5 percent of Guatemalan farms control over 65 percent of the arable land, while 88 percent of farms control only 16 percent. The *gini* index for land distribution is 0.859 (where 0 = perfect equality, 1 = perfect inequality, and anything above 0.45 is considered destabilizing), putting it in the same class as Haiti, Brazil, and Sierra Leone.

Pan-Mayanists argue that such structural inequalities must be combated through equal opportunity and ethnically targeted affirmative action programs. These projects, in turn, demand a unified Maya front that can only be forged through cultural valuation and ethnic pride, not the postmodern hybridity of Morales' intercultural *mestizaje*.

Maya Activism between the Wars, 1945–1979

Guatemala's civil war temporarily halted a productive, though not so revolutionary, social movement organized around cultural and ethnic pride. This Maya cultural activism – promoting the use of native languages and dress, revitalizing customs, promoting civil rights – had its start at least as early as the 1940s with the work of Adrián Inéz Chávez (1904–87), a native K'iche' Maya schoolteacher and autodidactic linguist and ethnohistorian. Chávez translated the sacred K'iche' text the *Popol Vuh*, he developed an alphabet for Mayan languages that replaced Latin characters with ones based on an imagined precolumbian iconography, and he organized Indian teachers and encouraged them to promote bilingual education.

Chávez's influence was wide reaching, and he inspired a range of Mayanist activism. By the late 1960s and early 1970s, local and regional grassroots Maya organizations were forming all over the highlands of western Guatemala. Their power was most visible in the K'iche' and Kaqchikel linguistic regions. In 1972 a group of K'iche' professionals living around Quetzaltenango formed a political party, *Xel-hú* (the K'iche' name for Quetzaltenango). In 1976, their candidate became the first indigenous mayor of San Juan Ostuncalco. Xel-hú had to abandon its political aspirations during the violence, but reemerged with vigor in the 1990s. In a major 1995 victory, the party's candidate, Rigoberto Quemé, was elected mayor of Quetzaltenango, Guatemala's second largest city. Quemé's election was significant not only for the progressive reforms he brought to governance, but also for the symbol he became for

Edward Fischer

Maya people across Guatemala. He showed that grassroots Maya political organization was not only possible, it was feasible–that working within the existing legal framework, profound changes could be achieved. His tenure has not been without problems. Not long after his election there were a series of protests against his policy initiatives that involved racist shouting and graffiti. Quemé was re-elected in 1999, although voting results were hotly contests by his ladino opponents.

Similar political movements had developed in towns in the Kaqchikel region, most notably Comalapa and Tecpán, both of which elected indigenous representatives to congress in the 1974 elections. In Tecpán the group Patinamit, in alliance with the Partido Revolucionario (PR, the Revolutionary Party) elected Fernando Tezaguic Tohón, who served a one-term tenure, and then kept a low profile during the violence. In 1994 Tezaguic revived his political career along with his idea of forming an indigenous political party. The group that he founded, the *Comité Proformación del Partido Político Sociedad Ixim* (the Formation Committee of the Political Party Sociedad Ixim), aligned itself with the moderate-left *Partido Reformador Guatemalteco* (PREG, the Guatemalan Reform Party) and presented Tezaguic and Edwin Domingo Roquel Calí as candidates for congressional seats in the 1994 elections. Sociedad Ixim's campaign, whose slogan was *Hombres de Maíz al Rescate del País* (Men of Maize to the Rescue of the Country), updated the pro-indigenous platform Tezaguic had promoted twenty years earlier, and stressed his acceptance of the ideas of pan-Mayanism and the notion of "harmony in diversity." Though neither candidate won, the fact that they organized a viable campaign based on cultural issues opens the door for future Indian-based political initiatives.

Whereas the early to mid-1970s had ushered in an era of increased Maya participation in national and local politics as well as the widespread emergence of peasant leagues and economic agricultural cooperatives, the civil war of the late 1970s brought a virtual end to such forms of organization and collective action. With war raging between revolutionaries and the US-backed military, there was little political room in Guatemala for the pursuit of Maya identity politics during the early 1980s. While trying to reach out to Maya peoples, most of the Guatemalan revolutionaries stuck to a rather orthodox Marxist-Leninist approach to ethnicity, seeing it as obscuring class alliances (which is not to say that there were not Mayanist sympathies within some revolutionary groups). For their part, the state and military largely saw the Maya as barriers to the development (economic, social, and cultural) of the nation and as susceptible prey for the revolutionaries (see Richards 1985).

88

Maya Activism in "Post-war" Guatemala

It is impossible to exhaustively describe the organization of the pan-Maya movement in Guatemala. It is by design and by chance a fluid network of organizations and individuals who share broadly similar visions of a future Guatemala in which Maya are equal citizens.

With the democratic opening in 1985 (and the country's first free election in over thirty years) and the concurrent scaling down of the violent counterinsurgency campaigns in the mid to late 1980s, Maya cultural activists began to pursue their agendas with renewed vigor. Their initial efforts concentrated on linguistic issues. This is partly because a number of young Maya active in the movement had trained with foreign linguists; partly because language is the most powerful public identity marker for Maya males (see Cojtí Cuxil 1997:12); and partly because of strategic concerns (language issues were seen as largely non-threatening to the powers that be).

The stage for this renewal was set by the *Segundo Congreso Lingüístico Nacional* (the Second National Linguistic Conference) held in 1984, a follow-up to Chávez's event some 35 years earlier. A follow-up meeting was held in 1986 to try and coordinate the efforts among the growing number of groups working in Mayan linguistics in Guatemala. The two key players at these meetings took opposed positions. The *Proyecto Lingüístico Francisco Marroquín,* a collective of Maya and foreign linguists working on a long-term project to produce dictionaries and grammars for Mayan languages, led the call for the creation of a scientifically-based yet culturally appropriate unified alphabet for writing all Mayan languages. The *Instituto de Lingüístico del Verano* (the Summer Institute of Linguistics, or SIL as it is known by its English acronym), a group of Christian linguists supported by Protestant churches in the United States, argued for maintaining the Spanish-based, language-specific alphabets they had developed over their decades of work in Guatemala. In the end, the pan-Mayanists won the day and founded the *Academia de las Lenguas Mayas de Guatemala* (ALMG, the Acacdemy of Mayan Languages) to promote the unified alphabet and to coordinate linguistic conservation efforts.

Through the ALMG, pan-Mayanists embarked on an ambitious program of research, documentation, and political lobbying. Working on a shoe-string budget, but fueled by the passion of conviction, Maya activists were able to negotiate substantial legislative reform. In a move that energized a spectrum of Maya activism, in 1988 the ALMG pushed through legislation making the unified alphabet for Mayan languages the legally recognized orthography. While this law legalized the new Mayan alphabet, it did not raise Mayan languages to the official status of Spanish. Furthermore, the victory has turned out to be a mixed blessing: as linguistic research turns up subtle differences in vowel lengths, for example, it has proven impossible to get legislators to update the statue. Nonetheless, the 1988 victory galvanized support for the ALMG and vindicated its strategy of working for incremental legislative reform.

By the late 1980s, there were a growing number of pan-Mayanist organizations advocating a variety of interests. The 13 Deer Maya Writers were conducting technical linguistic research; *Cholsamaj*, a nonprofit editorial house, was publishing indigenous perspectives on culture, society, and politics; the *Centro de Documentación e Investigación Maya* (Maya Center for Documentation and Investigation) began a university scholarship program and a library of cultural texts. —These efforts continued to focus primarily on issues language and culture. To the powers that be, demands were presented as a matter of folkloric preservation–tapping into a familiarity with the genre of tourist promotion–and were seen as a cheap concession to the impoverished Maya population.

By 1989 the bourgeoning number of Maya groups began to chafe at the limited linguistic focus of the ALMG, which had served as a de facto umbrella organization for a wide range of Mayanist activism. Ironically, the ALMG's position of moral authority within the movement was further eroded by its most dramatic victory: in 1990 then President Vinicio Cerezo signed into law a bill making the ALMG an independent policy-recommending body of the government. The ALMG's budget grew to hundreds of thousands of US dollars, its workers became civil servants, and, while it expanded its impressive research and lobbying projects, a number of pan-Mayanist leaders began to see the ALMG as compromised by its increasingly close links to established national politics. Thus it was that leaders of a number of Maya groups, including the ALMG, formed the *Consejo de Organizaciones Mayas de Guatemala* (COMG, the Council of Maya Organizations of Guatemala) to act as a non-governmental coordinating body for national pan-Mayanist cultural, linguistic, and political efforts.

Throughout the 1990s there was an explosion of groups loosely affiliated with pan-Maya activism (see Fischer and Brown 1996; Fischer 2001, Gálvez and Esquit 1997, Warren 1998). By the late 1990s Maya leaders were bolder in the scope and substance of their demands for political reforms to promote ethnic equality within Guatemalan society (calls that would have been met with death threats not so many years earlier). Making public what had previously been confined to private meetings and whispered conversations, COMG developed an explicit set of demands, outlined in *Rujunamil ri Mayab' Amaq'* [Specific Rights of the Maya People] published in 1991. This new range of Maya proposals called for, among other things, official recognition and protection of Maya sacred sites (modern altars as well as archaeological sites); a recognition of indigenous legal traditions, and their incorporation into

the national system; and, most radically, some sort of political autonomy for ethno-linguistic regions and proportionate national
representation.

By the mid-1990s, tensions had emerged between pan-Mayanist organizations and Maya-led *grupos populares* (popular groups) Grupos
populares range from the CUC peasant league to CONAVIGUA (an association of widows of victims of the violence), and most of their leadership
and grassroots support is Maya. Yet, there is a great ideological divide
between pan-Mayanists and popular groups rooted in their respective
emphases on ethnicity and class. In the mid-1990s, many popular groups
began to adopt Maya cultural symbols and incorporate Mayanist
concerns into their agendas. New groups, such as *Majawil Q'ij*, were
formed that sought to meld indigenous cultural activism with peasant
demands. Initially, in the eyes of many pan-Mayanists these groups were
simply putting an indigenous veneer on their old message in order to sell
it to funding organizations and rural Maya alike. The main umbrella
organization of these hybrid popular/culturalist groups is the suggestively
named *Instancia de Unidad y Consenso Maya* (IUCM, the Instance of
Maya Unity and Consensus). IUCM affiliates range from more traditional
leftist Maya organizations, such as *Comité de Unidad Campesino* (CUC,
Committee of Campesino Unity) and the *Comunidades de Población en
Resistencia* (CPR, the Communities of Populations in Resistance) to more
culturalist groups such as *Majawil Q'ij* and regional beauty pageant
committees. Fernando Tezaguic's political group *Sociedad Ixim* is associated with the IUCM.

As a sign of their growing political power, pan-Mayanist organizations
were invited to participate in the negotiation of Peace Accords. In 1994,
Maya groups created the *Coordinación de Organizaciones del Pueblo
Maya de Guatemala* (COPMAGUA, the Coordination of Organizations
of the Maya People of Guatemala, also known by its Maya name,
Saqb'ichil) to represent indigenous interests at the negotiating table.
COPMAGUA at first included only pan-Mayanist representatives from
COMG, the ALMG, and other similar groups. Soon thereafter, however,
representatives of the popular/culturalist *Asemblea de Pueblos Mayas*
(Assembly of Maya Peoples) joined. COPMAGUA proved successful in
forging a consensus to draft a peace accord. Their wide-ranging Accord
on the Identity and Rights of the Maya People was ratified by government, military, and guerilla leaders as part of the peace process in March
1995, and constitutes a binding component of the final Peace Accord
signed in December 1996.

Discouragingly, a 1999 popular referendum to approve constitutional
changes mandated by the Peace Accords and beneficial to the Maya population was defeated. The defeat was a major setback for Maya
organizations, even if the government remains at least nominally
committed to their implementations. In part, the "no" vote on the refer-

endum can be attributed to the well-funded campaign orchestrated by business groups and the low voter turnout in Maya-dominated regions (Warren 2000). But it also highlights the inability of the largely urban-based pan-Maya leaders to mobilize support among the rural Maya masses. In contrast to the cases of Bolivia and Ecuador (discussed by Postero and Zamosc in the present volume), Maya leaders do not have an active base of grassroots support that they can call on to protest and demonstrate – or even vote. Guatemala's pan-Mayanist leaders have been much more effective in harnessing international support for their projects, and thus placing external pressure on the state for reforms. But this is a tenuous basis for sustained reforms.

All major international assistance groups working in Guatemala give top priority to helping the indigenous population. It is USAID's explicit policy to develop poverty reduction and education programs with a Maya focus. Working through the Institute of Linguistics at the Universidad Rafael Landívar, USAID underwrote a massive project of bilingual and bicultural textbooks and teacher training. The European Union has likewise favored indigenous groups, and helped set up an umbrella organization of Maya NGOs (the *Mesa Nacional Maya de Guatemala*, MENMAGUA) through which they could channel major funding (supporting grassroots Maya efforts without dealing with hundreds or thousands of proposals at a time). Nordic countries and the Netherlands were also particularly generous in funding Maya projects throughout the 1990s. Even the Inter-American Development Bank (IADB), the World Bank, and other generally neoliberal multilateral organizations have instituted formal mechanisms to ensure that projects are culturally sensitive – and produce the sort of development that people will want and embrace. A report from the Indigenous Peoples and Community Development Unit of the IADB calls for a series of measures such as "direct transfers to the poor (of particular relevance to underprivileged groups such as the indigenous population)" and land reform (Lustig and Deutsch 1998; Plant 1998).

Pan-Maya groups now wield a degree of political clout in Guatemala, and their accomplishments are impressive: legislative reforms that favor Mayan languages; a large number of their demands recognized in the Peace Accords; and a burgeoning body of linguistic, cultural, and political research and analysis. In 2000, one of the earliest and most eloquent proponents of pan-Mayanism, Demetrio Cojtí Cuxil, was appointed Vice-Minister of Education; at the same time, Olitilia Lux was appointed Minister of Culture and Sports; a growing number of Maya work within various government ministries; and there are 15 (out of 113) self-identified Indian congressional deputies. Optimistic observers point out that this represents a radical positive change in Guatemalan society over the last 10 years; pessimists remind us that these are still very low absolute and relative numbers. The Defensoría Maya states plainly that "it is necessary and fundamental that 50 percent of congressional deputies be indigenous"; that figure is presently 13 percent. This returns us to the tenuous power base of pan-Maya activists. While most Maya I know *who are aware of it* support the broad pan-Maya agenda, most have not been exposed to Maya activism. In this light, the next imperative for pan-Mayanists will be to expand their base of support out into the countryside.

Pan-Mayanist Messages

In the "post-war" context of Guatemala, pan-Mayanist groups have developed a remarkably savvy and effective political agenda, deftly employing the tools of "strategic essentialism" in pursuit of their progressive ends. Since its early days, the leaders of the Maya movement have stressed the need to foster cultural unity among all Guatemala's Maya peoples (over 5 million, or about half of the total population) as a necessary base for political and economic power and greater social equality. Presented as a nonviolent third way in the wake of the country's devastating civil war, the pan-Maya movement opened up new democratic spaces within Guatemala's political structure and garnered the support of western governments and the United Nations. Critics have attacked Maya leaders of being self-serving opportunists, and indeed the greatest challenge facing the movement today is to solidify and unify grassroots, rural support (a daunting task given the state of transportation and communication in many Maya areas).

A fundamental tenet of pan-Mayanist political philosophy is that the Maya peoples of Guatemala (speaking 21 different languages and living in hundreds of often isolated villages) must come to recognize and pursue their common interests–for only through unity can they wield political power proportionate to their numbers. Fostering such unity within a diversity borne of geographic and historical distance requires what is often described as an ethnic awakening. This implies the presumption that ethnicity (and here specifically Maya-ness) is in some way innate; the work of cultural activism, then, is to raise ethnic consciousness and awaken dormant sentiments. It also implies a return to presumptively more pure and authentic cultural forms and symbols.

In this regard, the widespread usage of hieroglyphic symbols within the pan-Maya movement is significant. For Maya scholars, hieroglyphs act as powerful symbols of the splendor and literacy of that culture. In the late 1980s and 1990s, noted epigrapher Linda Schele offered hieroglyphic workshops in Guatemala for Maya groups. The materials she produced are widely circulated among Maya activists, and there is an intense interest among activists to learn Classic Maya numeration, the calendrical system, and the basic Maya glyphic syllabary. The Maya publishing house *Cholsamaj*'s policy is to use Maya bar-and-dot numeration for page numbers, and to date their publications using the Classic Maya long count notation. Maya activists also employ a modified version of the ancient Maya hieroglyphic syllabary to write their adopted names and the names of their organizations.

Maya revitalization efforts are also seen at the grassroots level. A growing number of individuals have adopted Maya names for themselves (e.g., Pakal in place of José) and some young parents are legally naming their children for pre-contact historical figures or their date of birth in the sacred Maya calendar. A few young Maya men are growing their hair long and wearing it in a ponytail, a style that recalls Classic Maya portraits as well as trendy foreigners.

> October 1993, Tecpán Guatemala. I should not have been surprised, but I was. Tecpán's patron saint is San Francisco de Assisi, and the titular festival in his honor is held every October 4th. A central event of the festivities is the election and crowning of a new town queen. Rather queens, as I learned. In late September, as our friends and neighbors began to propose candidates and plan float themes, my first reaction was an incredulity based on my perceptions of beauty pageants in the United States – wasn't the earnestness of my Tecpaneco friends a bit tongue in cheek, did they not also see the kitsch value? For the most part, no. I learned that beauty pageants are highly charged political events, where interpersonal, inter-ethnic, political, and economic rivalries were played out – the sort of "deep play" of which Jeremy Benthem and Clifford Geertz write. What shocked me most was the fact that two queens would be crowned, a ladina as the Reina Franciscana and an Indian as the Princesa Ixmukane. I further was surprised that my Maya friends were not more offended by the separate and unequal conditions of the elections. But, they were more concerned with showing up the ladinos with their float decorations and pageant presentations. People worked for weeks designing and constructing elaborate floats on the back of flatbed trucks, liberally employing Classic Maya iconography and idyllic scenes of traditional Maya lifeways. The Mayanist floats were amazing, their skits poignant, their candidates eloquent multiculturalists. But, in the end, the Indian candidate put forth by the local military base won the day.

Pan-Mayanists have produced a wealth of scholarship and political analyses, and they have simultaneously had to develop new outlets for disseminating their work. The largest barrier to effective Maya mass communication is an extremely high illiteracy rate among Maya peoples in Guatemala and the lack of technological infrastructure. For these and other social reasons, Maya culture places a high value on oral skill and dexterity; indeed, local political systems are traditionally based on a consensus model which favors persuasive orators. Building on this cultural bias, early pan-Maya activists distributed teachings and lectures about the value of Maya culture on audio cassette tapes; families and small groups would listen to these and pass them along informal social networks within and between communities throughout Guatemala. And as televisions and video recorders have become more common, these same sorts of materials are being distributed on video tape. One Maya group has bought time on several regional radio stations and broadcasts a weekly radio program, *Mayab' Winäq*. Airing on Sundays from 4:30 am until 7:30 am, *Mayab' Winäq* combines music, political commentary, public service announcements, and short radio plays, all with a pan-Mayanist message. As intoned by the booming voice of the program's host, Jolom B'alam:

> *Mayab' Winäq* brings together the roots of Maya culture: identity, music, and history. It is the voice of the people, of Maya sentiment and expression. It is the pure and sincere song of a peoples that hold dear the hope of future peace, equality, brotherhood, and justice for all. It is the musical expression of these words that carries our message of fraternity. It is the thought transmitted from our ancestral parents *Xpiapok* and *Ixmukane*.

Several pan-Mayanist organizations have also begun to produce newspapers, magazines, and other printed materials for the Maya public. Notable here is the work of *Cholsamaj*, the non-profit Maya editorial and publishing house established in the late 1980s. *Cholsamaj* has been a pioneer in the computerization of Guatemalan publishing; they have even developed proprietary software which allows them to quickly and easily set type in Maya hieroglyphs. Although many of its titles sell well by Guatemalan standards, *Cholsamaj* remains reliant on grants from international organizations, and, increasingly, publishing contracts from these same groups. Recognizing the vulnerability brought about by this reliance, *Cholsamaj* spun-off a for-profit subsidiary press, *Maya Wuj*; the non-profit *Cholsamaj* owns 51 percent of Maya Wuj and employees of the press own the other 41 percent. *Maya Wuj* does a lively trade in private printing jobs, including books, diplomas, posters, and wedding announcements. Its best-selling item is an annual date book (*Cholb'al Q'ij*/Agenda Maya) which combines the hieroglyphic symbols for traditional Maya day names with Gregorian calendar dates and short essays about Maya cultural values and political demands.

Laws, Treaties, and Lasting Impunities

The legal basis for many pan-Maya political demands comes from the 1985 Guatemalan Constitution and international treaties to which Guatemala is a signatory. The Constitution ensures the right of individuals and communities to have their own customs and languages (Article 58), promises to protect the cultures of native ethnic groups, especially the Maya (Article 66), and notes that, while Spanish is the official language of the country, indigenous languages are part of the cultural patrimony of the nation (Article 143) and should be taught in schools in areas populated mostly by Maya (Article 76). In addition, the International Labor Organization's Convention 169, which Guatemala ratified, requires that indigenous groups be given the greatest degree of self-control over development programs possible. Finally, the 1996 Peace Accords (particularly the Accord on the Identity and Rights of the Maya People) establishes a legal framework for directly addressing a broad range of pan-Mayanists demands. Although the constitutional reforms required by the Peace Accords were rejected in the 1998 referendum, the Accords provide powerful moral and legal leverage for Maya activists pushing for reform. And, implementation of the Accords has remained a government commitment (with a variety of sticks and carrots provided by international donors).

Bold in its aim, scope, and language, the Accord on Identity and Rights of the Maya People is largely based on an agenda set by pan-Mayanist organizations (for further detail on the 1996 accords and their impact on Maya activism see Warren 1998 and Brown *et al.* 1998). The Accord first clarifies and strengthens rights provided for by the 1985 Guatemalan Constitution in regard to education, language, and religion. Indeed, the greatest success of the accords has been in promoting bilingual and bicultural education through the Ministry of Education. Language and education issues play a central role in the pan-Maya movement, and a number of Maya leaders now work within the Ministry developing curricular materials and training teachers. Ironically, the most significant resistance to bilingual education has come from rural communities, where many Maya parents want their children to focus on learning Spanish (the traditional language of upward mobility) rather than K'iche' or Kaqchikel or Mam. (María Elena García and Jose Antonio Lucero's chapter in this volume provides a similar case in highland Peru.) But attitudes are slowly changing as more and more Maya have come to take new pride in their native heritage: take, for example, the scores of new private and state-chartered Maya schools opening in larger towns across the country.

More radically, the Accord calls on the state to undertake legal reforms and affirmative action programs to ensure that Maya gain proportional representation in political offices. To believers in a unified Guatemalanness, this broaches the most threatening portion of pan-Mayanist demands. It plays to the notion that the pan-Mayanists are radical separatists that would like to see the downfall of the Guatemalan state. In fact, the most extreme Maya proposals have called for political autonomy for ethno-linguistic groups, represented by a Maya Parliament that would form half of a federal bicameral legislature. But this language did not make it into the Peace Accords, and even the advocates of such views admit their slim chances of ever being considered, much less implemented, by the Guatemalan state.

The Peace Accords do call for much greater accommodation and representation of indigenous peoples and traditions within the existing legal and political frameworks–providing translators and native language legal counsel to indigenous defendants, incorporating traditional legal practices of the community into the local court system, ensuring more proportionate Maya representation in the national government. In such ways, the Peace Accords outline what we may call a neoliberal approach to affirmative action: devolving power back to communities in order to allow for greater self-determination for the majority of indigenous peoples. Implementation, however, has been nonexistent, thwarted both by the 1999 defeat of the Consulta Popular (a popular referendum to amend the constitution in ways mandated by the Peace Accords) and the unwillingness of government administrations to enact reforms that would diminish their power and authority. The moral superiority of local governance has also been called into question following an epidemic of lynchings in rural communities in recent years.

The Peace Accords also call for some taxation authority to be devolved from the central government to municipal authorities–the notion being that indigenous peoples could then participate more directly in the governmental decision-making processes (Nancy Postero's chapter on Bolivia and Theodor Rathgeber's chapter on Colombia give examples of this type of participation). This fails to account for the fact that many rural Maya distrust their local government officials as much as the state bureaucracy. In June 2002, thousands of residents turned out in Tecpán for a demonstration against a new municipally collected tax; protests turned violent and the mayor and the police force were both run out of town. Continued opposition led the city council to renounce the tax collection, which local residents were unwilling to entrust to local officials. Even in post-war Guatemala, political violence continues. Human rights workers are threatened, kidnapped, and assassinated; activists' offices are ransacked and files stolen; and the perpetrators almost inevitably escape with impunity.

The Movement's Leadership

It would be a mistake to characterize the pan-Maya movement as monolithic. Like all such movements, pan-Mayanism is actively and dynamically constructed by individuals, each with their own agendas, brought together because of perceived ideological affinity and the pursuit of a broad common cause. The pan-Maya movement is broad based and made up of numerous organizations, many, but not all, of which are formally tied to one or more of the umbrella groups mentioned above. The fundamental ideological goals of these groups are largely convergent.

In those domains where community and individual interpretation vary greatly, such as religion, the pan-Maya movement takes its least strident, least controversial positions (although this too varies between pan-Maya groups and individual leaders). Indeed, one of the secrets to the success of the movement lies in the fact that its ideology appeals to individuals across religious boundaries – Protestant, Catholic, and traditionalists alike. Of course there is some religious tension, and a number of recently formed Maya groups have dedicated themselves to the promotion of traditional Maya religious values. Most often this takes the form of sponsoring and advertising ceremonies to commemorate Maya religious holidays, but Maya priests have also successfully pushed for legislation to protect sacred Maya archaeological and ceremonial centers. Most pan-Maya leaders are nominally adherents to Maya religion and/or syncretic Catholicism, although a few are practicing Protestants. There is, nonetheless, a notable absence of religious fervor, partly attributable to strategic bridge-building, but also due to the sort of skepticism that is everywhere associated with higher education. At the local level, however, pan-Mayanism seems to appeal to both Catholics and Protestants, each of whom interpret the meaning of cultural valuation and development in slightly different ways.

Pan-Maya activism has no single charismatic leader. In part this reflects a Maya model of group consensus building that diffuses decision making and power, and an abiding respect for age and experience as the primary sources of authority (at present the movement's elders are but in their early fifties). It also reflects the political reality in which the movement has had to operate. In the mid-1980s, and even today, being labeled as a Maya leader in Guatemala could have deadly consequences. A few pan-Maya leaders have confided that they are sometimes followed, that their phones are tapped, and that they live in fear of being shot, or worse kidnapped, by either state security forces or private paramilitary death squads. In this context Maya leaders do not feel that they have the luxury of pursuing apolitical scholarship, even if such were possible. Yet, this does not mean that Maya scholar-activists are activists first and scholars second. The two roles are mutually constitutive and reinforcing in an integrated methodology of intellectual praxis.

Leaders of the pan-Maya movement mostly come from rural Maya communities, but have, often at first to take advantage of educational opportunities (or fleeing the violence in their communities), moved to Guatemala City and have formed a number of non-governmental, non-profit organizations that promote cultural rights. They come from a growing class of professional Maya scholars, businesspeople, and activists. In many ways these leaders are an atypical sector of the Maya population: they are well-educated, with most at some stage of university studies; they are overwhelming urban; and they are relatively affluent, and increasingly so as the market for self-identified Maya professionals grows, fueled by demand from international organizations and even a few Guatemalan state agencies. There are, of course, exceptions to this "essentializing" trait list of characteristics of pan-Mayanist leaders, but it well describes the general pattern found in leaders' biographies.

Most pan-Mayanist leaders have been trained in a social science. Programs in linguistics at the Universidad San Rafael Landívar (funded through USAID) and the Universidad Mariano Gálvez (funded by the SIL) are aimed specifically at young Maya scholars. The *Centro de Documentación e Investigación Maya* (CEDIM, Maya Center for Documentation and Investigation) established a grant program for Maya women to study in national universities in the early 1990s, and other scholarship programs have since emerged. Informal ties with foreign scholars have enabled a small but prominent group of Maya to study at universities in North America and Europe, and programs in indigenous Fourth World studies have increased the demand for in-house natives in foreign universities.

Within the movement itself we may identify three distinct generations of activists. First, there are the "the elders" born in the 1940s and 1950s. Many of these individuals were exposed to academics and identity politics through work with the SIL and Catholic Action groups, and a smaller number through the work of the *Instituto Indigenista Nacional* (National Indigenist Institution). Many members of this generation studied at one of the Catholic Church's Indian boarding schools, the *Instituto Indígena Nuestra Señora de Socoro* (Our Lady of Help) for girls located in Antigua and the *Instituto Indígena Santiago* (Santiago Indigenous Institute) for boys in Guatemala City. Funneled mostly through connections with rural parish priests, these two schools accepted promising indigenous youths from across the country for training as teachers. It appears that the Church was motivated by a sincere desire to promote development among the Maya. The goals were modernist: development through education. The result was postmodern: appropriating the tools of Western education for ethno-nationalistic ends through Indigenous seminars, political parties, beauty pageants, and other cultural events.

A few members of this generation earned scholarships to study abroad at universities in Europe and the US (particularly in the late 1960s), and these experiences are often recalled as galvanizing an Indian ethnic consciousness. They often recall the ethnic awareness that accompanied living abroad, a context that both accentuated difference and romantically valued the novelty of being Maya. One man recalls studying English in Canada, the lone Maya among a group of ladino exchange students, and the English teacher who regaled students with the fallacies of the Spanish grammatical gender system ("stupid, stupid, stupid," he would repeat, arguing that objects have no natural gender). While his ladino classmates became indignant at this attack on their language, the young Maya man chimed in to agree, explaining that Maya languages, like English, did not have such an illogical gender system. It seems that such foreign contexts, especially academic ones, are propitious for the development of ethnic self-consciousness. Living and studying abroad in a radically different cultural context accentuates ethnic difference, and the distance from the hegemonic structures in which one was socialized allows for a revaluation of subaltern alternatives.

A second generation is composed of those born in the 1960s and early 1970s. These men and women, and in this generation there is a growing minority of women leaders, occupy most of the movement's formal and informal leadership roles. Often younger siblings to the elder generation, these activists benefited from the advances of their predecessors. They were generally quicker to start and pursue studies, encouraged by the elder brothers and sisters. They also were exposed to a culturalist ideology early on by their elder siblings, often participating peripherally in the cultural groups active in the early 1970s. There was less influence from the SIL and Catholic Action (although these factors were not absent), and more contact with secular groups such as the PLFM, and later OKMA, in one of their ongoing training seminars. Links to foreign scholars are better established, and a larger number than in the previous generation have studied abroad and hold graduate degrees from prestigious institutions. Both those who studied abroad and those who studied at home were instrumental in establishing the movement's momentum in the mid-1980s, and among them they formed a number of pro-Maya organizations.

Finally, there is now a third generation of Maya activists, largely the children of the elder generation, born in the late 1970s and 1980s. This is the first generation of children to come of age being exposed from their earliest years to the philosophy of pan-Mayanism. A large number seem to be following in the footsteps of their parents, pursuing studies in the social sciences and seeking jobs either with the government or non-profit organizations. A significant minority have chosen to pursue careers in business, medicine, computer programming, architecture, and other professional fields. I asked one father what he thought of his son's deci-sion to study architecture. He replied that the movement has plenty of social scientists – what the Maya people need now are more self-identi-fied Maya professionals, both as role models and as foundations of a Maya economic base not dependent on foreign assistance. Why, he asked, should a ladino architect be hired to create the impressive neo-Maya design of *Tikal Futura*, a luxury mall, hotel, and office complex built on the outskirts of Guatemala City in 1994? Would not a Maya architect such as his son, who has not only studied archaeology and iconography in school but who was also socialized in the Maya aesthetic, be better qualified? This same father explains that as his son was growing up he often worried about raising him in Guatemala City, removed from the traditional Maya values that permeated daily life in his home town of Tecpán. To quell his fears the father developed a number of neo-Maya socialization techniques, which he has since promoted among his peer group. When his son started working at odd jobs at about age nine, for example, the father made him contribute all of his wages to a household pool used for living expenses. As he grew older, the son could receive larger and larger disbursements from the common pool, but he still had to symbolically give all of his earnings to the family first. Such self-conscious socialization methods were reinforced through formal education, and the boy in question, along with his siblings, was sent to a cooperative Maya school run by pan-Maya activists for their children living in Guatemala City. Complementing a standard western fare for primary schools, students were taught about Maya history, learned to write using the unified orthography for writing Maya languages, and learned of the struggle of Maya identity politics. As a result the man's son and the other classmates have a much less self-conscious internalization of pan-Mayanist ideological precepts and symbols and will be an important source of change.

Pan-Mayanists leaders in Guatemala are in the awkward position of having several constituencies, often with competing interests, to which they are beholden. Their primary obligation is to the country's Maya population, the vast majority of whom live in remote rural areas. Thus initial efforts have focused on raising the cultural consciousness of the masses, demonstrating and reinforcing the value of Maya culture, arguing for its role in the modern world, and recognizing it as a basis for concerted political action. Second, pan-Mayanist leaders must appeal to the powers that be in Guatemala – challenging racist opinions and lobbying for legal changes, certainly, but also portraying the pan-Mayanist agenda as primarily cultural rather than political (and thus non-threatening and undeserving of violent reprisal). Finally, pan-Mayanists must also court the attention and favor of international academics and policy makers. Playing on the recent global valuation of all things indigenous, the recognition of indigenous rights as a subset of fundamental human rights, and the ideological commitment of many academics to support the empowerment of marginalized peoples, pan-Mayanists have been very successful at gaining material support for the movement from international organizations.

The greatest challenge facing the national pan-Maya movement is reconciling local concerns with the broader goal of fostering pan-Maya unity and ethnic consciousness. Maya leaders themselves acknowledge that the movement speaks only for "organized Maya" and not all Maya (Gálvez and Esquit 1997: 88–90). At the same time, Demetrio Cojtí writes that, with the exception of those thoroughly assimilated into ladino society, "the Maya pueblo is entirely Mayanist and thus anti-colonialist, just with different degrees of consciousness and forms of action" (1997: 51). He divides Maya ethnic consciousness into three categories. First, there is the mostly illiterate Maya peasantry who has a fundamental (yet largely untapped) sense of themselves as part of the Maya pueblo, reinforced through the constant lived experience of ethnic discrimination and social marginalization. Second, there are the Maya peasants and workers incorporated into popular (i.e., class-based) organizations whose ethnic awareness is subsumed to class consciousness. Finally, there are the educated middle- and lower-class Maya promoting pan-Maya unity through "more authentic Maya practice" in their "initiatives in the fight against colonialism" (1997: 52–2). Cojtí concludes that the pan-Maya movement seeks:

> the development of a Maya consciousness in, of, and for itself and to fight for the rights of the Maya pueblo. Its primary obligation is logically to achieve clear and complete ethnic consciousness among all Indians, and too realize this it has to resolve the problems of communication and the diffusion of ideas encountered in a multilingual country such as Guatemala. (1997: 53)

Beyond Victimization

Conceptions and discourses of victimization are simultaneously empowering and disempowering. To the sensitive observer, victimization may embolden political activity. Such was the case with the 1980s Central American solidarity movement in the United States and with the worldwide anti-globalization movement of the late 1990s and first few years of the twenty-first century. This is well, good, and necessary; international pressure certainly forced the Guatemalan government to scale back human rights abuses and to negotiate a settlement with the guerrillas. Victimization may also be used as moral leverage for political reform by victimized peoples, as pan-Mayanist have strategically deployed it in this age of globalized multiculturalism.

Yet, at the same time, it is too easy to reduce victims to nothing more than victimhood, thus losing sight of the rich complexity of their motivations and actions. Discursively reducing the Maya to victimhood situates blame for the their situation on structural conditions. Again, this is well, good, and necessary: Maya peoples clearly suffer from structural iniquities in Guatemalan society. And, as I have shown above, pan-Mayanist leaders are promoting creative and concrete alternatives to the present system. But here they are not mere victims, but protagonists in the creation of their own futures.

Victimhood is a negation of power. Yet to understand Maya cultural activism we must take a more Foucauldian approach, seeing power as diffuse, contingent, and widely distributed. This lead us to view the Maya as active rather than merely reactive – as power brokers and bricoleurs, structurally disadvantaged and yet still able to create and exert power. I do not mean to suggest that the Maya should be blamed for their oppression or that activists should cease to use the language of victimhood to press for social justice; but rather, that reducing the Maya to nothing more than their victimization adds symbolic insult to violent injury by negating the complex intentionality of their humanity. As always, anthropologists should take their cue from the peoples they study, and I think we have a lot to learn from the Maya. In the West, we tend to essentialize the self, reducing individuals (and groups) to one or more definitive (and presumptively innate) characteristics. Such a view subtly underlies discourses of victimhood espoused by the human rights movement. In contrast, Maya tend to view the self as much more malleable and multifaceted, grounded not only in 'self' interest but also in communal relations. Such a perspective makes mute the debate over whether Maya leaders are self-serving or altruistic–they are, of course, both and their power lies in the balance. Such a perspective also allows us a clearer understanding of the complex practices of Maya political agency: hybrid constructions incorporating both, traditional cultural symbols and international discourses, materially underwritten by small-scale farming and foreign NGOs, organized through word of mouth and Internet mailing lists.

The Maya perspective on the self and its implications for political activism and social analysis are perhaps most poetically expressed in the words of Sub-comandante Marcos, the leader of the Maya zapatistas of Chiapas, Mexico. Like pan-Mayanists, the zapatistas employ identity politics to validate their claims against the Mexican state, although theirs is a more militant call for political, economic, and social reform. But Marcos is not Maya, leading critics to call into question the movement's legitimacy and authenticity. Disparaged for not being Indian and accused of being gay, Marcos deftly resists such tidy categories in characteristic Maya fashion by stating that he is: "gay in San Francisco, a black in South Africa, Asian in Europe, a Chicano in San Isidro, an anarchist in Spain, a Palestinian in Israel, an indigenous person in the streets of San Cristóbal . . . In other words, Marcos is a human being in this world. Marcos is every untolerated, oppressed, exploited minority that is resisting and saying 'Enough!'" Here Marcos, in his own poetic way, effectively captures a widespread sentiment among Maya activists who steadfastly refuse to be pigeonholed by dehumanizing essentialisms and categories of social containment.

Notes

1   The commission's 1999 report, Guatemala: Memoria del Silencio, is available online <http://www.hrdata.aaas.org/ceh/report/>.
2   The "thirty-six year war," as journalist are apt to refer to it, has a certain ring to it. But I would divide this into two distinct wars: one in the eastern highlands that started in the early 1960s and was decidedly defeated by the end of that decade, and another, initially led by some of the veterans of the previous conflict, in the Maya dominated highlands of western Guatemala. Back in conventional step, I would date this war (or phase of the conflict) to the massacre of 34 Maya farmers at Panzós on 29 May 1978, and the rise to power of Gen. Romeo Lucas García.

Edward Fischer

References

Brown, R. McKenna *et al.* 1998: Mayan visions for a multilingual society: The Guatemalan Peace Accords on Indigenous Identity and Languages. *Fourth World Bulletin on Indigenous Law and Politics* 6: 28–33.

Browning, John 1996: Un obstáculo imprescindible: el indígena en los siglos XVIII y XIX. *Memoria del Segundo Encuentro Nacional de Historiadores.* Guatemala: Universidad del Valle.

Cojtí Cuxil, Demetrio 1997: *Ri Maya' Moloj pa Iximulew; El Movimiento Maya.* Guatemala: Editorial Cholsamaj.

Fischer, Edward F. 2001: *Cultural Logics and Global Economies: Maya Identity in Thought and Practice.* Austin: University of Texas Press.

Fischer, Edward F. and R. McKenna Brown (eds.) 1996: *Maya Cultural Activism in Guatemala.* Austin: University of Texas Press.

Gálvez, Víctor and Esquit, Alberto 1997: *The Mayan Movement Today: Issues of Indigenous Culture and Development in Guatemala.* Guatemala City: FLACSO-Guatemala.

Lustig, Nora and Deutsch, Ruthanne 1998: The Inter-American Development Bank and Poverty Reduction: An Overview (IADB working paper). Washington: IADB.

Morales, Mario Roberto 2000: Sujetos interculturales. *Siglo XXI*, June 10.

Plant, Roger 1998: Indigenous Peoples and Poverty Reduction: A Case Study of Guatemala (IADB working paper). Washington: IADB.

Richards, Michael 1985: Cosmopolitan world-view and counterinsurgency in Guatemala. *Anthropological Quarterly* 58 (3), 90–107.

Stoll, Davis 1993: *Between Two Armies in the Ixil Towns of Guatemala.* New York: Columbia University Press.

Warren, Kay B. 1998: *Indigenous Movements and their Critics: Pan-Maya Activism in Guatemala.* Princeton: Princeton University Press.

—— 2000: Lessons from the 'failure' of the 1999 referendum on indigenous rights in Guatemala. Paper presented at the Advanced Seminar, School of American Research, Santa Fe, New Mexico, October 22–26.

Indigenous Struggles in Colombia

Historical Changes and Perspectives

Theodor Rathgeber

The indigenous movement in Colombia pioneered the continent-wide trend of indigenous organization. Since colonial times, Colombian indigenous peoples have resisted domination and economic exploitation. The current wave of indigenous activism began in the 1970s, focusing on the recovery of ancestral lands. Over time these struggles expanded to include issues of control and protection of the environment, the desire to reduce dependency on the capitalist economy, the protection of culture and identity, and struggles for human rights and a truly pluriethnic constitution. In the process, indigenous groups and organizations arose at community, regional, national and international levels.

As in other countries in Latin America, these issues were intensified by indigenous participation in the international conferences surrounding the 1992 Colombus Quincentennial. Indigenous organizations used these meetings to push debates about social emancipation and pluriethnic reality of their nations onto the national agendas. Indigenous groups have participated in other international meetings since then – from the United Nations Working Group on Indigenous Peoples and the Vienna Conference on Human Rights to the World Population Conference in Cairo. Such international events have fostered a sphere of legality and legitimacy in which indigenous claims can be contested. Indigenous movements have used these new openings in a variety of ways. This chapter offers an overview of the growth and current situation of the indigenous movement in Colombia, which is one of the most remarkable movements of its kind in Latin America.

Theodor Rathgeber

Overview: Colombia's Indigenous Peoples

It is estimated that the total number of indigenous people in Colombia fluctuates between 700,000 and 800,000, or 2–3 percent of the country's population. This estimate is based on official census figures that do not include the indigenous people living in the cities. Some *cabildos* (indigenous councils) are actually funcioning in large cities, such as Cali, where they have their governing offices. All in all, there are 81 indigenous groups with 64 languages, located in 27 of the 32 departments (Colombian equivalent to states or provinces).

Fifty-six groups live in the Amazonian Basin and in the Llanos region. In some regions, such as the Cauca Department (which has 1.2 million inhabitants and an indigenous population of 150,000 to 200,000), indigenous populations constitute a majority in many municipalities. The largest group are the Nasa (formally known as Páez) in southern Colombia; also numerous are the Embera in the northwestern part of the country, the Wayúu in the Guajira peninsula, and the Zenú on the Atlantic Coast (Pineda Camacho 1995).

Two national and 36 regional organizations were formed as a result of the indigenous struggles of the last thirty years. The revival of the indigenous movement in Colombia started in 1971 with the formation of CRIC, the Regional Indigenous Council of the Cauca Department. ONIC, the Colombian National Indigenous Organization, was established as an umbrella federation in 1982, representing the vast majority of the indigenous groups. OPIAC, the Organization of the Indigenous Peoples of the Colombian Amazon, was formed in 1995. It represents the indigenous peoples of the Amazonian Basin and is part of COICA, the Coordination of Indigenous Organizations in the Amazonian Basin. Two national political parties were also formed in the 1990s: ASI, the Social Indigenous Alliance, and MIC, the Colombian Indigenous Movement.

To a great extent, the organizational fragmentation can be attributed to the patterns of settlement throughout what is now Colombia. The indigenous peoples were largely organized on the basis of small communities and were only marginally aware of imperial regimes such as the Inca. This constellation made it difficult for the Spanish to impose their regime evenly across all the regions. Only in emergency situations or in the case of war did people organize themselves at the regional level. Instead, the Indian groups were organized at the local or community level, often based on traditional structures such as the *minga*, collective work performed by all the members of the community. The *minga* continues to be recognized as an institution that helps to maintain the indigenous collective identity. Even today, territorial dispersion is a factor that complicates the processes of social and political organization beyond community levels (Lindig and Münzel 1985).

Historical, Social and Political Context of the Contemporary Indigenous Struggles

Until the early 1960s the system of ownership of large holdings in Latin America, known as *latifundismo*, was the economic institution that structured social and political interests. Through this system, societal values were articulated and cultural identities were placed into a hierarchical structure. The indigenous – and peasantry – were forced into marginalization, where their existences were little above the level of survival.

Latifundismo has given way to neoliberalism as the main force and ideology structuring Colombian society today. The eagerness to commodify all aspects of life, and to exploit natural resources without bounds affects even the most remote communities. According to this ideology, society must be regulated only to the extent that the free flow of capital is not hindered. Goods and services are valued on strictly economic criteria. Political and social questions are subsumed to these values, which requires the adaptation of the country's social, political and cultural conditions to a market ideology. One prime example is the acceleration of exploitation of the natural resources, even in environmentally sensitive areas. Colombia is one of many countries in Latin America that is rapidly expanding the extraction of raw materials as a result of this neoliberal push.

The results of this assault on the environment could be seen during the 1990s. The government of César Gaviria (1990–4), gave private companies, especially those investing in raw materials, the green light in spite of the legal restrictions that protected communal lands. Crude oil became one of the most important materials for export and foreign revenue. The Andres Pastrana administration (1998–2002) modified the mining law, implementing a Mining Code that weakened the established mechanisms of consultation and participation with the affected communities. Previously, every phase of a project required an environmental license that allowed for the presentation of concerns by those affected. Since 2000, however, all impact evaluation procedures have been reduced to a single environmental license, transforming what was once a coordinated and participatory process into a simplified pro-forma process. This threatens the provisions of the national constitution and international agreements (such as Convention 169 of the International Labor Organization), which protect indigenous territorial autonomy.

At the political level, the scenario presents itself less unilaterally, although it follows similar lines. The *latifundismo* structure was a factor that helped sustain the authoritarian regime that culminated in the civil war known as *La Violencia* (the violence), which ravaged the country during the 1940s and 1950s. Murder, intimidation, and eviction of those who disagreed with the system became the official instruments for solving the social crisis. None of the main actors responsible for the crimes have, thus far, been brought to justice. Nor did this system come to an end with the agreement signed by the politicians to end the civil war. The National Front, in effect between 1958 and 1974, was a pact between the liberal and conservative parties to share political power in order to pacify the country. Under the formally democratic National Front regime, elections were openly manipulated, discrediting the most fundamental participatory institution: the vote.

Political violence became endemic. With the pretext of containing the guerrillas, the government of Julio Cesar Turbay (1978–82) imposed a wave of repression that ended most social protest. In the second half of the 1980s, the electoral participation of the *Unión Patriótica* (Patriotic Union, a leftist party formed by former guerrillas) ended in disaster: death squads and paramilitary groups annihilated most of its leaders. Similarly, during the presidential campaign of 1989–90, three of the presidential candidates with the best chances of being elected were killed.

In 1991, as we discuss below, there was an important political process which resulted in reforms granting rights to indigenous and peasant groups. Yet, the current president, Alvaro Uribe (2002–6) seems to have taken on the authoritarian style of President Turbay. According to declarations made by the Home Affairs Minister Fernando Londoño, the rights granted by the 1991 constitution will be restricted. It appears that only the actors of the "dirty war" have changed. Instead of the state acting as the main source of repression, as was the case in the time of the Turbay regime, now the paramilitary or self-defense groups are crushing what they consider subversion. They are not alone, of course, since they receive support from the state forces as well as the whole social environment which allows the repression. The Uribe administration is also bent on creating a rural militia composed of peasants and a network of informers and vigilantes.

It is also clear that guerrilla groups also act with the same rationality, and that they are an integral part of the problem. Due to the basis of their income – especially that coming from "taxes" on drug-trafficking, kidnapping, and blackmailing of oil companies – there is little need now for them to try to reach an understanding with the rest of society. They pressure communities into supplying them with food and fuel, recruiting youngsters by force. Thus, the military logic of solving the crisis through armed conflict appears to have been adopted by all actors. The war is directed now at the society as a whole, and protesting this brings substantial risks. The state of emergency has become routine, and participation is increasingly being restricted to activity within clientelist networks. In Colombia, authoritarianism has been a historically common approach to managing the relationship between state and society, and is always considered as a first option when it is necessary to deal with a crisis (Guzmán *et al.* 1977; Pizarro 1985; Sánchez and Peñaranda 1986; Sánchez Gómez 1991, Human Rights Watch 1996, 1998; Pecaut 2002).

The Reforms of the 1990s

Under the slogan of "modernization" of the state, a legal framework was established to allow for wider articulation between sectors of the society. Several important reforms were made to the constitution and the political structure which proved helpful to Colombia's indigenous peoples.

During the administration of Virgilio Barco (1986–1990), the implementation of the initiatives taken by the government of Belisario Betancur (1982–1986) continued, especially state decentralization. According to Boisier (1999), the "winds of decentralization" were blowing all over Latin America by then. More than 100 years after the first attempt (in 1863), the first direct elections for town councilors and mayor took place in 1988. The Gaviria government also extended the direct vote to the election of departmental governors.

The number of town councilors and majors who presented themselves as "independent" increased greatly with the opportunity for direct voting for local representatives. However, the expected break-up of the hegemony of the two traditional parties and the clientelist system was not achieved. One important result, however, was that the electoral reform allowed indigenous groups to elect their own local authorities and obtain representation in departmental assemblies and the national Congress. In the 2000 elections an indigenous candidate, Floro Tunubalá, was elected governor of the Cauca department. Together with five other governors, he openly opposed the national government's policy of fumigation of illegal drug crops (Fals Borda 1989; Restrepo 1991; Rathgeber 2001c; Fajardo 2001).

With the new constitution of 1991 (Art. 103), the Gaviria government added more participatory elements, particularly at the local level. One example is the transfer of funds to the municipalities, which is now an important item in the budget of indigenous organizations. Under this scheme, the municipality (or another public entity of the same type such as the indigenous councils) presents projects for the improvement of public education, public health, or other local services. Once the project is approved, the municipality has the right to receive transfers from the central state to cover most of the costs of the project. Another factor that opened the way for more participation was the provision of legal instruments that allow citizens to claim their rights *vis-à-vis* the state. In the case of the indigenous groups, it is particularly important that they can exercise their *derecho de tutela*, their right to use injunctions, to make sure that they are consulted before projects are carried out in their areas of residence. However, an injunction does not guarantee that the government will comply, especially when the projects have to do with oil extraction or the exploitation of other natural resources. For all its importance as a mechanism that seeks to promote participatory, democratic, and transparent procedures in government, the fact is that the *tutela* right has become a conflict-ridden legal issue.

Why did the government make these changes? There were important factors behind these reforms. On the one hand, the Gaviria government was keen on modernizing the institutional apparatus of the state. It was evident that, apart from the violence, Colombia's political system was undergoing a crisis of governance. Even industry had complaints about the inefficiency of the administration, underscoring the need to improve the management and regulation of the state. In the same way, international institutions – at the bilateral as well as the multilateral level – called for an innovation of the traditional political structures and emphasized the need for "democratization" and participation in decision-making. To this end, the state's regulatory capacity at the national level was reduced in some sectors, especially in relation to the welfare question, and at the local level it had less influence *vis-à-vis* the economy. In other areas, for example the issuing of licenses for mining and oil production, there was a concentration of transactions at the state level in order to "increase" efficiency. These "modernizing" efforts also paved the way for the sacking of employees and workers of national institutions, thus complying with the neoliberal challenge of a minimized state. In this sense, the modernization of society is not limited to the free trading of goods (Nolte 1996).

On the other hand, modernization reforms provided political openings for social movements, which had demanded increased direct participation since the beginning of the 1970s. They used the reforms to revitalize the political field at the municipal level, push for full participation for all citizens, and search for ways to regulate the social crises with civil (that is, non-military) methods. Colombia's history is characterized by the struggle against structures imposed by the ruling classes: the centuries-long indigenous resistance; the commoners' rebellion that preceded the independence movement in 1781; the craftsmen's struggle for democracy in 1854; the social protests of the 1930s; the radicalization of agrarian reform in the 1960s and 1970s; the regional and urban civic movements that started in the second half of the 1970s; and the confluence of the indigenous and civic movements advocating for a multicultural nation. Despite the pervasiveness of armed conflict and repression, these social forces and their debates and activities showed that there were actors with the potential to dissent within democratic frameworks. Their protests forced governments to adjust their programs and develop new instruments that would facilitate negotiations with the dissatisfied sectors. A case in point were the mobilizations – with intense involvement of indigenous groups– that contributed to the establishment of a special State Attorney office that monitors human rights violations and commits the

Colombian government to cooperate with the International Commission for the Protection of Human Rights. Once again, however, there is no guarantee that state agencies will comply with their constitutional duties (Meschkat *et al.* 1980; García 1981; Zamosc 1986; Chaparro 1989; Rathgeber 1991; Huhle 2000).

These legal and political changes now make it possible for the indigenous movement to expand its power, representation, and participation. This is happening on a number of levels. Some of the decentralization reforms now allow the *cabildos*, or indigenous councils, to direct funding for bilingual schools, to build health centers with traditional and western medicine, and to set in place a water and energy infrastructure within a communal regime (not privatized). The indigenous population also invested in small industries and other income-generating ventures. They were also able to regain some of their traditional legal jurisdiction, which allowed room, once again, for the institutionalization of indigenous conflict resolution processes. This has not been without tensions, however, as some community members (for example, those who saw a physical punishment as a violation of individual human rights) questioned this indigenous jurisdiction. Others conflicts emerged. In the past, it was hard to find a new governor for an indigenous *resguardo* (reservations allocated to the indigenous peoples in colonial times). Since the posts at the *cabildo* of a *resguardo* imply access to funds, there is now stiff competition for these jobs.

Thus, while in other countries decentralization was often implemented in a half-hearted manner, in Colombia, decentralization reforms were taken as a serious challenge. In a sharp departure from past practices, in the 1990s, social movements and organizations were able to transform administrative reform into a real revitalization of politics, especially at the local level. The indigenous organizations in several regions of the country were among the most committed players in this process.

Indigenous Groups as Social Actors

When referring to the indigenous movement as a social actor in the current period, we cannot forget the history of indigenous resistance against domination since the Spanish conquest, or the other complex processes that have allowed their culture to be maintained, in particular in remote regions with a difficult topography and thus difficult access. Furthermore, indigenous peoples developed a surprising capacity to adapt some colonial institutions to their own purposes. The *cabildos*, or local councils, were instituted in Spanish colonial times with the goal of having communities manage their own poverty. This type of "self-government" was reformulated by national and departmental laws passed in the 1890s. In the 1970s, the indigenous movement took advantage of the provisions of these laws, transforming the *cabildo* into the institutional basis for winning autonomy.

The main indigenous protagonist of that period, CRIC, emerged fighting alongside peasant organizations for a change in the distribution of rural land and for democratization of society. CRIC advocated not only indigenous territories, but also for traditional rights, the maintenance of indigenous customs, and the importance of cultural diversity in the country. It became the model for regional indigenous organizations. From its beginning in 1971, Cauca's indigenous movement attracted attention because of the strength of its mobilizations even in times of repression. The great capacity of its leaders to convoke gatherings generated its own dynamic, which – according to conservative estimates – resulted in the reclaiming of more than 35,000 hectares of land that had been previously occupied by large landowners and the church. (CRIC estimates are on the order of 60,000 hectares.) They also did away with other duties such as the poll tax, eliminating the bases for the political dominance exercised by the landowners.

In the 1980s, the indigenous population of the Amazon basin succeeded in obtaining guarantees to approximately 18 million hectares. This expansion of indigenous territories was deeply criticized by previous governments and investors because it hampered exploitation of natural resources in the region. The recovery of ancestral land meant not only the further availability of additional land to satisfy the needs of the families of the indigenous population, but also local governance, control, and utilization of the indigenous territories according to their own rules and methods. These achievements did not come about without losses: between 1971 and 2000, approximately 600 indigenous leaders were killed, and for the most part their assassins remain unpunished (Rathgeber 1994; Pineda Camacho 1995; CRIC 1997, 2000).

From 1980 onward, the political platform and discourse of the CRIC and the national indigenous organization ONIC promoted the autonomy of the indigenous councils. In 1985 the *cabildos* in the Cauca region presented the Vitoncó resolution, which would become a landmark for the autonomy of indigenous communities. The concept of autonomy consisted of the management of natural resources by the communities, the election of their indigenous representatives according to their traditions, and the development of their own rules, all financed by funds available from the public budget (so-called "transfers") and backed by a system of justice based on their customary law (Rathgeber 1994; Pineda Camacho 1995; Bonilla 1995).

The indigenous movement also touched on the issue of seeking civil solutions for social conflicts. One of the most notable successes was the 1984 CRIC agreement with the regional chapter of FEDEGAN, the Cattle Raisers Federation, whose members had traditionally used paramilitary bands to repress the groups that tried to occupy their lands. In this highly violent situation, both parties put emphasis on a dialogue to safeguard their own interests. The cattle raisers agreed to peacefully solve the land conflicts involving indigenous communities, while CRIC promised to use its influence to put an end to the land invasions. Some groups on the political left denounced the agreement as treason, but most of the indigenous communities supported it, since it allowed them to consolidate their territories in a time of war. The CRIC/FEDEGAN agreement became one of the few examples in Colombian history in which civilian actors were able to solve a major social conflict without the intervention of state authorities. Still, in many other regions of the country, indigenous groups suffered the consequences of the dirty war that developed in the second half of the 1980s.

Using the same approach, Cauca's indigenous movement opted for establishing a dialogue with state institutions. After the mid-1980s – when the armed conflict became more acute and the Cold War crushed many social movements and trade unions – the CRIC tried to convince the government, the Catholic Church, and even the military to implement the civil option to solve the conflict. At the national level, it achieved the creation of a Department of Indigenous Affairs at the Attorney General's Office for the investigation of abuses committed by the military and the police on indigenous territories. Since 1996 the indigenous peoples in the Antioquia region have been trying to reach an agreement with the armed groups – the guerrilla and the paramilitary – under which their autonomy within their territories is to be respected, as is their neutrality *vis-à-vis* the ongoing battle for power. The guerrillas rejected the agreement and it seems that the Uribe government will do the same; yet, the state is now trying to induce the indigenous groups to collaborate with state security forces, even though they do not share the same notion of national security. The dialogues contributed to the precarious balance between those in favor of, and those against, militarization.

The continued militarization threatens to bring social and political activity in the indigenous communities to an end. It obstructs the supply of food and medicine and restricts tasks carried out in the different climatic zones (open-air religious ceremonies and communal assemblies) and even in central urban areas. The indigenous authorities recognized by law need permits from the military or guerrilla commanders to move within the region or to call meetings. The guerrillas of the FARC (Colombia's Revolutionary Armed Forces), have at times impeded indigenous efforts to recuperate territory because it is not convenient to their strategic objectives. The fighting between of the state's forces, the paramilitary, and the guerrillas is threatening the physical existence of the indigenous communities. The indigenous group "Quintín Lame," was formed in 1984 as a self-defense group against the landowners' paramilitary groups. It had little military action, but was supported by the local people. Nevertheless, most of its indigenous leaders realized that the armed approach did not suit the needs of the communities, or the concept of autonomy, and so the group was dissolved at the beginning of the 1990s (Rathgeber 1994, 2002; Bonilla 1995).

Despite the militarization of the country, and the difficulties it causes them, indigenous organizations have still been able to accomplish significant change. Probably the most important have been the constitutional reforms in 1991. The indigenous movement brought its impressive discursive abilities to the debates of the 1991 Constituent Assembly, which came as the country took a brief interlude from the war to try to bring the armed conflicts to an end. Indigenous organizations were represented by three elected assembly members who were able to get some significant provisions passed into the new constitution. Under the reforms, the state has the following obligations: to recognize and protect the ethnic and cultural diversity of the country (art. 7); to ensure equality and safeguard the dignity of the different cultures (art. 70); to recognize traditional indigenous institutions (art. 72); to guard the collective property of the indigenous territories and grant them the status of Indigenous Territorial Entities (art. 63, 286 and 329); to guarantee ancestral religion (art. 18 and 19); to respect the right to a sustainable development and to consult with the indigenous communities when a proposed project relates to indigenous territory (art. 79, 80 and 330); to give official status to the indigenous languages and establish bilingual education in the indigenous territories (art. 10, 68.5); to guarantee autochthonous systems of justice within the indigenous territories (art. 246); and to ensure a minimum of indigenous representation at the parliamentary level (art. 171 and 176). The indigenous population witnessed the enshrinement of their fundamental rights in the constitution; an event without precedent in the history of Colombia (Bonilla 1995; Pineda Camacho 1995; ONIC 1996a; Muyuy Jacanamejoy 1997).

The other arena in which indigenous peoples have been active is in the search for peaceful solutions to the war. In 1996, the indigenous movement mobilized at national level to push this issue. The government of Ernesto Samper (1994–8) had not complied with the various agreements, and the number of leaders killed had increased dramatically. In the Cauca region, the Páez, Totoró, and Yanacona groups had secured their land rights with the handing over of more than 20,000 hectares between 1992 and 1994. With the occupation of the Episcopal Conference headquarters and of other public buildings and the blocking of the Pan-American Highway and other important roads, the indigenous population pressured the government into signing two decrees. The first one (No. 1396/96) created the Human Rights Commission for the Indigenous Peoples. The second (No. 1397/96) created the National Commission for Indigenous Territories. This latter decree had the task – amongst others – of defining the timeline for the issuing of titles and the expansion of indigenous lands. A Permanent Council of Agreement and Consensus with the Indigenous

Peoples and Organizations were also established. The participation of regional and national organizations did not preclude the involvement of local organizations in the negotiations. The Human Rights Commission and the Permanent Council still exist. The provision that created the Commission for the Indigenous Territories was abolished later by the Pastrana government.

In the past three years, the indigenous population in the Cauca region established a "territory of coexistence, dialogue and negotiation" in the community of Piendamó, next to the Pan-American Highway between Cali and Popayán. This public space has been set up with the aim of fulfilling several objectives: to discuss alternative proposals to Plan Colombia (the United States' drug eradication assistance program), to exchange alternative experiences, and to build on the relationships of solidarity with the international community. It seeks to gather those groups of civil society not wishing to place themselves within the bipolar schemes set by the government and the guerrilla group, FARC. The indigenous population did not trust the dialogue process between the two parties; nor did they feel represented by either side. They were seeking a new relationship between the indigenous groups, the other actors, and the government, emphasizing the necessity of civil options for solving social conflicts.

Surrounded and threatened on several occasions by the FARC and the paramilitary, the indigenous population has managed to maintain their "territory of coexistence" in Piendamó. While the government and the guerrilla groups have not paid much attention to this initiative, it has generated substantial interest at the international level. Even the president of the Italian Parliament participated in one of the meetings in 2000 (CRIC 1996, 1999; ONIC 1996b; Rathgeber 2000, 2001a, 2001d).

However, there are limits for indigenous actors trying to neutralize negative forces and influence institutional changes. Since the mid-1990s, they have not been able to prevent the intensification of the conflict or the militarization within the borders of indigenous territories. Those responsible for the massacre in the Nilo hacienda in 1991 (in the municipality of Caloto, Cauca region), in which 20 indigenous Nasa people were killed, have not been punished. However, the CRIC's investigations have revealed that the responsibility lies with members of the national police and drug-dealers. The Inter-American Human Rights Commission recommended that the Colombian government pass a decree allowing the indigenous people to acquire the lands they have claimed for more than a decade, the conflict over which was the underlying reason for the massacre. The government still refuses to issue the decree (ONIC 1996b, 1999c; Rathgeber 2001a, 2001b, 2001d).

More importantly, the government has not implemented the laws or decrees necessary to put the constitutional provisions in practice. The seizures of land by white settlers, landlords, and drug-traffickers continue in spite of the Constitution. Such basic needs as health, education, food, and housing are not met. In the areas of oil exploration – above all in Arauca, Boyacá, North Santander, and Putumayo departments – the right to consultation and participation is limited to mere attendance to a pro-forma public event. According to the indigenous organizations, they are dealing with a new form of colonization. Those who oppose the indiscriminate exploitation of gold, coal, wood, or medicinal plants are accused of belonging to the guerrillas, which in some areas is equivalent to a death sentence. Cultural aggression is practiced daily by a variety of state institutions, as well as by the church, missions, settlers, landlords, drug-traffickers, the paramilitary, and the guerrillas.

If we compare the current situation to that of the 1970s, the impact of the indigenous movement on socio-political reality in Colombia is remarkable. They have successfully strengthened the processes of democratization, extended citizen participation, and renounced violence as a method of conflict resolution. They have managed to translate the state's rules into instruments that they are now using to meet the needs of their communities, protect their territories, promote improvements in their living conditions, and experiment with new forms of social links. The indigenous movement has emerged as one of the loudest critics of the Colombian state, even though they defend the existence of the constitution as a core standard and as an indispensable condition for the development of a different culture. They have come forward as a major force promoting the opening of political spheres, in addition to articulating their own model of development (Rathgeber 1994; Ströebele-Gregor 1994).

Shaping the Future from an Indigenous Perspective: Three Case Studies

Globalization processes imply an acceleration of the flow of capital. In the process, the activities of extractive industries have the effect of spreading insecurity, threatening the cultural and physical survival of indigenous peoples (Hardt and Negri 2000). In the previous sections of this chapter, we have considered broad processes of change at the national level, paying attention to the ways in which the indigenous movement has been adapting and trying to influence politics. In the following sections we review three examples of local and regional struggles focused on the defense, recovery, and development of indigenous identities and territories.

The U'wa: Defending an Ancestral Territory

The approximately 5,000 members of the U'wa people have traditionally lived in the foothills of the Eastern mountain range and the Sierra Nevada del Cocuy. In the department of Boyacá, the U'wa share the territory with peasant families. They maintain a land management strategy on their territory that distributes land in certain areas, according to the agricultural calendar. This strategy, which provides basic food security, has already been negatively affected by the loss of land and dissociation within the territory. The Cobaría community lacks access to land in the lower regions, which means that they go hungry during certain times of the year. Plans for oil extraction in their territory imply an additional threat to the food security and cultural integrity of the U'wa people. The oil company Oxy, Occidental of Colombia, planned to carry out exploration activities in the so-called Bloque Samoré, on which the U'wa ancestral territory lies. The Gaviria government signed a contract with Oxy and Ecopetrol (the Colombian state oil company) allowing both companies to explore the entire area of Bloque Samoré for 28 years. The Samper government (1994–8) decided to license the Oxy project (in 1995) without prior consultation with the indigenous communities.

At the beginning of the 1990s, the government licensed areas surrounding the Cobaría *resguardo*, Aguablanca indigenous reserve, the Curipao *resguardo* and an area not yet appointed as *resguardo*. *Resguardos* are collectively owned lands that, since colonial times, have had the status of indigenous territorial reservations. Since 1994, the U'wa had been demanding the expansion and unification of their *resguardo* from INCORA, the National Institute for Agrarian Reform. The inspection and cartographic studies of the territory had already been carried out, but INCORA was undecided on whether to grant the changes because of the oil interests. The case of the Nukak territory was also instructive. The size of their territory had been reduced at the time of its establishment, the northwestern part being taken away from them. As a semi-nomadic people of roving farmers in the Amazon jungle, this area was indispensable for their survival. It was later discovered that on this particular land there were potential oilfields.

Other indigenous peoples in Colombia have also experienced the catastrophic impact of oil exploration and exploitation on their culture and territories, including the Yariguí and Aripí peoples from Magdalena, the Barí from Catatumbo, the Kofan from Putumayo and the Hitnü, Hitanü, Betoye, and Jiwi from Arauca. All these groups live in the vicinity of the U'wa, who were also aware of the negative experiences of indigenous communities in Ecuador and Peru through reports from the environmental organization Oil Watch. The U'wa people decided to defend their ancestral territory at all costs (ONIC 1997a, 1997b, 1999b; Rathgeber 1997).

According to the Colombian constitution, the *resguardos* and the other communal lands of ethnic groups are collective property of the native communities and, as such, they cannot be sold or confiscated by the government. Moreover, the agrarian reform regulation 160 / 1993 established that those land sites determined as communal land are also regulated. The U'wa succeeded in ensuring that the area for oil exploration be dealt with according to the provisions established by Convention 169 of the International Labor Organization. This meant that the project could not have been carried out without prior consultation with the community and their expressed approval. It required them to agree on the indemnity, reparations, and benefits the communities should receive as compensation for their rights of usufruct. In addition, it required specific studies regarding the impact on the social, economic, and cultural integration of the communities.

The environmental license issued in 1995 by the Ministry for the Environment for the exploration in the Bloque Samoré conditioned Oxy's activities to a previous process of consultation and agreement with the indigenous population in the region. However, this condition should have been decided before the authorization of the seismic activities was issued, thus verifying the possibilities of negative impacts on the indigenous community. Oxy carried out the first seismic activities on part of the U'wa territory without complying with these obligations, arguing that no exploration within the *resguardo* was to take place, and that they did not have the cartography of the U'wa territory. The company went on to suggest that the guerrillas were acting on the Bloque Samoré region and influencing the indigenous population. Of course FARC was active in the area and favored oil exploration, because they hoped to gain an additional source of funds. Three foreign activists who worked for the U'wa cause were killed in 1999 as a result. The U'wa communities denounced this lack of compliance by Oxy with various authorities. They presented a *tutela* before the court and agreed with the Foreign Affairs Minister – whose duty is to ensure compliance of the rights of indigenous peoples – on the establishment of a commission to review complaints. They also sought to capture the national and international public's attention in order to stop Oxy's activities. Various non-indigenous social sectors, including some of the blue-collar workers from Oxy and Shell, backed the U'wa cause.

The Commission verified seismic activities in the U'wa territory, but sanctions against Oxy never materialized. Besides, the government insisted that the U'wa people did not have a unified position and that a considerable proportion of them were in favor of oil exploration. The U'wa communities responded that they were all against the project, declaring this in multiple opportunities through the *cabildos* and their traditional authorities. They underlined the importance of consulting these representative institutions and not any other U'wa group.

At the legal level, the U'wa did not achieve a favorable verdict. The Constitutional Court passed judgment that in 1997 the government had granted the license in accordance with the legislation. Only one appeal in the same year before the Inter-American Commission of Human Rights could slow down the project in Bloque Samoré. Based on the conclusions of a Harvard University study, the commission recommended putting an immediate stop to all oil exploration on U'wa territory and restarting the consultation process. However, the recommendation left open the possibility of restarting oil exploration activities in Bloque Samoré outside U'wa territory and after consultations with the U'wa had taken place. It also proposed that the Colombian government continue to recognize U'wa's ownership of their ancestral territory. The study emphasized the importance of recognizing and showing respect for the representative structures of the U'wa people, their traditional authorities and their *cabildo*. It condemned the negative rumors that were circulating, particularly regarding the link between the U'wa and the guerrillas (ONIC 1997a, 1997b, 1999a).

After all these efforts, the government established the *resguardo único* (consolidated *resguardo*), but at the same time the Ministry for the Environment granted a new environmental license with a modification regarding the area, which now included a new region of exploration a few meters away from the *resguardo*. The indigenous representatives of the U'wa people then traveled to Oxy's headquarters in the United States to a shareholders' meeting in 1999, asking them to stop this project once and for all.

Escorted by the army, who on their way in crushed several demonstrations, Oxy brought in the technical equipment and team to start the exploration work at the beginning of 2001. Three children died as a result of the use of force. Work continued until the beginning of 2002, when the company decided to stop further activities, declaring the area inappropriate for exploration and bringing the project to an end. While the U'wa and their sympathizers celebrated the fact that they could keep their ancestral territory and began repairing the damage done as a result of the exploration, the Ministry for the Environment extended two new licenses to national companies for exploration on another part of the Bloque Samoré. The struggle of the U'wa has yet to find an end. Meanwhile the U'wa have reclaimed a large part of their territory and are resolute in their quest to preserve their culture (Rathgeber 2001a, Asociación U'wa 2001, 2002).

The Embera-Katío: Appealing to the rule of law

The Embera-Katío live in an indigenous *resguardo* (comprising the old Iwagadó and Karagabí *resguardos*), which has an extension of 203,290 hectares within the Paramillo natural park in the northwest of Colombia. The Embera-Katío belong to the Embera people consisting of around 57,400 members distributed in the departments of Choco, Antioquia, and Cordoba. In the latter, the Embera-Katío live side by side with Afro-Colombian communities, descendants of the Cimarron slaves who in the eighteenth century sought refuge in these rainforests. Currently, the Embera-Katío comprise 19 communities situated in the hydrographical basins of the rivers Sinú, Esmeralda, Verde, and Cruz Grande.

The region is a tropical jungle, well known for its richness in biodiversity due, in large extent, to the way the Embera-Katío have lived and managed the rainforest, which demands high mobility in times of scarcity. They live scattered along the rivers and streams, in family groups that exploit the environmental diversity available around their settlements. They have developed their own sophisticated systems of production, incorporating fruit tree seeds into the vegetable gardens distributed around the communities. They combine horticulture with fruit collection, hunting, and fishing depending on the season. This type of economy sustains the family and provides food security, but does not leave much excess production for trade. In general, the Embera do not have a centralized system or a hierarchical political structure. The family nucleus is autonomous in terms of decision-making, although advice provided by the other families is taken into account (Mueller-Plantenberg 1999; Rathgeber 1999).

The 1960s saw the beginning of a continuing process of colonization or settlement on Embera-Katío's land. These settlers did not know about rainforest management. At first they began with small-scale wood harvesting, which did not cause serious damage to the rainforest. Devastation really commenced with the use of the power saw. It is estimated that in the eighties around 95,000 hectares of primary forest were razed. A part of the Embera-Katío population also began to cut down the forest in order to get income to buy tools, motorboats, flashlights, and radios. The traditional indigenous sectors raised the alarm to prevent the destruction of their territory.

At the beginning of the nineties these traditional sectors began a process to elaborate an "ethno-development plan" that would recuperate part of the traditional economy and revitalize domestic relations between the communities. However, the plan failed due to differences of opinion regarding the use of the ecosystem. Balancing the different interests was the most important part of the plan because it had to take all proposals into consideration and still be sustainable. To this end, the plan included the creation of a political body whose function was to mediate between different interests according to its own previously agreed-upon regulations, and to establish a mechanism for compensation *vis-à-vis* different forms of authority and social relations. This was necessary because existing government institutions had lost all credibility.

The plan sought to increase food security, establish new forms of subsistence, improve existing medical care, and complete the transport infrastructure. On the basis of their model of subsistence they wanted to broaden their economic activities, gradually developing an economic model that would meet the needs of a growing population and generated income. New and adapted technologies were introduced which were to increase yields of traditional production. The plan also covered management of the Sinú riverbed to be used as drinking water reservoir, financed by funds from the water companies that supply approximately one million customers (Rathgeber 1999).

The entire process came to a halt with the construction of the hydroelectric plant Urrá I. Back in the 1950s, the political elite from the Córdoba department proposed the construction of a hydroelectric plant (Urrá I and II) in the Sinú River. For this purpose, at the beginning of the 1980s, feasibility studies were carried out and funding sources sought. The Urrá I project included the flooding of 7,400 hectares, mainly land from the Paramillo natural park that had been affected by the settlements. The first part of the dam was to include 100 hectares of Embera-Katío territory, and the second phase, Urrá II, planned the flooding of 70,000 hectares, affecting 475 Embera-Katío families. In addition, the project represented a threat to approximately 100,000 people (30,000 families) who lived on the areas below the dam, fishing and farming for their livelihood. All in all, it was estimated that about one million people would be affected by the project.

The electric plant in Urrá I was to produce 340 megawatts, or 2 percent of the country's energy production. The immediate beneficiaries of the project were planning commercial agriculture and cattle-breeding enterprises on 262,000 hectares, constructing an irrigation system that would turn 150,000 hectares into productive land. Among the hoped-for benefits were the creation of 3,500 jobs and the collection of income by the municipalities from the sale of energy. However, the cost-benefit studies also revealed that the project was not economically viable in the long term, that it would cause environmental damage to the rainforest, and would have a negative impact on the population living along the riverside, all reasons why the project was rejected in the first place.

In light of the power cuts that the country's capital, Bogotá, experienced during 1992, when the city suffered hours-long cuts on a daily basis, the government decided to consolidate the flow of energy with construction of additional electric plants like Urrá I. Works were started in 1993 by a Swedish company which used exclusively Canadian and Swedish funds, since the World Bank had decided to abandon the project given its negative impacts. A Russian company supplied the equipment to generate the energy needed during construction. The dam was completed in 1998 (Mueller-Plantenberg 1999; Cabildos Mayores Embera-Katío 1999a).

The inhabitants of the region occupied by Urrá I, including the Embera-

Katío population and other fishing and peasant families, did not have any idea of the impact that the plant would have on them. Thanks to the help of two experts from the Córdoba and Medellín University – both of whom were later killed – the population began to realize that their food security was being threatened. Their staple food, the local fish variety Bocachico – their main source of protein – disappeared within a period of five years. In the face such a tremendous negative impact, the Embera-Katío and the fishing families decided to oppose the second phase of the hydroelectric project.

In 1995, more than 600 indigenous people – men, women, children, and the elderly – embarked in wooden rafts on the Sinú River to say their farewell to the river. This first mobilization, known as the *Do Wa'bura,* attracted international and national public attention and forced the Urrá S.A. company into negotiations with the Embera-Katío. During the first meeting, the company committed itself to consult them regarding compensation amounts for damages and to implement the recommendations of environmental impact studies. However, 30 percent of the construction work had already taken place, and the indigenous population was still not clear about the damages.

The contracting company Urrá S.A. did not fulfill its various obligations. The Embera-Katío decided to resort to the *tutela* legal suit to safeguard their consultation and mitigation rights. In 1998, when the dam was concluded but not yet filled, the Constitutional Court, as final authority, granted the *tutela* to the Embera-Katío, ruling a temporary halt of the works. The court painstakingly explained the shortcomings of the proceedings and ordered the Ministry for the Environment – responsible for the issuing of licenses – and the Urrá S.A. company to comply with all the studies, consultations, consensus processes, and mitigations before work could be continued. The Court set a deadline of six months for settlement discussions to take place, and emphasized the fact that the Ministry and the company should respect the cultural unity of the communities, refraining from attempting to foster divisions when carrying out conversations with the Embera-Katío. The sentence was rather canny because, in fact, there was an attempt to divide the Embera-Katío in order to achieve an agreement for financial reparations instead of land compensation. Despite the encouragement of this division, the Ministry was forced into compensating the Embera-Katío with land as well, as a result of international protest and mobilizations (CCC 1998; Cabildos Mayores Embera-Katío 1999a; Mueller-Plantenberg 1999; Rathgeber 2001b).

During this time, the paramilitary killed a traditional leader of the Embera-Katío, a very important figure of the indigenous resistance, and six other leaders received death threats. Three consultants of the Embera-Katío who worked with ONIC were declared "military targets" and had to take refuge abroad. Before this event, three people who were committed to the indigenous resistance had already been murdered.

From 1999 to 2001, other indigenous leaders who had played a key role in the negotiations with the Ministry and the company died or disappeared. In addition, the Alto Sinú area had been turned into an epicenter of war, brought about by disputes over territorial control between the guerrillas and the paramilitary, involving the indigenous people and causing many deaths.

At the beginning of the negotiations at the end of 1998, the Embera-Katío presented an ethno-development plan they called the *plan de vida* (plan for life). They proposed several programs aimed at long-term food security for their people. The process of implementation of the court verdict took more than six months and was accompanied by several demonstrations, including a long march from the Sinú River to Bogotá (800 km) and the occupation of the quarters of the Ministry for the Environment. At the same time the Embera-Katío extended their support links, getting an international body to monitor the conversations. At the international level, the claims over delays and tricks played by the Ministry for the Environment forced the minister to travel to Europe twice to explain matters. The Vice-President and the Minister of Foreign Affairs were sharply criticized when they spoke in public on their European tours, emphasizing the need for compliance with the decision made by the Constitutional Court. The attitude of state officials suggested that the sentence would not be respected (Cabildos Mayores Embera-Katío 1999b, 1999c; ONIC 1998, 1999b, 1999c, 1999d; International Rivers Network 1999).

The conversations finally concluded, and the Embera-Katío opted for *plan Jenen*, which contained many of the demands included in their ethno-development plan. They had invoked the rule of law to make sure that the rights enshrined in the constitution were fulfilled. Meanwhile the Embera-Katío mobilized all civil means in their effort to guarantee their cultural survival. In all these stages, international solidarity networks kept supporting the struggle. However, this saga is not yet over and the future does not look promising. Although the Urrá S.A. may well be handing out food and other essentials such as medicine, the indigenous often remain empty-handed. Frequently, the paramilitary stop them and take away their goods upon return from Tierra Alta, the place appointed for distributing goods. In spite of multiple complaints, the state security forces have not intervened yet (Rathgeber 2001b).

Puracé: Searching for Economic Alternatives

The Puracé sulphur mine lies on the piedmont of the active volcano that bears the same name, about 40 km to the east of the department's capital, Popayán. Starting in 1940, members of the *resguardo* Puracé detected this source of sulphur. In 1946 operations were started in the mine, owned until 2000 by the company Industrias Puracé S.A. Most of the mining workers came from the *resguardo*. The mine is the largest source of employment in the whole region, providing jobs – direct and indirect – to approximately 300 families, or one-fourth of the population of the Puracé resguardo, comprising 1,129 families and approximately 4,200 inhabitants.

One of the consequences of the liberalization of the Colombian market after 1990 was that imported sulphur could be bought at lower prices than the domestic product. The Puracé S.A. company began to lose money and went through its first economic crisis in 1992. Threatened with the possibility of losing jobs and income for the region, the *cabildo* of the Puracé *resguardo* decided to talk to the company, proposing that the mining workers and indigenous community assume control of the operation of the mine. The negotiations concluded without a concrete result. However, a declaration of intent was signed in 1995 in the Piendamó *resguardo*. A year later Industrias Puracé S.A. went bankrupt and put an end to its activities. The trade union entered into negotiations with the company, both parties seeking a resolution which would allow them to continue operating, even without a profit for the company, but with the aim of generating enough revenue to cover the social obligations of the company to their workers and employees. Especially at stake were the pensions of 49 mining workers who had already gone into retirement. Their demands came to one million dollars.

They arrived at an agreement in 1998, which established that the Colombian state would oversee the proceedings of the contract. Industrias Puracé S.A. continued operating and its shareholders were now the workers. The management maintained its legal constitution as limited liability company until 1999. From then on, two companies operated parallel to each other. One was constituted by the management; the other a subsidiary formed by the miners whose responsibility was the running of operations. In August 2000 the management of the company reopened bankruptcy proceedings. It stated that it would stop all mining activities and stop paying wages. The *cabildo* of the Puracé *resguardo* took over the management together with the workers. The mine continued operating under a new name: *Empresa Minera Indígena del Cauca* (Cauca Indigenous Mining Company).

During the process of negotiations the *cabildo* relied on the CRIC on several occasions for information about the legal and economic context. A general assembly decided to continue on their own accord with the mine in spite of the concerns raised in meetings with the CRIC, with one important condition: the exploitation of the mine was to be adapted to suit the social and cultural interests of the indigenous community and to implement programs to improve the environment. It turned into a paradox of Latin American history in general, because mines have been a prime example of exploitation and annihilation of mankind and nature, and this one was now going to be turned into a source of income for survival. It was to guarantee pensions, employment, and benefits, in addition to maintaining good social relations with the members of the *resguardo*. There are hopes that through management of the mine by the *cabildo* and the miners, relations within the *resguardo* will be consolidated and the *resguardo* can become better established (Cabildo Indígena de Puracé 2001; Rathgeber 2001a, 2001d).

The *cabildos* had made strenuous efforts to bring together the miners and inhabitants of the *resguardo*, most of them peasants. For many years they had lived in separate worlds, miners usually in the urban areas, peasant farmers in rural areas. The lack of roads also fostered divisions. Tensions between trade union mining workers of indigenous origin and the *cabildo* surfaced from time to time. Before work was started in 1945, the *resguardo* had to sacrifice an area of 600 km. Years later they had confrontations over environmental issues. The processing of sulphur generates toxic gases, which caused damages to part of the land in the *resguardo*. At the same time, the mine contaminates stream water. With the support of the regional university and CRIC, the *cabildo* started researching the environmental damage in the 1970s, filing complaints before the courts.

They organized demonstrations, blocking the roads leading to the mine. The case came up in court in 1974 and the tribunal ordered payment for damages. The government interfered, however, arguing that the indigenous people may have bought weapons with the money, and payments were stopped. In order to keep minimum relations with the *cabildo*, the company would now and then donate some building materials for the construction of a house or some other structure in the *cabildo* (Meschkat 1983; Rathgeber 1994).

The production of sulphur during the first year under the *cabildo* regime was below the previous year's figures. In addition, demand for sulphur was higher than the mine's previous production capacity. The *cabildo* foresaw promising prospects, though, and set itself to the task of finding investors to modernize the mining equipment and diversify their supply with processed foods such as fine grains. They currently want to reduce the volume of production to prolong the use of the site and reduce environmental pollution, while attempting to mitigate the damages caused in the past. However, they require modern equipment and technology. It is estimated that this investment will require around $1.5 million. The previous company had not invested in machinery or technology for a long time. Looking for investors, CRIC approached some German non-governmental organizations in 2000. Ironically, the *cabildo* requires an environmental license from the Ministry to modernize and extend its line of products. Whereas before, the Ministry issued licences without much of a problem, it was now hesitant. Some environmental groups oppose the plans. Many other groups support this experiment and want to help the *cabildo* by putting them in contact with companies in the Valle del Cauca department, who are seeking to establish a regional network of organic production to bring to the market (Rathgeber 2000, 2001a, 2001d).

Conclusion

The processes currently taking place under the neoliberal model of globalization are characterized by the acceleration of the flow of financial capital. They require an autonomous economic regime, a re-organization of society and of the corresponding state, and a particular definition of the limits of politics. From an economic perspective, neoliberalism advocates the autonomy of market players, the modernization of the state, and the efficiency of the state's administration. At the social level, it has become synonymous with instability and insecurity for the majority of people. This chapter has shown that Colombian indigenous people are at the center of this loss of security, especially when exploration and drilling take place on their territories. I have argued that this economic model denies the basic structures necessary to maintain their food security and cultural identity. In defending and strengthening their identity, Colombian indigenous groups fighting for their rights have demonstrated their disagreement with the aims and rules of the dominating economy. Of course there are also indigenous communities in Colombia who are looking for other means of survival and who are subscribing to the rules imposed by the system. However, the indigenous people in the examples described in this chapter advocate an economy that will strengthen social relations and go beyond pure consumption. The U'wa, the Embera-Katio, and the Puracé *resguardo* have tried to build, consolidate, and develop an economic regime that is in line with their cultural identity. The U'wa and the Embera-Katío continue with the traditional norms that will preserve their unique cultures, which are defined along the path of indigenous resistance.

The Puracé *resguardo* provides an example of the co-existence of classic business objectives with sustainable aims like social and environmental care, a friendlier relationship with nature, and the development of culture. Contrary to the restructuring of the industrial areas in other parts of the world, which modify the regional economies according to world market aims, the indigenous mining company takes into consideration the geographic, environmental, and cultural criteria of the region. Contrary to the neoliberal trend which considers only the needs of the market, the indigenous company of Puracé understands the *resguardo* as a social fabric that requires initiating processes and making investments that will allow them to sustain their identity. The last two congresses of the CRIC (in 1997 and 2001) focused on this issue of becoming "entrepreneurs" in order to generate new productive cycles and to have enough resources available for an increasing indigenous population that seeks to maintain their culture. The introduction of some cultural guidelines into the capitalist trading economy is nothing new in the Cauca region. The CRIC started working in 1978 on projects that dealt specifically with recovered land for the revival of the *minga* institution and associative work as a way of rebuilding the indigenous community. The communities experimented with revolving funds for cattle and agricultural productions based on traditional and cash crops, like organic coffee. They started different forms of production and distribution oriented and managed by their own rules and institutions. The role of the *cabildo* would extend even more in this sense with the reconstruction of the regions through the *Entidades Territoriales Indígenas* (Indigenous Territorial Entities), implementing ethno-development plans that include bilingual education and health projects based on both traditional and western medicine. In Cauca there is already a network of more than 150 primary schools. In addition to the regular curriculum, these schools also teach the history of indigenous ancestors, myths, and legends.

Faced with circumstances that do not allow for a continuation of traditional life, the indigenous communities are defying the dominant economy, introducing their values into the market. These experiments have often failed, but have served to strengthen the indigenous institutions and organizational processes. Some indigenous reserves in North America are also experimenting in this area under the slogan of "new work." In countries like Brazil, and within non-indigenous groups, this challenge is being discussed under the terms of "economy of solidarity." This way of thinking takes some elements from discussions that have been taking place in Europe since the beginning of the 1930s (Polanyi 1944, 1997; Bergmann 2002; Singer 2002). These struggles belong to the world's laboratory and the continuous search for alternatives to the dominating economy.

Another theme of major importance is the struggle for autonomy. Within this context the indigenous movement has always tried to change the rules of the state as the necessary condition for their development and preservation as a unique culture. Thanks to their struggle and the new political constitution, the Colombian indigenous movement has gained considerable leverage to retrieve, consolidate, and develop their territories, their own forms of government and, once more, their identity. In addition, it has placed emphasis on the fact that self-reorganization based on identity could provide a valid answer to globalization and to the existing social insecurities surrounding the sustainability of cultural complexities.

Within the context of political mobilization, the indigenous movement contributed significantly to the erosion of some old forms of political dominance and to the defense and revitalization of the political field. It widened the spaces of civil society and advocated the rule of law and democratic and participatory principles. It defends the constitution, the decentralization of the state, the direct elections of governors, and self-management at communal level as minimum norms for local struggles. And even though the achievements in this area are sometimes small, the fact that the struggle is taking place at all shatters the image that the economic rules imposed on society are equivalent to natural laws that are impervious to any type of social change. The indigenous movement thus feeds the process of democratization, seeking new relations between citizens, indigenous groups, the government, and society.

To conclude, the Colombian indigenous movement also challenges the terms and concepts of the experts who define and analyze their reality. Until the 1990s their concept of autonomy was often criticized as a deviation from the class struggle. Moreover, they sought social emancipation at a time when most social scientists saw the struggle for identity as essentially regressive. In writing this chapter, my own perspective has been influenced by the conceptual approaches that have dominated the analysis of social movements since the 1980s. This, however, is not the end of the discussion. It is only the beginning of the debate on how to adequately understand the realities and aspirations of the indigenous peoples.

References

Asociacion U'wa 2001: *Boletín de Prensa* (April).
—— 2002: *Boletín de Prensa* (May).
Bonilla, V. D. 1995: Itinerario de una militancia paralela: la lucha por los derechos indígenas y la lucha por la democratización en Colombia. In G. Gruenberg (ed.), *Articulación de la Diversidad: Tercera reunión de Barbados*. Quito: Abya-yala.
Bergmann, F. 2002: New Work: Challenge for the Third Millenium. Paper presented at the Nuee Arbeit Initiative, Kassel University, Germany.
Boisier, S. 1999: *Teorías y Metáforas sobre el Desarrollo Territorial*. Santiago de Chile: Libros CEPAL.
Cabildo Indígena de Puracé 2001: Proyecto minero de la comunidad indígena de Puracé: mina de azufre natural "El Vinagre" (mimeo document).
Cabildos Mayores Embera-Katío 1999a: Reconstrucción económica y socio-cultural del pueblo Embera-Katío (mimeo document).
—— 1999b: Comunicado de prensa (August).
—— 1999c: Resolución del 3 de Septiembre.
CCC – Corte Constitucional de Colombia 1998: Sentencia No. T-652/98, Bogotá, Colombia.
Chaparro, J. 1989: Los movimientos políticos regionales; un aporte para la unidad nacional. In G. Gallón (ed.), *Entre Movimientos y Caudillos, Cincuenta Años de Bipartidismo, Izquierda y Alternativas Populares en Colombia*. Bogotá: CEREC.
CRIC – Consejo Regional Indígena del Cauca: 1996: Boletín de prensa (August).
—— 1997: *Nuestra Experienca Organizativa: 1995–1997*. Popayán: CRIC.

—— 1999: *Del Silencio a la Palabra: Territorio de Convivencia, Diálogo y Negociación.* Popayán: CRIC.

—— 2000: *Tejiendo una Propuesta de Vida.* Popayán: CRIC.

Fajardo, H. 2001: Sociedad civil, movimientos sociales y poder político en tiempos de globalización. In Natalia Caruso (ed.), *Colombia en el Forum Social Mundial.* Bogotá: Corporación Foro Nacional por Colombia.

Fals Borda, O. 1989: Filosofía de la Participación y sus Implicaciónes Políticas. In G. Gallón (ed.), *Entre Movimientos y Caudillos, Cincuenta Años de Bipartidismo, Izquierda y Alternativas Populares en Colombia.* Bogotá: CEREC.

García, A. 1981: *Los Comuneros en la Pre-Revolución de Independencia.* Bogotá: Plaza & Janés.

Guzmán, G. *et al.* 1977: *La Violencia en Colombia: Estudio de un Proceso Social.* Bogotá: Punta de Lanza.

Hardt, M. and Negri, T. 2000: *Empire.* Cambridge: Harvard University Press.

Huhle, R. 2000: Kolumbien: noch kein friede in sicht. *Lateinamerika: Analysen und Berichte* 24.

Human Rights Watch 1996: *Colombia's Killer Networks: The Military-Paramilitary Partnership and the United States.* New York: HRW.

—— 1998: *Guerra sin Cuartel. Colombia y el Derecho Internacional Humanitario.* Bogotá: HRW.

International Rivers Network (Berkeley, CA) 1999: Press releases (December).

Lindig, W. and Münzel, M. 1985: Die Indianer: Kulturen und Geschichte. Munich: Deutscher Taschenbuch Verlag, 1985.

Meschkat, K. *et al.* 1980: *Kolumbien: Geschichte und Gegenwart eines Landes im Ausnahmezustand.* Berlin: K. Wagenbach.

Meschkat, K. 1983: Umweltzerstoerung und widerstand: fallstudien aus dem suedwesten kolumbiens. *Lateinamerika: Analysen und Berichte* 7.

Mueller-Plantenberg, C. 1999: Información básica sobre el proyecto hidroeléctrico Urra I. (mimeo document, Kassel University).

Muyuy Jacanamejoy, G. 1997: Los indígenas colombianos y su relación con el estado. Paper presented at the International Congress of Americanists, Quito, Ecuador.

Nolte, D. 1996: Descentralización en América Latina: conceptos, tendencias y problemas. *Desarrollo y Cooperación* 5, 8–11.

ONIC – Organización Nacional Indígena de Colombia 1996a: La libre determinación: una construcción y una conquista. Document presented at the Conference Visiones de Abya-Yala, Copenhaguen.

—— 1996b Boletín de prensa (July).

—— 1997a: El caso U'wa – Bloque Samoré: observaciones de la ONIC al informe del proyecto en Colombia de la Organización de los Estados Americanos y la Universidad de Harvard (mimeo document).

—— 1997b: El caso U'wa – Bloque Samoré: respeto por la integridad y la territorialidad indígenas (mimeo document).

—— 1998: Planes de Vida de los Pueblos Indígenas. Fortaleciendo la Pervivencia (mimeo document).

—— 1999a: Boletín de prensa (February).

—— 1999b: Defendiendo la sangre de Kerachikará: breve resumen del caso del pueblo U'wa (mimeo document).

—— 1999c: Boletín de prensa (July).

—— 1999d: Boletín de prensa (September).

Pécaut, D. 2002: *La Guerra Contra la Sociedad*. Bogotá: Editorial Planeta.

Pineda Camacho, R. 1995: Pueblos indígenas de Colombia: una aproximación a su historia, economía y sociedad. In ONIC and CECOIN (eds.), *Tierra Profanada, Grandes Proyectos en Territorios Indígenas de Colombia*. Bogotá: Disloque Editores.

Pizarro, E. 1985: Colombie: Entre Démocratie et Autoritarisme. *Amerique Latine* 21, 5–11.

Polanyi, K. 1944: *The Great Transformation*. Boston: Beacon Press.

—— 1977: *The Livelihood of Man*. New York: Academic Press.

Rathgeber, T. 1991: Bewegende ohn-macht, neue soziale bewegungen in Kolumbien. In Reusch, W. and Wiener, A. (eds.), *Geschlecht, Klasse, Ethnie: Alte Konflikte und Neue Soziale Bewegungen in Lateinamerika*. Saarbruecken und Fort Lauderdale: Verlag Breitenbach Publishers.

—— 1994 *Von der Selbsthilfe zur Selbstbestimmung? Chancen Autonomer Lebensproduktion in Indianischen und Kleinbaeuerlichen Organisationen in Kolumbien*. Münster: LIT Verlag.

—— 1997: Interview: CRIC president (Cologne).

—— 1999: Interview: Embera-Katio advisor (Goettingen).

—— 2000: Interviews: CRIC activists (Hannover, Goettingen, and Berlin).

—— 2001a: Interviews: CRIC and ONIC activists (Bogotá and Popayán)

—— 2001b: Interviews: Embera-Katio indigenous activists (Bogotá).

—— 2001c: Interview: governor of the Cauca Department (Berlin).

—— 2001d Notes: CRIC's 11th Congress (La María, Piendamó).

—— 2002: Movimientos indígenas y revitalización de la política para la regulación de la sociedad: el caso de Colombia. Paper presented at the conference Globalización, Resistencia y Negociación en América Latina, Universidad de Granada, June 25–29.

Restrepo, L. A. 1991: Kolumbien: Bedeutet die Verfassungsgebende Versammlung das Ende der Nationalen Front? *Lateinamerika: Analysen und Berichte* 15.

Sánchez, G. and Peñaranda, R. (eds.) 1986: *Pasado y Presente de la Violencia en Colombia*. Bogotá: CEREC.

Sánchez Gómez, G. 1991: *Guerra y Política en la Sociedad Colombiana*. Bogotá: El Ancora.

Singer, P. 2002: Globalización y economía solidaria: experiencias del Brasil. Paper presented at the Nuee Arbeit Initiative, Kassel University, Germany.

Ströebele-Gregor, J. 1994: Abschied von stief-vater staat: wie der neoliberale rueckzug des staates die politische organisierung der ausgeschlossenen befoerdern kann. *Lateinamerika: Analysen und Berichte* 18.

Zamosc, L. 1986: *The Agrarian Question and the Peasant Movement in Colombia*. Cambridge: Cambridge University Press.

The Ecuadorian Indian Movement

From Politics of Influence to Politics of Power

Leon Zamosc

Between 1992 and 2002 Ecuador had five presidents. Three of them were elected to the office. The other two replaced elected presidents deposed by coups. Although the removals of Abdalá Bucaram in 1997 and Jamil Mahuad in 2000 transpired under different circumstances, what is striking is the similarity in the processes that brought them about. Both Bucaram and Mahuad tried to introduce drastic measures to complete the neoliberal program in Ecuador, but neither of them was able to secure enough political backing in congress. In both cases, the coups took place at the height of acute national crises, following massive mobilizations that had been organized by the Indian movement. The previous elected president, Sixto Durán, had experienced a similar squeeze. Battered by popular opposition and abandoned by his political allies, he had been forced to shelve his program of reforms, finishing his term as a figurehead devoid of effective power.

Political crises and precarious presidencies have defined Ecuador as one of the most, if not *the* most, unstable country in Latin America. In this chapter, I will take this feature of Ecuadorian reality as a starting point for examining three aspects of special interest. The first aspect has to do with the relationship between neoliberalism and political volatility. Some analysts argue that political instability poses great obstacles to the successful implementation of neoliberal reforms (Haggard and Kaufman 1995). But this is an uninteresting truism, since it seems obvious that political volatility is as counterproductive to neoliberalism as to any other government program. Addressing the Ecuadorian situation, it is more appealing to me to invert the presumed causal relationship and explore the hypothesis that, depending on the context of social conflict, attempts to establish a neoliberal agenda can act as factors of political destabilization.

The second aspect is linked to the incidence of class struggle. In Ecuador, the turbulence of public life is nothing new. Since the return to democracy in 1979, the political scene has been confusing, with presidents from different parties succeeding one another, forever handicapped by the lack of parliamentary support. Analysts studying Ecuador highlight the existence of a political culture of discord that is rooted in regional, ideological, and personal rivalries (Conaghan 1989; Thoumi and Grindle 1992). They also point out that the rules of the electoral game, which favor the proliferation of parties and the two-round system of presidential election, generate fragmented congresses and permanent conflicts between the executive and legislative branches (Conaghan and Espinal 1990; Schuldt 1994, 105–6). These arguments offer us an image of institutional instability, confirming that presidential systems do not function well in conditions of party fragmentation (Mainwaring 1993; Shugart 1995). But what remains to be explained is precisely that which, in recent times, appears as the most salient factor: the veto power of the masses that go out to protest in the streets. The Ecuadorian case calls attention to the fact that class conflict continues to be a relevant factor in Latin American politics. My approach to the study of Ecuador's political instability recognizes that relevance, paying attention to structural determinations that are systematically ignored by analyses focused on institutions.

The third aspect has to do with the Ecuadorian Indian movement, which in recent years has assumed leadership in the popular struggles. As we know, the new social movements approach has become popular in Latin America. Its adherents favor the analysis of identities and the cultural aspects of social mobilization, disdaining class conflicts and openly political battles (Foweraker 1995; Hale 1997). Proponents of this view would suggest that, because of their specificities of identity and culture, Indian movements should be seen as the archetypes of the new type of social movements. But what is taking place in Ecuador reveals a different story: Indian struggles have not been limited to cultural affirmation or the securing of ethnic rights. While these goals have been important, the Indian movement has transcended them, involving itself in broader battles over social issues and becoming a player in the contest for political power. My study is an attempt to shed light on these dynamics.

In the first part of the chapter I will review the social and political conflicts related to successive attempts to impose the neoliberal agenda in Ecuador. I will present the material as a three-act drama, starring three governments facing off against a popular opposition led by the Indian movement. In the subsequent sections I will offer an analysis of the three aspects mentioned above, ending with some observations about the political developments of the last few years.

Act One: Sixto Durán, or the Radicalization of Neoliberalism

Sixto Durán came from the Social Christian Party, the main conservative force in Ecuadorian politics. Due to personal conflicts with León Febres, the historic leader of the party, Durán and some of his followers decided to run independently in the 1992 election (Notisur 1992). When Durán was elected, it was expected that he would continue the policies of gradual adjustment that had been followed in the country since the 1980s. But it quickly became clear that Durán and his economic czar, vice president Alberto Dahik, wanted to do away with gradualism. Their Structural Adjustment Plan, prepared with the assistance of the International Monetary Fund (IMF), proposed drastic steps to deregulate trade and capital flows, reduce social spending, and eliminate subsidies for essential services and basic consumption items. In addition, the plan defined goals that had never been pursued in Ecuador, such as reducing the payroll of public employees and privatizing the state's enterprises and social security program (CORDES 1992; Viteri Díaz 1998, 89–95).

Durán wanted to radicalize neoliberalism. But the task proved to be more difficult than he imagined. At the economic level, the adjustment policies lost credibility when it became clear that neither the initial package of reforms nor those that followed would reactivate the economy (Viteri Díaz 1998, 164–7). Politically, despite the neoliberal consensus of the center-right, Febres' personal animosity toward Durán led his Social Christian Party to join repeatedly in the opposition against the reforms. As a result, few of Durán's initiatives were passed in congress. The privatization law, which became permanently mired in the legislature, was also opposed by the military, who viewed state enterprises as one of the most positive legacies of the military governments of the 1960s and 1970s (Notisur 1994; AGAFA 1993). Finally, corruption became a central issue. The critical point was the accusations against vice president Dahik, whose resignation and embarrassing flight from the country left the government with scant credibility (Notisur 1995a; Flores 1995).

There were significant changes in civil society, too. Most important, the Indian movement rose to the leadership of popular struggles, a position from which it has been exercising social and political influence that goes well beyond the demographic weight of the population it represents. In the 2001 national census, Indians accounted for less than 10 percent of the total Ecuadorian population (INEC 2001). While it is true that the formulation of the census questions was restrictive from the point of view of ethnic self-definition, it would be unrealistic to presume (as some activists do) that the Indian population exceeds the 15–20 percent range (Zamosc 1995). Elsewhere, I have given a detailed account of how the process of Indian organization, initiated in the 1960s, gained momentum, allowing local community associations to expand their activism to regional and provincial levels (Zamosc 1994). In the Amazon, this process came in response to the arrival of colonists, oil companies, and state agencies. In the valleys of the Sierra (highlands), where the bulk of the Indian population is located, the main stimulus for organizing was the fight for agrarian reform. After the limited achievements of the land struggles, Indian peasant organizations had continued to work for community development, against discrimination, and in defense of their culture. These parallel processes led to the creation of umbrella Indian federations in the Sierra and in the Amazon and, toward the end of the 1980s, the establishment of CONAIE, the National Confederation of Indian Nationalities. There are few Latin American countries that have unified Indian confederations, and no other Indian organization has demonstrated the power to paralyze a country again and again, as is the case with Ecuador's CONAIE.

During the Durán government, CONAIE displaced the trade union federations as the main referent for popular opposition. Despite the worsening conditions of workers and employees, the trade unions had lost the power to mobilize their membership. Their weakness was more than an expression of the crisis of the political left. In Ecuador, only one-third of salaried workers are unionized, and the labor movement has a long history of political division (León 1988; Saltos 2001, Tamayo 1993). At the beginning of Durán's term, labor conflicts were declining sharply in number.[1] The latest protest mobilizations of the FUT (the United Workers Front, integrated by the main trade union federations) had ended in failure, and the national strike was discredited as an effective form of struggle (Tamayo 1993). By contrast, CONAIE's star was on the rise. In 1988, it had obtained important concessions from Social Democrat president Rodrigo Borja, who agreed to establish a national bilingual education program in all the Indian areas of the country (Moya 1990; Walsh 1994). In 1990, CONAIE had coordinated its first Indian uprising, a massive mobilization that paralyzed the country for days, protesting the high cost of living, the low prices for peasant products, and the lack of solutions to land conflicts (Zamosc 1994; León 1994). Borja's government had no choice but to negotiate with CONAIE, eventually endorsing a land acquisition program coordinated by an NGO of the Catholic Church. Two years later, CONAIE sponsored a march of Amazon Indians who occupied a park in Quito until Borja agreed to demarcate and title their lands (Sawyer 1997).

The first skirmish with Durán took place in 1993, over a government plan to liquidate the *Seguro Campesino*, the health service for rural areas. CONAIE supported the mobilization of beneficiaries of this service until, after two days of demonstrations and highway blockades, Durán was forced to restore the budget and promise that the state would continue the service (Kipu 1993; CPSSC 1993). Next came the battle over the Law of Agrarian Modernization, a bill sponsored by the government and the Chamber of Agriculture to eliminate the legal basis for land expropriation, direct all state support toward entrepreneurial production, abolish communal property, and privatize irrigation water. CONAIE called for the formation of the *Coordinadora Agraria*, a coalition that included smaller Indian and peasant organizations such as FEINE (the Federation of Evangelical Indians, which embraces Protestant communities) and FENOCIN (the Federation of Peasant and Indian Organizations, influenced by the Socialist Party). By 1994 the *Coordinadora Agraria* had organized workshops to discuss the legislation and proposed an alternative bill of its own (CAN 1993a, 1993b, 1993c). When Congress passed the government's bill, the *Coordinadora Agraria* called a national uprising, paralyzing the country again for several days. The military refused to repress the uprising, and the government was forced to negotiate every chapter of the law with the Indian representatives. The revised law defined peasant agriculture as a rightful beneficiary of state support, reaffirmed that water was a public resource, and recognized the legality of communal and cooperative forms of property ownership (Kipu 1994).

Resistance to neoliberalism became the basis for a popular front when CONAIE and its agrarian allies began to coordinate positions with the unions of state companies slated for privatization and with other urban organizations. This led to the formation of the *Coordinadora de Movimientos Sociales*, a broad coalition that included the Indian and peasant organizations, independent unions from the public sector, and a large number of grassroots and neighborhood associations, feminist groups, human rights activists, and development NGOs (Tamayo 1996). The decisive battle was waged in November of 1995. When it became evident that it would be impossible to reform the constitution in congress, Durán decided to appeal directly to the citizenry, holding a referendum with questions aimed at strengthening the executive power, approving the privatization of state enterprises and social security, and weakening the unions. Big business supported the "yes" campaign, making substantial investments in advertising. The *Coordinadora de Movimientos Sociales* and the trade union federations organized public debates, presented alternative ideas for constitutional reform, and carried out an intense grassroots campaign to promote the "no" vote. On the day of the referendum, all eleven questions were voted down (Notisur 1995b).

Act Two: Abdalá Bucaram's Neoliberal Populism

The failure of the referendum delivered the final blow to Durán's plans. He ended his term as a lame duck president in the midst of an electoral campaign in which the candidates avoided any talk of adjustment and privatization. The success of the campaign against the referendum had reinforced the position of the Indian activists who advocated for electoral participation. In its December 1995 assembly, CONAIE decided to launch a political movement that would be based on the Indian movement and other groups from the *Coordinadora de Movimientos Sociales* (CONAIE 1995). The party, the Pachakutik Movement of Plurinational Unity (Pachakutik means "time of resurgence" in Quechua), made its debut in the electoral campaign of 1996, in alliance with an independent movement led by Freddy Ehlers, a popular television commentator (Beck and Mijeski 2001). Ehlers did not qualify for the second round of the presidential vote, but Pachakutik's results were fairly good, obtaining 10 percent of seats in the national congress and a significant representation at the level of provincial legislatures, local councils, and mayorships (Kipu 1996). Although I cannot go into detail here about the performance of Pachakutik, it is worth pointing out that in the elections since 1996, its support has oscillated between a minimum of 6.5 percent and a maximum of 10.7 percent of the total vote, which indicates that the party has been relatively successful in obtaining the backing of the Indian population (Zamosc 2001). An important consequence of this is that Pachakutik has served as a vehicle for securing positions of local and regional power in the districts in which the Indian population is concentrated.

The electoral triumph of Abdalá Bucaram set the stage for the second act of the neoliberal class struggles in Ecuador. Bucaram, a clownish politician, was the leader of the Roldocista party, a populist force whose base of support was in the suburbs of the coastal capital Guayaquil, the largest city in the country. As its mayor, Bucaram had earned a reputation for corruption, but he had also succeeded in extending his web of clientelist influence (de la Torre 1997). In the 1996 campaign, his populist discourse was more strident than ever, denouncing the "politicians of the oligarchy" and making fun of Durán's frustrated reforms. For the political and business elite in the country, Bucaram's victory was a veritable torment. However, as soon as he assumed power, the new president launched an aggressive plan to divide the Indian movement, creating a Ministry of Indian Affairs, going around CONAIE's back to appoint one of their Amazonian activists as minister, and distributing money to gain the support of Indian groups in the Amazon and some provinces in the Sierra (Kipu 1996). Bucaram had filled his government with relatives and friends and, as the accusations piled up, it became obvious that the country was sinking to unprecedented depths of corruption. The president continued to sing in public and dance on tabletops in front of television cameras, but he had changed his discourse. Now he spoke of the virtues of capitalism and the necessity for structural adjustment, trying to ingratiate himself with the IMF, and finally inviting Domingo Cavallo, the architect of Argentina's neoliberal reforms, to serve as consultant for his economic plan (Notisur 1996).

Bucaram announced his adjustment package at the beginning of 1997, at a moment when CONAIE and the *Coordinadora de Movimientos Sociales* were preparing a large mobilization against corruption and the creation of the Ministry of Indian Affairs. Bucaram's proposals included draconian reductions in the budget, cuts in subsidies to electricity and gas, labor and tax reforms, and an Argentine-style convertibility plan to fix the local currency to the dollar (Notisur 1997a). The mobilization against corruption became a mobilization for the removal of Bucaram. As the streets of Quito filled with protesters, the political enemies of the president conspired in congress until, meeting in an extraordinary session, they declared Bucaram mentally incompetent, removed him from his post, and named the head of congress as the new president (Notisur 1997b).

In the process of Bucaram's removal, CONAIE and its allies extracted the promise that the new president would convene a constituent assembly to reform the constitution. In the elections for the assembly, which took place toward the end of 1997, Pachakutik obtained 10 percent of the seats (Andolina 2003). The delegates from Pachakutik pushed through several reforms, including the definition of Ecuador as a multicultural state and a series of social, cultural and political rights. Together with provisions on territoriality and participation in state entities, these rights provided a legal basis for Indian groups to exercise a certain degree of autonomy over their lands (CODENPE 2000).

Act Three: Jamil Mahuad and the Paroxysm of Crisis

A well-known analyst of the nineteenth century wrote that, in politics, history tends to repeat itself; first as tragedy, then as farce. In Ecuador, history also repeated itself, but in reverse. First came the farce, starring Bucaram and the congressmen who removed him from power. Then came the tragedy, in the form of the country's economic collapse and the military-Indian coup against Jamil Mahuad.

Mahuad won the elections of 1998 as a candidate of the Christian Democrats, whose party had moved from its original center-left position toward the right of the political spectrum. Mahuad's political capital came from the image of efficiency he had earned as mayor of Quito. That would not prove enough for him to handle the situation he would have to face, however. From one side, there were increasing pressures from IMF officials who were scandalized by the stagnation of Ecuador's neoliberal program. From the other side, there was a popular coalition on war footing, which was determined to get in the way of reforms and had repeatedly proven its oppositional power. To top it off, the economy plunged into the worst crisis since the depression of the 1930s (Notisur 1998a; *Economist* 1998).

The Ecuadorian economy depends on exports, principally oil from the Amazon and bananas from the coast. The immediate causes of the collapse of 1998 and 1999 were the fall of oil prices and the devastation of the coast by the El Niño phenomenon. Financial deregulation had allowed banks to concentrate their loans in the coastal business sectors. When these exporters could not repay their loans, the banks plunged into crisis and, despite the government's billion-dollar bailout program, public trust in the banking system plummeted. Since deregulation had also facilitated the mobility of money, the crisis generated a massive flight of capital, with account holders trying to withdraw all they had from their accounts and financial sharks orchestrating a frontal attack against the national currency. The economy contracted by 7 percent, unemployment and the state deficit shot upward, and it became evident that the country would not be able to pay its external debt (Notisur 1998b, 1998c, 1999a).

Mahuad introduced new austerity measures, devalued the national currency, froze bank accounts, and concentrated on approving a series of reforms through an alliance with the Social Christian Party, the traditional champion of the interests of exporters and bankers from the coast (Notisur 1999b, 1999c; *Economist* 1999a). At the same time, he tried to negotiate a deal with the IMF that would open the door to obtaining more loans. The IMF set out its conditions: dollarize the economy to guarantee stability; cut the deficit by eliminating subsidies on electricity, gasoline, and gas; privatize public enterprises; reform the tax structure by placing direct taxes on income and rent; and abstain from saving the failing banks (Notisur 1999e; *Economist* 1999b, 1999c).

These demands put Mahuad between a rock and a hard place. The IMF's insistence on eliminating subsidies and privatization guaranteed that the popular sectors would fight back. During 1998 and 1999, Mahuad had to deal with three large mobilizations, whose details are summarized in table 4.1. Significantly, participation in the protests broadened, starting with CONAIE's coalition, and later including middle-class sectors such as truckers and associations of small and medium entrepreneurs. The process took the form of a bargaining sequence in which the popular sectors negotiated each adjustment measure with Mahuad, who progressively weakened until, in the mobilization of July 1999, he had to back down completely.

But the IMF's conditions did something more: they left the president without allies. Mahuad counted on the political right to approve reforms in congress, but the pressure of the IMF to implement tax reform and leave banks to their own fate alienated bankers and large businesses. The Social

Table 4.1 Main protest mobilizations against president Jamil Mahuad, 1998 and 1999

Mobilization	Participants	Demands
1998 (September 9–October 8) National protest against the first package of measures	CONAIE, other Indian and peasant organizations, trade union federations, other social movements	Restore subsidies to electricity, fuels, and gas Broaden criteria for Bono Solidario (cash subsidy for poorest families) Fair tax reform, consider the set of budget-reduction measures proposed by popular organizations Create a permanent forum for discussion and negotiation of adjustment measures
1999 (March 16–20) National protest against further austerity measures proposed by the government	CONAIE, other Indian and peasant organizations, trade union federations, other social movements, transport coops (buses and taxis)	Reconsider raises of fuel prices Lift restrictions on small savings accounts No bailout, close failed banks Withdraw ten bills submitted by government to congress Lift the state of emergency
1999 (July 7–17) National protest demanding fulfillment of the agreements on the March austerity measures	CONAIE, other Indian and peasant organizations, trade union federations, other social movements, transport coops (buses, taxis, trucks), associations of small and middle entrepreneurs, Association of Municipalities	Fulfill agreements reached in previous negotiations Freeze prices of fuel, gas, and public services Shelve privatization plans Reduce payments for foreign debt service

Sources: Notisur (1998c, 1999d), Kipu (1998, 1999a, 1999b).

Christian Party pulled out of the negotiations, leaving the president alone (Notisur 1999d, 1999f; *Economist* 1999d). When that happened, it became clear that Mahuad's presidency would not last much longer. The question was how the end would come about.

In the final days of 1999, when Mahuad announced the dollarization and the other IMF measures, Indian groups began to flock to Quito demanding his removal from office (Notisur 2000a). On January 21, 2000, in one of the most singular moments in Ecuadorian history, young military officials and Indian leaders embraced one another in congress, proclaiming a "government of national salvation." Following frenetic consultations between stammering generals, disconcerted politicians, and American diplomats who let it be known that their country opposed the coup, General Carlos Mendoza assumed command and immediately announced that he would restore constitutional order by installing vice president Gustavo Noboa as the president. Colonel Lucio Gutiérrez and the other officials involved in the coup were arrested, while CONAIE's leaders ordered a peaceful retreat of the protestors.[2] In the following months, all those detained were granted amnesty. While dollarization was maintained, most of Mahuad's other measures were annulled. President Noboa continued negotiations with the IMF, but the talks were eventually abandoned without reaching an agreement (Notisur 2002a).

Neoliberalism, Social Conflict, and State Legitimacy Crisis

Figure 4.1 synthesizes an analytical vision of the recent political instability in Ecuador. The economic crisis and the IMF pressures are my points of departure. In Ecuador, as in other countries of the region, neoliberalism took the form of a hegemonic mandate; that is, it was accepted by governments of different parties as the only viable alternative (Hey and Klak 1999). But it quickly became evident that the attempts to implement that model passed the costs of adjustment to the popular sectors. Moreover, the reforms did not improve the economic situation, and some of the measures actually made it worse. This resulted in a dual political crisis: a *crisis of representation*, grounded in the fact that none of the traditional parties took the interests of popular sectors into account; and a *crisis of state legitimacy*, as the state lost respect and authority because its initiatives were viewed as unjust and inefficient. Popular rejection took two forms: the vote for populist leaders like Bucaram, and protest mobilizations. Both alternatives, however, resulted in a vicious circle. Bucaram turned out to be a neoliberal populist, and the mobilizations, as successful as they were in thwarting the successive governments' initiatives, could not prevent politicians and the IMF from coming back with a new neoliberal offensive.

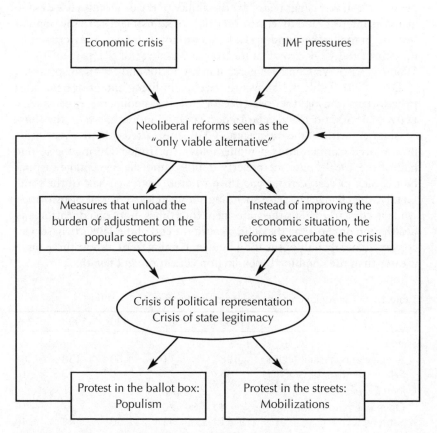

Figure 4.1   The cycle of political instability in Ecuador

To understand the relationship between the reforms and political processes, it is important to point out that the core of the matter is not whether adjustments are necessary in Ecuador. First of all, budget deficits and indebtedness have created a situation in which fiscal discipline, tax reform, and renegotiation of debts are unavoidable. Second, in a context in which Ecuador's development will continue to depend upon exports and the global market, liberalizing trade and encouraging capital investment appear to be basic elements for any economic policy. Finally, the reform of the Ecuadorian state is also imperative, not only because of institutional and bureaucratic deficiencies, but also because, since the return of democracy, particular interests of pressure groups have dominated public policy.[3]

There is no doubt, then, that Ecuador needs reforms. The real question has to do with the content of these reforms and the distribution of their costs. From this point of view, the Ecuadorian case has illutrated a situation in which the repeated attempts to implement a radical variant of

Leon Zamosc

neoliberalism were aggravated by the ability of the economic elite to safe-guard its interests and divert the sacrifices of adjustment onto the popular sectors. In the background was a failed economic model, as evidenced by the fall of the GDP growth rate from an average of 9.1 percent in the 1960s to 3.9 percent and 1.8 percent in the 1980s and 1990s, respectively (ILDIS 2003). Table 4.2 shows the decline in living conditions for most Ecuadorians during the two decades of the neoliberal experiments. Between 1980 and 1999, salaries decreased by more than half, the share of salaries within the aggregate GDP contracted in an even more pronounced manner, and open unemployment tripled. During the second half of the 1990s, extreme poverty doubled and the percentage of poor households increased from one-third to more than one-half of the total. Finally, the changes in state spending show a clear reversal of priorities: while in the early 1980s the state spent four times more on education and health than on repaying the debt, toward the end of the 1990s debt service consumed nearly half of the total budget, coming to be almost three times greater than the combined spending on education and health.

Table 4.2 The social cost of adjustment in Ecuador, 1980–1999

	1980	1985	1990	1995	1999
Salaries					
Average annual salary (US$)	198	111	60	138	88
Salaries as share of GDP (%)	35	24	16	17	10
Unemployment					
Open unemployment (%)	4	20	6	7	15
Sub-employment	31	42	50	46	46
Poverty					
Consumption poverty (%)	34	56			
Extreme poverty (%)	12	21			
State expenditure					
Education (%)	33	24	16	14	13
Health (%)	7	7	7	5	4
Service of public debt (%)	9	21	37	41	45
Public debt					
Total debt (US$ billions)	4.6	8.1	12.2	13.9	15.0
As proportion of GDP (%)	39	68	116	77	95

Sources: Pérez (1994), BCE (2001), SIISE (2002), ILDIS (2003).

It is no secret that state policies determine the manner in which the costs of an economic adjustment are distributed among different sectors of the population. Citizens will accept sacrifices if they agree they are needed, if they are convinced that state policies will help restore equilibrium, and if they sense that the distribution of costs is equitable. None of these conditions was present in Ecuador, where the public was never consulted, where the neoliberal policies actually aggravated the crisis, and where inequity reigned from the beginning. In the early 1980s, the first adjustment measures included a scandalous scheme of debt nationalization, by which the Central Bank assumed responsibility for the entire private sector debt, at a cost of $1.2 billion for the Ecuadorian state (Younger 1993). Later, fiscal reform increased the value-added tax and other indirect taxes, allowing the business sector and more powerful groups to benefit from low income taxes (Salgado 2001). During Mahuad's term the income tax was eliminated altogether while the government, in addition to freezing and devaluing savings accounts, invested about four billion dollars (equivalent to one-quarter of the annual GDP of the country) toward saving private banks (Salgado 2002).

We thus arrive at the core of the problem: the fact that the neoliberal reforms, by openly favoring the economic elite and systematically harming the popular sectors, exacerbated social conflict and eroded the basis of state authority. Instead of acting as an impartial entity that protected the interests of the entire nation, the state appeared to the majority of Ecuadorians as an agent of the most powerful groups. Defined this way, the crisis of state legitimacy laid the groundwork for the outbursts of social protest that would come to play a central role in Ecuadorian political life.

Crisis of Representation, Class Struggle, and Political Instability

In contemporary democracies, the political party system is the routine channel by which citizens express their preferences. Social groups that are not represented by the parties are politically excluded, in the sense that the interests of their members are not taken into account in public policies. A crisis of representation occurs when the political system is incapable of resolving conflicts because stakeholders in the conflict are not represented within the system. The classic symptom is the massive protests through which excluded sectors express their demands or try to influence the political decisions. This was the situation in Ecuador when all the parties joined in the neoliberal consensus. Civil society protest emerged as the only way of expressing opposition, becoming a means by which the popular sectors acquired power to negotiate or veto the neoliberal reforms. What elements of organization and articulation made it possible for the protests to take this direction? And on what basis did the organizers of the protests claim to represent the popular sectors?

Clearly, the success of the popular struggles was a function of the Indian movement's ability to provide leadership. In the fights of the first half of the 1990s, CONAIE's leaders were able to frame Indian demands as part of a discourse that denounced the anti-peasant nature of the neoliberal agenda, and thereby resonated with the interests of other agrarian organizations. In the second half of the 1990s, when CONAIE formed a front that included the unions and other urban sectors, it broadened its discourse to include the demands of the entire popular camp under the slogan of national resistance to neoliberalism. Discourses, however, are not enough to create and lead alliances. The decisive element is the movement's ability to show potential allies that it has the power to act on the discourse and achieve concrete results. In the 1990s, the power of the Indian movement came from its capacity to carry out mobilizations that had an effective impact on government policies. Opposition to neoliberalism offered the key for a politics of popular resistance and, in a context in which the labor movement had lost its capacity to mobilize, CONAIE emerged as the only civil society actor that could lead that resistance.

Class was a fundamental factor in the struggles of the 1990s, in the sense that the identities and interests of the protagonists were defined as a function of their position in the country's economic structure. In the previous section I emphasized that the antagonism revolved around the costs of adjustment, demonstrating that the conflict was triggered by the initiatives of a state that systematically sided with the interest of big business. In that context, the organized opposition took the shape of a broad popular alliance led by the Indian movement. It is worth making two observations here. The first is that, in Ecuador, the content of the popular struggles has been much less than radical. So far, they have not questioned private property, the class structure, or the capitalist organization of the economy. It cannot even be said that the popular groups are trying to gain a larger slice of the national "pie." In essence, then, these are defensive struggles, focused on preventing further deterioration of the situation of the weakest sectors. The second observation is that the conflict could have proceeded in a very different manner if the Ecuadorian politicians and the IMF had been more realistic. Above all, they seemed unable to gauge the power of the opposition, persisting in their plan to implement an agenda that was simply unattainable in the existing correlation of forces.

This final point brings me to the conclusion that political instability in Ecuador has been, in large part, an effect of the equilibrium of the forces at play in the class struggle. The key manifestations of the phenomenon – the political breakdown of Durán and the overthrows of Bucaram and Mahuad – leave no doubt about the fact that actions of the opposition played a decisive role. On each occasion, the shakeup of the political scene and the interruption of the reform process were the direct results of the veto power of the popular alliance. But that power was not sufficient to resolve the conflict because the state continued under the control of the economic elite, whose politicians would invariably re-take the initiative. In this way, the deadlock in the class conflict came to regulate the dynamics of political instability, through a vicious cycle in which each attempt for reform provoked a popular response, and each setback to neoliberalism gave rise to a new effort to implement it.

The Trajectory of the Indian Movement

Why did CONAIE, which could have limited its struggles to the rights of the Indians, gravitate toward assuming leadership in the popular resistance against neoliberalism? To understand this, we must remember one of the central points in our introductory chapter, that many Indian movements cannot be seen as purely ethnic phenomena. Insofar as most Ecuadorian Indians are peasants, their position in the class structure is another fundamental element in the definition of the character of their movements. It is not surprising, then, that from the very beginning the Indian organizations combined the demands characteristic of the peasantry with their aspirations as an ethnic group. As far back as 1988, in its second congress, CONAIE's demands included improvements in the social and economic situation of Indian communities, protection of their lands, support to small agriculture, infrastructure development, and programs in education, health, and other types of assistance. At the same time, it raised aspirations that related to the status of the Indians in society. These included the definition of Ecuador as a plurinational state, representation within state institutions, officialization of native languages, territorial autonomy, recognition of CONAIE as the representative of all Indian groups, and control over education, health, and development programs (CONAIE 1988).

But a social movement's project is not determined solely by its objectives. Another critical element is the formulation of a strategy for action. From the beginning, it was clear that the Indian movement viewed the establishment of its own spaces within the state as critical to achieving its goals. The question was: how should the movement act to conquer these spaces? The key guidelines came from the Organization and Policy Committee of the second congress, whose resolutions included the following strategic prescriptions: negotiate demands with incumbent governments, take the initiative in national mobilizations to pressure the state, have a permanent public presence by taking stands on all relevant issues, combine forms of struggle, and put CONAIE at the center of a broad front of all exploited and marginalized sectors (CONAIE 1988).

We can say, then, that the rise of CONAIE to the leadership of the popular struggles had two sources. On the one hand, because of its power to mobilize, CONAIE appeared as the appropriate agent to rally the generalized discontent and coordinate the expressions of protest. On the other hand, CONAIE had an effective vocation for popular leadership. Originally, this calling reflected the strategic idea that the Indian struggles should be linked to the more general struggles of all Ecuadorians, and that the movement should take the lead. But in light of its subsequent development, it would be too simplistic to view CONAIE's calling to leadership as a purely ideological effect. In my opinion, what came to matter most was the fact that leadership in the class struggles proved highly instrumental for the Indian movement.

This point can be demonstrated by examining CONAIE's tactics in the mobilizations. Returning to table 4.1, a striking aspect of the protests is that the lists of demands did not include specific Indian issues, despite the fact that CONAIE called the mobilization, provided the bulk of the protesters and conducted the negotiations with the government. This, however, does not mean that ethnic demands were not present in the fight. The agreements that ended the protests included agendas for subsequent negotiations, and it was there that, invariably, CONAIE included demands related to Indian aspirations. Thus, the national mobilizations became an effective means for achieving the goals of the Indian movement. In the cases that appear in table 4.1, the negotiations led to agreements on legalization of traditional medicine, creation of a special investment fund for Indian areas, reorganization of PRODEPINE (the Development Program for Indian and Black Populations) according to CONAIE's blueprint, budget increases for Indian agencies within the state, and even the assignment of radio frequency bands for Indian organizations (Kipu 1998, 1999a, 1999b).

More generally, the instrumentality of CONAIE's leadership in the popular struggles was reflected by the fact that, thanks to the political capital earned in the mobilizations, CONAIE was able to achieve some of its most significant goals without the need for further protest. This points to another component of the successful strategy of the Indian movement: the combination of forms of struggle. Throughout the 1990s, CONAIE supplemented oppositional mobilization with intense activity on other fronts. One of them had to do with institutional initiatives. In addition to filing lawsuits in the courts, CONAIE's activists mounted aggressive lobbying campaigns that led to several agreements, including the establishment of the previously mentioned PRODEPINE program with financing of 50 million dollars from the World Bank, as well as the creation of CODENPE (Ecuadorian Council of Indian Nationalities and Peoples), the coordinating agency for state programs for Indian and Afro-Ecuadorian groups (García 2002; Uquillas 2002). The other important front was electoral participation, which, as we have already seen, served to secure Indian rights in the new constitution, obtain representation in the legislature, and win political office at the local level.

What I have just described is an impressive picture of accomplishments on the part of the Ecuadorian Indian movement. It is difficult to imagine that such a feat would have been possible if CONAIE had behaved according to the expectations of new social movements theorists; that is, focusing mainly on issues of cultural identity, avoiding class conflict, and shunning politics. What we see in this case is a social struggle which became increasingly politicized. At the beginning, CONAIE exerted pressure from outside the system in order to influence state policies. With the launching of Pachakutik, however, the movement made a transition from the "politics of influence" to "the politics of power," seeking to capture positions within the state as a means for direct participation in decision making. The most dramatic expression of this ambition for power was the coup against Mahuad, which also revealed the naïve opportunism of those who were leading CONAIE at the time. The cost of that blunder was minimized by the magnitude of public anger toward Mahuad and by the fact that the conspirators did not hold on to power. It could even be said that, in the short-term, the coup reaffirmed the political clout of CONAIE, preparing the ground for the electoral result that, two years later, would sweep Pachakutik into the government.

The PSP-Pachakutik Alliance: From Hope to Frustration

In the 2002 electoral campaign, efforts to form a center-left alliance were not successful. CONAIE considered proposing one of its leaders for the presidency, but the idea was discarded when two Indian candidates emerged and it was felt that competition could cause divisions within the movement. Meanwhile, Lucio Gutiérrez and his followers had founded the Patriotic Society Party, PSP, with the colonel as its presidential candidate. In a fateful move, the leaders of CONAIE and Pachakutik agreed to an improvised alliance with the PSP (EC 2002a, 2002b, 2002c). In the November elections, Gutiérrez benefited from the Indian vote and the fact that there were eleven candidates on the ballot, winning the first presidential round with 20.4 percent of the vote (Notisur 2002b). In the second round, which took place in December, Gutiérrez defeated the banana tycoon Alvaro Noboa, who had run independently as a conservative populist, by a margin of 9.6 percent. As with previous presidents, Gutiérrez could not count on majority support in congress, since the PSP-Pachakutik alliance won only 17 of 100 delegate seats (Notisur 2002c).[4]

Since the coup, Gutiérrez had presented himself as a radical populist. He talked "with rage" about the utter poverty of the masses, denouncing the foreign debt as a looting mechanism, and arguing that the dominant classes had surrendered national sovereignty. To counter these evils, he promised to reject the neoliberal model and wage war on corruption (Gutiérrez 2002; PSP 2002). However, as the elections neared, the colonel toned down his discourse and included figures from big business and the banks in his team of advisors. Gutiérrez visited Washington to talk with

IMF and US government officials and, immediately after his election, he began to speak about the inevitability of further austerity measures (EC 2002d, 2002e). The change was reflected in the makeup of his cabinet, which was announced on January 15, 2003. Gutiérrez assigned the ministries of Foreign Affairs, Agriculture, Education, and Tourism to Pachakutik (two of these posts were occupied by prestigious Indian leaders). But the Ministries of Government and Finance, which controlled economic policy, were assigned to neoliberal technocrats who had been functioning as links between Gutiérrez, the IMF, and the business sectors (Notisur 2003a).

Gutiérrez's main priority was an agreement with the IMF, which made the elimination of Ecuador's fiscal deficit the condition for approving a standby loan. Knowing that the agreement would pave the way for substantial World Bank loans that could be used for social investment and development projects, the representatives of Pachakutik accepted the austerity measures, doing their best to moderate them. But the only real thing they managed to prevent was the elimination of the gas subsidy. The end result was a package of measures that, among other things, included a salary freeze in the public sector and significant increases in the prices of fuel, transportation, and electricity (Notisur 2003b). At the same time, the government's letter of intent to the IMF set deadlines for reorganizing the customs agency, unifying the salary scale of public employees (to increase their contributions to social security), and submitting a tax reform bill to congress (MEF 2003). In the eyes of many activists, all of this amounted to a betrayal. The Indian federation of the Sierra, Ecuarunari, withdrew its support for the government and demanded the resignation of the ministers responsible for the measures (Ecuarunari 2003). CONAIE echoed Ecuarunari's condemnations, but instead of breaking with the government, called for a rectification of the economic policies (CONAIE 2003a).

In May, two powerful unions went on strike: the teachers, who demanded payment of overdue salaries; and the oil industry workers, who opposed the terms of joint venture contracts with foreign companies. Disagreements over how to handle the strikes sharpened tensions between the PSP and Pachakutik. The labor disputes ended with concessions to the teachers and a postponement of the oil contracts, but Gutiérrez retaliated against the oil workers' union by firing its leaders (Notisur 2003c). One by one, the other organizations took a stand against the government, pressuring CONAIE to assume a more combative attitude. Finally, CONAIE's assembly decided to distance itself from the government and draw a clearer line between itself and Pachakutik. As a social movement, CONAIE would adopt an independent, critical attitude toward the state. As a political party, Pachakutik would have autonomy to decide whether it would stay or not in the government (EC 2003a, 2003b). Later, in the middle of June, CONAIE organized a "summit" of activists to prepare a list of demands for the president. The economic proposals were reminiscent of the policies of "inward development" from the classic era of Latin American reformism. At the social level, emphasis was placed on education, health, and assistance programs. The specifically Indian demands called for greater investments in existing programs and legislative initiatives to make Indian constitutional rights effective in practice (CONAIE 2003b).

The agreement with the World Bank was signed at the end of June 2003. The Assistance Strategy for Ecuador included loans for one billion dollars, and provided that half of the funds would be used for social programs during 2003–7 (World Bank 2003). The availability of resources for social programs could have helped consolidate the government alliance. However, during the month of July the symptoms of breakdown continued. The proselytizing activities of the PSP in rural areas irritated Indian activists, who viewed them as part of a plan to weaken their movement and establish clientelist networks for Gutiérrez. In the cabinet, there was no political coordination: the ministers acted on their own, mutual accusations abounded, and resignations and dismissals commenced. In congress, the "allies" maneuvered in opposite directions: while Pachakutik's delegates negotiated to form a center-left block, the PSP delegates courted the Social Christian Party. The clearest signs came from Gutiérrez himself, whose public declarations implied that he did not care about the fate of the alliance (Notisur 2003d). The breakdown took place in the first week of August, when Pachakutik congressional delegates refused to support a bill to modify employment conditions in the public sector. In response, president Gutiérrez dismissed Pachakutik's ministers (EC 2003c, 2003d).

With the collapse of the alliance, the internal divisions of the Indian movement rose to the surface. The leaders of CONAIE and Pachakutik were caught in the crossfire between the Amazonian groups, who criticized them for leaving the government, and the radical sectors from the Sierra, who reproached their delay in breaking with Gutiérrez (EC 2003e, 2003f). At the same time, Gutiérrez made efforts to weaken CONAIE. He issued an executive decree that allowed him to unilaterally appoint the officials of CODENPE and the other Indian state agencies. Since the creation of the bilingual education program, the directors of these agencies had been proposed by CONAIE and then officially ratified by the president. This implied that CONAIE, in addition to effectively controlling these state enclaves, monopolized the representation of all the Ecuadorian Indians, which was always opposed by smaller organizations like FEINE and FENOCIN. Gutiérrez's decree sought to aggravate the differences among the organizations in order to divide the Indian–peasant front and, above all, to neutralize CONAIE by threatening to take away its privileges. When CONAIE demanded the cancellation of the measure, the president agreed not to implement it, but he left open the possibility of doing so in the future if the conflict with CONAIE escalated (EC 2003g, 2003h). In fact, Gutiérrez was beginning to exploit a vulnerability of the Indian movement: the need to defend the achievements of its past struggles.

By December, the president had not yet succeeded in securing political support. The prestige of the military was called into doubt in an arms sale scandal, and Gutiérrez himself faced accusations of nepotism and corruption (Notisur 2003e). Reading the situation as similar to that which had lead to the fall of Bucaram, CONAIE's leaders called its members and other organizations to plan a large mobilization and demand the dismissal of Gutiérrez. But the Indian groups from the Amazon opposed the mobilization, and old allies like FEINE and FENOCIN were unenthusiastic. As a result, the protest had to be deferred (EC 2004a). Meanwhile, Gutiérrez arrived at an informal agreement with the Social Christian and the Roldocista parties, which offered support in exchange for ministries and preferential funding for the regional and local governments that they controlled (EC 2003i; EIU 2004).

During January 2004, CONAIE was unable to bring about the mobilization it had announced. Disagreements with the other organizations continued. FEINE and Gutiérrez were negotiating infrastructural works and social programs for the Protestant Indian communities. More troubling still for CONAIE was the fact that some of its own organizations, particularly in the Amazon, were involved in similar dealings (EC 2004b, 2004c). But despite these warning signs, CONAIE seemed determined to reaffirm its combative credentials. Finally, after three postponements, the call to mobilization came in response to an incident in which the president of CONAIE and his relatives were assaulted by armed men (EC 2004d, 2004e). Although the Indian leader was unharmed, and it was never clear whether the attack had a political motive or was just common delinquency, CONAIE accused the government and called for a protest on February 16. The list of demands was vague. Instead of raising concrete, negotiable issues, it set forth general themes related to repression, poverty, free trade agreements, and the foreign debt. On the day of the mobilization, the grassroots response was decidedly weak. The Amazonian Indian federation announced publicly that it would not participate, and none of the other popular organizations joined in the protest. After just one day, CONAIE was forced to admit failure and call off the mobilization. Instead of reaffirming its cohesion and capacity for opposition, this episode underscored that the Indian movement was in crisis (EC 2004f, 2004g).

Conclusion

In this chapter I have argued that, in Ecuador, the fundamental conflict has revolved around the costs of the neoliberal reforms. I identified two crises: a crisis of representation, rooted in the political exclusion of the popular sectors; and a crisis of state legitimacy, which resulted from the fact that the neoliberal policies were widely perceived as ineffective and grossly unjust. In these respects, the victory of the PSP-Pachakutik alliance in the 2002 elections was an important opening because the popular opposition gained a foothold within a government that was also open to the influences of the IMF and the local elite. For the first time since the beginning of the adjustment, there were favorable conditions for institutionalizing the conflict and forging compromises on the process of reform. Since the popular struggles had focused on fending off the inequities of the reforms rather than calling for radical changes, it was unlikely that Pachakutik would derail the search for agreements. At the same time, it seemed logical to expect that the pressures of the IMF and big business would be subject to bargaining, and that the state would therefore be able to act with greater autonomy *vis-à-vis* these actors.

Thus, the reconfiguration of the political scene was a significant step toward overcoming the double crisis that plagued the country. This highlighted a critical question: would Gutiérrez provide the political leadership that was needed to convert what seemed possible into a reality? Here it is worth remembering that leadership is an interactive process that does not depend solely on the leaders' charisma. The effectiveness of leaders hinges upon their ability to take the initiatives that are best suited to the imperatives of a given situation (Blanchard *et al.* 1993). Under the circumstances prevailing in Ecuador, charismatic appeal is much less important than the other classic functions of leadership: articulating a project and consolidating loyalties. In essence, Gutiérrez's success depended on his ability to become the architect of a national accord. To define his government's project, he had to negotiate the exchange of concessions among the relevant political actors. To consolidate his position, he needed to win the trust of those actors, making clear that their interests and concerns were taken into account and that he, as president, would not take sides.

It is important to stress these tasks because it allows us to better understand Gutiérrez's approach to the politics of compromise. During the electoral campaign, the president spoke frequently of a social and political pact. However, his actions revealed that his notion of compromise was not based on the goal of defining a common ground, but on the idea that it was possible to maintain an equilibrium by handing out shares of power. Instead of building a consensus and striking deals, Gutiérrez compartmentalized the executive branch, handing out ministerial positions so that each sector could pursue its respective agenda in limited areas of state policy. The goals of this strategy were obvious from the beginning: leaving the economy in the hands of the neoliberal technocrats to gain support from the IMF and the business elite and, at the same time, neutralizing CONAIE by allocating to Pachakutik some programs in which the Indians were supposed to have a special interest.

Gutiérrez's gambit presented the Indian movement with a dilemma. To understand this dilemma, we must keep in mind the two main elements in CONAIE's trajectory: its evolution from the "politics of influence" to the "politics of power" and its dual role as representative of the Indians and leader of the popular struggles. In theory, Pachakutik's presence in the government offered an opportunity to leave the mobilizations behind and achieve objectives by participating in the decisions of the state. In practice, however, the extent of that participation depended on the president, who had the authority to define the composition of the cabinet and its *modus operandi*. That asymmetry of power proved deadly for CONAIE and Pachakutik, which were unable to prevent Guitierrez's political reversal. Ultimately, the Indian movement had to face the reality that, to stay in the government, it would have to accept its exclusion from economic policy making, resigning itself to the exercise of "fragments" of power. The inducement was the possibility of consolidating its achievements and making the Indians' constitutional rights effective. The cost of that option, however, was the taming of the movement, which would have to restrict its agenda to Indian issues, and accept and legitimize the neoliberal reforms.

Pachakutik's withdrawal from the government was a reaffirmation that CONAIE was not willing to sever the connection between ethnic and class struggles. However, it is was immediately clear that the organization had been seriously weakened and that it would be an uphill battle to resume its contestatory role again. The main symptoms of CONAIE's crisis were the internal divisions, the loss of political capital *vis-à-vis* other popular organizations, and the vulnerabilities which had became apparent in the confrontations with Gutiérrez. The failure of the February 2004 mobilization demonstrated that the Indian movement would have to give priority to its internal overhaul, and that it would need time to restore its own unity and rearticulate the popular front.

Still, it would be a mistake to presume that the current difficulties of CONAIE signal the end of its political influence. In the short-term, Gutiérrez will intensify his clientelist offensive and try to secure the support of the traditional political forces. But his maneuvers are unlikely to provide a basis for political stability. Since the commitment of his new conservative allies is flabby, the president will have trouble keeping his government afloat. Moreover, CONAIE has survived the divisive offensives of previous presidents, and it is doubtful that Gutiérrez, lacking a suitable party apparatus, will be able to consolidate a base of social support through clientelism alone. In fact, the only certainty is that the end of the PSP-Pachakutik alliance and the government's turn to the right signal a return to the previous deadlock, that is, to the crisis of representation. Since the determinants of the crisis of state legitimacy also remain unresolved, what we see in Ecuador is a new scenario of political instability. Sooner or later the tensions will manifest themselves in popular protest, presenting opportunities for the comeback of the Indian movement.

Notes

Many colleagues and friends provided useful comments on earlier versions of this work. In particular, I would like to thank Jorge León for his critiques and suggestions. I am also deeply indebted to Nancy Postero for her assistance in the final editing and, above all, for her patience.

1   According to data from the Ministry of Labor, the number of conflicts decreased as follows: 362 in 1989, 186 in 1992, and 93 in 1995. The number of strikes showed an even steeper decrease: 167 in 1989, 47 in 1992 and 7 in 1995 (BCE 1999).
2   Notisur (2000b). For detailed accounts of the January 21 coup see Hernández *et al.* (2000), Lucas (2000), and Ponce (2000).
3   Cesar Montúfar (2000) uses the notion of "political praetorianism" to describe the process by which different factions of the Ecuadorian elites fight for the spoils of a "privatized state."
4   The coalition's members of congress included eight delegates from Pachakutik, three from the PSP, and six from joint lists (Notisur 2002c).

References

AGAFA – Asociación de Generales y Almirantes de las Fuerzas Armadas. 1993: Puntos de vista sobre la Ley de Modernización del Estado. *Espacios* 2, 137–41.

Andolina, R. 2003: The sovereign and its shadow: constituent assembly and indigenous movement in Ecuador. *Journal of Latin American Studies* 35 (4), 721–51.

Beck, S. H. and Mijeski, K. J. 2001: Barricades and ballots: Ecuador's Indians and the Pachakutik political movement. *Ecuadorian Studies* 1.

BCE – Banco Central del Ecuador. 1999: Anuario. Quito: BCE.

——. 2001: Anuario. Quito: BCE.

Blanchard, K. *et al.* 1993: Situational leadership after 25 years: A retrospective. *Journal of Leadership Studies* 1 (1), 22–36.

CAN – Coordinadora Agraria Nacional. 1993a: Por la tierra, la paz y el desarrollo (March 10).

——. 1993b: Carta a Carlos Vallejo, presidente del Congreso Nacional (June 23).

——. 1993c: Proyecto de ley agraria integral (July 5).

CODENPE – Consejo de Nacionalidades y Pueblos Indígenas del Ecuador. 2000: *Nuestros Derechos en la Constitución.* Quito: Génesis Ediciones.

Conaghan, C. 1989: Ecuador: the politics of locos. *Hemisphere* 1 (1), 13–15.

Conaghan, C. and Espinal, R. 1990: Unikely transitions to uncertain regimes? Democracy without compromise in the Dominican Republic and Ecuador. *Journal of Latin American Studies* 22 (3), 553–75.

CONAIE – Confederación de Nacionalidades Indígenas del Ecuador. 1988: Memorias del segundo congreso de la CONAIE.

——. 1995: Resoluciones de la asamblea extraordinaria (December 3).

——. 2003a: Resoluciones de la asamblea (February 18).

——. 2003b: Mandato de la primera cumbre de las nacionalidades, pueblos y autoridades alternativas (June 16).

CORDES – Corporación de Estudios para el Desarrollo. 1992: La nueva política económica. In P. L. Paredes (ed.): *Paquetazo: Las Medidas de Sixto y Dahik.* Quito: El Conejo, 1992.

CPSSC – Comisión Permanente del Seguro Social Campesino. 1993: *Jornada Nacional de Lucha Campesina.* Quito: Ediciones Especiales.

de la Torre, C. 1997: Populism and democracy: political discourses and cultures in contemporary Ecuador. *Latin American Perspectives* 24 (3), 12–25.

EC – *El Comercio* (daily newspaper, Quito). 2002a: El centro-izquierda lucha por su unidad (May 30).

——. 2002b: Sin mayores resultados la cita de centro-izquierda (February 27).

——. 2002c: Tres factores jugaron en favor de Lucio Gutiérrez (July 10).

——. 2002d: Los encuentros de Gutiérrez en Washington calmaron los ánimos (November 3).

——. 2002e: Gutiérrez: el pinchazo va (December13).

——. 2003a: La Conaie marca más distancia con el régimen (May 27).

——. 2003b: Pachakutik y la Conaie marcan sus territorios (May 28).

——. 2003c: Pachakutik se quedó fuera del poder (August 7).

——. 2003d: La alianza de Gobierno cayó por su propio peso en 6 meses (August 10).

——. 2003e: La Conaie y Pachakutik con una táctica defensiva (August 16).

——. 2003f: La relación Conaie-Pachakutik está en crisis (September 3).

——. 2003g: Gutiérrez busca cambios en el Codenpe (October 10).

——. 2003h: Lucio Gutiérrez gana un 'round' a la Conaie (October 18).

——. 2003i: El Gobierno se fortalece en el Frente Político (December 19).

——. 2004a: La Conaie pone pausa a su protesta contra el Gobierno (January 12).

——. 2004b: Los amazónicos en paz (January 20).

——. 2004c: La Feine hace la paz con Gutiérrez (February 1).

——. 2004d: El atentado a Leonidas Iza conmociona (February 3).

——. 2004e: La Conaie acusa al Gobierno y prepara movilizaciones (February 3).

——. 2004f: Indígenas suspenden las protestas (February 17).

——. 2004g En las movilizaciones se evidenció la crisis de la Conaie (February 21).

Economist (weekly magazine, USA). 1998: Picking up the pieces (December 12).

——. 1999a: The furies wait (March 6).

——. 1999b: Awaiting rescue (August 7).

——. 1999c: Jamil juggles (September 4).

——. 1999d: Under the volcano (November 27).

Ecuarunari – Confederación de Pueblos de la Nacionalidad Quichua. 2003: Resoluciones de la asamblea extraordinaria (February 14).

EIU – The Economist Intelligence Unit. 2004: *Ecuador Country Report* 1, 7–8.

Flores, T. 1995. Corrupción y democracia: El caso Dahik. In N. Saltos (ed.): *Corrupción: Epidemia de Fin de Siglo.* Quito: ILDIS.

Foweraker, J. 1995: *Theorizing Social Movements.* London: Pluto Press.

García, F. 2002: Política, estado y movimiento indígena: nuevas estrategias de negociación en tiempos de dolarización. Paper presented at the annual meeting of the Ecuadorian Studies section of the Latin American Studies Association, Quito, July 18–20.

Gutiérrez, L. 2002: Breve síntesis de la revolución civil-militar del 21 de Enero del 2.000 en el Ecuador y algunas reflexiones al respecto. Online <http://www.sociedadpatriotica.com>.

Haggard, S. and Kaufman, R. R. 1995: The *Political Economy of Democratic Transitions*. Princeton: Princeton University Press.

Hale, C. R. 1997: Cultural politics of identity in Latin America. *Annual Review of Anthropology* 26, 567–90.

Hernández, J. *et al.* 2000: *21 de Enero: La Vorágine que Acabo con Mahuad*. Quito: El Comercio.

Hey, J. A. and Klak, T. 1999: From protectionism toward neoliberalism: Ecuador across four administrations *Studies in Comparative International Development*, 34 (3), 66–97.

INEC – Instituto Nacional de Estadística y Censos. 2001: *Sexto Censo Nacional de Población*, 2001. Quito: INEC.

ILDIS – Instituto Latinoamericano de Investigaciones Sociales. 2003: *Economía Ecuatoriana en Cifras, 1970–2003*. Online <http://www.ildis.org.ec/estadisticas>.

Kipu – El Mundo Indígena en la Prensa Ecuatoriana (press reports). 1993: Press reports on the mobilization to defend the rural health service (January 9–18).

——. 1994: Press reports on the Agrarian Modernization Law, the mobilizations against the bill, and the subsequent negotiations (May 7–July 16).

——. 1996: Press reports on Pachakutik's electoral results (May 20–30).

——. 1998: Press reports on protest mobilizations (September 9–October 21).

——. 1999a: Press reports on protest mobilizations (March 11–25).

——. 1999b: Press reports on protest mobilizations (July 7–August 3).

León, J. 1988: *Composición Social y Escena Política en el Sindicalismo Ecuatoriano* (monograph). Quito, CEDIME.

——. 1994: *De Campesinos a Ciudadanos Diferentes: El Levantamiento Indígena*. Quito: Abya-Yala.

Lucas, K. 2000: *La Rebelión de los Indios*. Quito: Abya-Yala.

Mainwaring, S. 1993: Presidentialism, multipartism, and democracy: the difficult combination. *Comparative Political Studies* 26 (2),198–230.

MEF – Ministerio de Economia y Finanzas del Ecuador. 2003: Letter of intention and memorandum of economic policies (February 10).

Montúfar, C. 2000: Crisis, iniquidad y el espectro predatorio del estado ecuatoriano: interpretación política de la coyuntura 1998–2000. Paper presented at the conference Ecuador 2000, Universidad Andina, Quito, August 16–18.

Moya, R. A. 1990: A decade of bilingual education and indigenous participation in Ecuador. *Prospects* 20 (3), 331–43.

NotiSur – South American Political and Economic Affairs (newsletter). 1992: Sixto Durán elected president in runoff (July 7).

——. 1994: President Durán battles congress over constitutional reforms (October 21).

——. 1995a: Criminal charges against vice-president Alberto Dahik deepen political crisis (September 1).

——. 1995b: President Sixto Durán suffers defeat in referendum on constitutional reforms (December 1).

——. 1996: Controversy permeates president Abdalá Bucaram's tumultuous first three months in office (November 15).

——. 1997a: Government economic plan continues to generate broad opposition (January 10).

——. 1997b: Congress votes to oust president Abdalá Bucaram (February 7).

——. 1998a: President-elect Jamil Mahuad must walk political and economic tightrope (July 24).

——. 1998b: President Jamil Mahuad introduces unpopular economic measures (September 18).

——. 1998c: Protests intensify against government austerity measures (October 2).

——. 1999a: President Jamil Mahuad says country is in financial crisis (January 22).

——. 1999b: Ecuador devalues its currency as crisis continues (February 26).

——. 1999c: Congress approves president Jamil Mahuad's economic package (April 30).

——. 1999d: President Jamil Mahuad battered by protests (July 16).

——. 1999e: International Monetary Fund approves standby loan (September 3).

——. 1999f: Crises plague administration (November 5).

——. 2000a: Cabinet resigns after president Jamil Mahuad adopts dollar as local currency amid protests (January 14).

——. 2000b: Indian Protests topple presidency of Jamil Mahuad, vice-president Gustavo Noboa takes over (January 28).

——. 2002a: Economy minister resigns amid scandal (June 28).

——. 2002b: Presidential elections go to runoff (October 25).

——. 2002c: Lucio Gutiérrez wins presidency in Runnof (December 6).

——. 2003a: Lucio Gutiérrez takes office as president (January 17).

——. 2003b: Indigenous cabinet members walk tightrope between administration and communities (February 14).

——. 2003c: President Lucio Gutiérrez hit by more strikes, dissention within coalition government (June 20).

——. 2003d: President Lucio Gutiérrez' authoritarianism creates problems with indigenous members of coalition (August 1).

——. 2003e: Narco-scandal threatens government of president Lucio Gutiérrez (December 5).

Saltos, N. 2001: Movimiento indígena y movimientos sociales: encuentros y desencuentros. *Boletín ICCI-ARY Rimay* 27.

Pérez. A. 1994: Distribución del ingreso y pobreza. *Revista Economía* 7.

Ponce, J. 2000: La *Madrugada los Sorprendió en el Poder*. Quito: Editorial Planeta.

PSP – Partido Sociedad Patriótica. 2002: Declaración de Principios. Online <http://www.sociedadpatriotica.com>.

Salgado, W. 2001: Economía ecuatoriana y tendencias recesivas de la economía mundial. *Ecuador Debate* 54.

——. 2002: Financiamiento del gasto público: entre el FMI y las cuentas pendientes del salvataje bancario. *Ecuador Debate* 57.

Sawyer, S. 1997: The 1992 Indian mobilization in lowland Ecuador. *Latin American Perspectives* 24 (3), 65–83.

Schuldt, J. 1994: *Elecciones y Política Económica en el Ecuador*. Quito: ILDIS.

Shugart, M. S. 1995: The electoral cycle and institutional sources of divided presidential government. *American Political Science Review* 89 (2), 327–43.

SIISE – Sistema Integrado de Indicadores Sociales del Ecuador. 2002: La Década en Cifras. Online <http://www.siise.gov.ed>.

Tamayo, E. 1996: *Movimientos Sociales: la Riqueza de la Diversidad*. Quito: ALAI.

Thoumi, F. and Grindle, M. 1992: *La Política de la Economía del ajuste: La Actual Experiencia* Ecuatoriana. Quito: FLACSO.

Uquillas, J. E. 2002: Fortalecimiento de la capacidad de autogestión de los pueblos indígenas y afroecuatorianos: el caso PRODEPINE. Paper presented at the annual meeting of the Ecuadorian Studies section of the Latin American Studies Association, Quito, July 18–20.

Viteri Díaz, G. 1998: *Las Políticas de Ajuste: Ecuador 1982–1996*. Quito: Corporación Editora Nacional.

Walsh, C. 1994: El desarrollo sociopolitico de la educación intercultural bilingüe en el Ecuador. *Pueblos Indígenas y Educación* 7 (31–32), 99–164.

World Bank. 2003: *Country Assistance Strategy for the Republic of Ecuador.* Report No. 25817 EC (April 29).

Younger, S. D. 1993: The economic impact of a foreign debt bail-out for private firms in Ecuador. *Journal of Development Studies* 29 (3), 484–503.

Zamosc, L. 1994: Agrarian protest and the Indian movement in the Ecuadorian Highlands. *Latin American Research Review* 29 (3), 37–68.

——. 1995: *Estadística de las Areas de Predominio Étnico de la Sierra Ecuatoriana*. Quito: Abya-Yala.

——. 2001: Implications of Pachakutik's electoral gains for Indian territoriality and autonomy in the highlands. Paper presented at the congress of the Latin American Studies Association, Washington, September 6–8.

Un País Sin Indígenas?

Rethinking Indigenous
Politics in Peru

María Elena García and *José Antonio Lucero*

Not long ago, Peruvian anthropologist Luis Millones reports, the World Bank decided to provide funds to indigenous people from "Mexico to Tierra del Fuego." "To do so, the Bank went in search of the representative indigenous institutions in all of the Latin American countries. And it found itself with the surprising discovery that between Ecuador and Bolivia, there was a country without *indígenas* (indigenous people)" (Millones 1999: 79).[1] In the larger picture of the region-wide "return of the Indian" (Albó 1991), Peru – where indigenous people constitute approximately 40 percent of the national population, but which claims no representative national indigenous confederation – has been considered an exception at best, a failure at worst. Scholars and activists have pondered the "absence" of indigenous organizing in the country, and they have lamented the lack of ethnic identification among Quechua and Aymara *campesinos* (peasants). Compared to indigenous organizing in other Latin American countries, where indigenous federations are actively promoting the revival of indigenous language and culture, demanding collective rights, and forcing issues of sovereignty and self-determination into discussions about citizenship and nationalism, Peru remains a question mark in the literature.

In this chapter, however, we suggest an alternative interpretation. We argue that Peruvian "failure" is a product of the frameworks and models used by scholars and advocates of indigenous movements, rather than an accurate description of the complex dynamics of indigenous politics in the country. We agree with Carlos Ivan Degregori's under-appreciated contention that "perhaps it is not a matter of being behind or ahead, but rather of the distinct forms through which ethnicity is expressed in different countries" (Degregori 1993: 128). Additionally, we echo Kay Warren's (1998) warning of the limitations associated with privileging a single, unified model of social movement, obscuring the multiplicity of actors, spaces, and voices that constitute contemporary indigenous struggles. In this paper, we argue against a reading of Peruvian movement "failure" and explore the dynamic ways in which indigenous mobilization is taking place at local, national, and transnational levels. Accordingly, we first interrogate various views of Peruvian absence or failure. Then, after a brief historical overview, we explore the different forms and various scales at which indigenous struggles have made themselves present in ways that sometimes diverge, and at other times converge, with developments throughout the region. Finally, we discuss the recent emergence (since the fall of President Alberto Fujimori) of new actors and the openings of new spaces that are full of both possibilities and dangers. We conclude by re-thinking Peruvian indigenous politics and what the Peruvian case suggests about indigenous movements more generally.

Peruvian Indigenous "Failure" in Comparative Perspective

With the uneasy transitions to democracy that took place in many Latin American countries during the 1980s, as well as the influence of world-wide economic and cultural global trends, states throughout Latin America have been increasingly concerned with the reformulation of nations as multiethnic or multicultural spaces (Stavenhagen 1992; Brysk 1996; Van Cott 2000). Because of their appeals for ethnic, cultural, and political autonomy and recognition, indigenous groups throughout the region are now prominent actors in discussions about national identity and citizenship in Latin America. In the 1990s particularly, the region saw a surge of indigenous political and cultural activity.[2]

In regards to this regional and indeed global trend, indigenous movements in Peru have been widely described as "marginal" (Albó 1991), "largely non-existent" (Yashar 1998), and "a profound failure" (E. Mayer cited in Yashar 1998). In other Latin American countries, such as Bolivia, Ecuador, and Mexico, the 1980s and 1990s saw the emergence of powerful national indigenous organizations. Yet, in the same period, Peru had no "national," that is, pan-regional, indigenous organization.[3]

Scholars and advocates of indigenous movements lament the lack of indigenous political activity in Peru, and offer three main explanations for this "absence" of ethnic mobilization. First, many scholars point to the legacies of the populist and corporatist government policies of General Juan Velasco Alvarado (1968–75). The Velasco regime organized indigenous populations around class-based labels and social programs, and prohibited the use of the term Indian by promoting instead identification as campesinos or peasants. Privileging a class-based idiom over an ethnic one (what some have called "de-indianization"), the Velasco regime pursued a strategy of populist reform and of leftist mobilization that, according to some scholars, made ethnic identification unlikely (Gelles 2002). However, other Andean states saw comparable efforts to "re-baptize Indians as peasants," but still boasted a resurgence of explicitly indigenous political identities (Albó 1994). Moreover, while the histories of agrarian struggles are undoubtedly important to understanding Peruvian indigenous politics, it is probably a mistake to view class and ethnic identities as mutually exclusive options.

A second explanation, then, looks to the lack of political opportunity and capability in building supra-communal organizations, due largely to the disastrous effects of civil war (Albó 1991, Yashar 1998). The war that raged in the 1980s and early 1990s made Peru a much less hospitable environment for the organization-building activities of non-governmental organizations (NGOs), missionaries, unions, and indigenous activists that took place in other Andean republics. During this time, political violence, repression, and persecution – both on the part of the Peruvian government and of Sendero Luminoso and the Túpac Amaru Revolutionary Movement (MRTA)[4] – had (and in some cases continues to have) a devastating impact on the spaces available for grass-roots organizing in Peru. Sendero militants eliminated all rival sources of political power, and government forces interpreted any sort of gathering as potentially subversive. Because Sendero originated in the highlands, the government (especially in the early 1980s) often assumed a link between terrorism and Andean indigenous communities, making it particularly difficult to organize around ethnic banners.[5]

We agree that the Peruvian political context is quite different from other Andean countries where indigenous organizations have been more visible. Nonetheless, this kind of structural view of political opportunity and capacity, while valuable, tends to assume a rather static notion of indigenous struggle, one that seems simply to be awaiting the right conditions in order to emerge through the cracks of uneven states. A political/structural approach may say much about the conditions for protest, but it says very little about the complex cultural dynamics that are part of making collective identities and collective action. However, this does not necessarily mean that "cultural" explanations are necessarily preferable to "structural" ones, as an examination of the third view of Peruvian failure illustrates.

Thirdly, then, we turn to the argument advanced most forcefully by Peruvian anthropologist Marisol de la Cadena regarding the cultural force and particularity of *mestizaje* (racial and cultural mixture) in Peru. De la Cadena rejects earlier contentions that Peruvian Indian identity has been erased by national projects of mestizaje. She emphasizes instead the significance of historical conditions that have led Peruvian Andeans (Cuzqueños specifically) to appropriate and redefine the term *mestizo* as a way "to develop de-Indianization as a decolonizing indigenous strategy" (2000: 325). De la Cadena examines primarily the lives of urban Cuzqueño intellectual elites, university students, mestiza market-women, and others who, she argues, expand their mestizo identity to include indigenous practices. In doing so, these individuals (whom she labels "grass-roots indigenous intellectuals") have redefined dominant notions of indigenous identity. Defying perceptions of indigenous identity as "exclusively rural, essentially backward, irrational and illiterate," indigenous mestizos present indigenous culture as both rural and urban and compatible with literacy and progress. Thus, for Cuzqueño grassroots intellectuals, "indigenous culture exceeds the scope of Indianness and includes subordinate definitions of the mestizo/a" (2000: 316). Moreover, becoming mestizo does not necessarily mean "erasing" indigenous cultural identity. In other words, indigenous practices do not disappear when indigenous people learn Spanish and move to the city. In fact, one strategy of empowerment employed by indigenous intellectuals in Cuzco, is to embrace an identity as *indigenous* mestizos.

Examining perceptions of race, culture, and ethnicity in Peru historically, de la Cadena contends that the "lack" of *recognized* ethnic mobilization in the country is due to the fact that indigenous mestizo activism is not usually considered "ethnic" activism (de la Cadena 2000, 2001). While there is much to de la Cadena's valuable examination of Peruvian identity politics, it neglects important rural and transnational spaces where Indianness is emerging in complex and important ways that often are constructed *in opposition* to mestizo identity. De la Cadena argues that indigenous politics in the city of Cuzco are about the politics of mestizaje. However, it would be a mistake to take the dynamics of urban Cuzco to stand for the entire Andean region, not to mention Peru as a whole.

In the following pages, rather than suggest an alternative diagnosis for the "failure" of Peru, we seek to explore the particular patterns of indigenous politics in the Andean highlands, the Amazonian lowlands, and in transnational spaces. Arguing against "failure" and "absence," we do not mean to simply invert the image and declare the triumph of indigenous politics. Instead, by sketching a more complex picture of Peruvian indigenous politics – full of contradictions, risks, and hopes – we seek to understand both the range of indigenous activism and reflect on the frameworks that the state, scholars, and development agencies have used to evaluate the varieties of indigenous experiences.

María Elena García and José Antonio Lucero

Historical and Political Background

The Latin American "Indian" began as a colonial construct that was instrumental to the fiscal and political ordering of Spanish America. As with most colonial encounters, the construction of new forms of domination combined elements from the repertoires of both colonizing and colonized societies. Spanish colonizers left many native structures in place and grafted the colonial state onto complex networks of tribute systems that predated the Conquest (Spalding 1984; Stern 1987). This political syncretism was ostensibly abandoned during liberal periods in the nineteenth century and populist ones in the twentieth as national leaders attempted to redefine the "Indian" politically as "citizen" and socioeconomically as "peasant." It is helpful to provide some detail on how the re-baptism of Indians into peasants took place in "revolutionary" Peru.

Corporatism, Populism, and Social Reform

General Velasco's "Revolutionary Government of the Armed Forces" (1968–75) emerged in reaction to social unrest and the rise of peasant and guerrilla movements in the highlands in the 1950s and '60s. Declaring the necessity of transforming Peru's basic economic and social structures as the only way to counter instability and a future insurgency, and proclaiming an anti-imperialistic, anti-oligarchic and fervently nationalistic ideology, Velasco launched a series of social reforms aimed at ameliorating the conditions of peasants and indigenous peoples. These reforms fundamentally challenged the existing power dynamics throughout the country.[6]

Velasco's radical agrarian reform – most often cited as a turning point in Peruvian history – was officially initiated throughout the highlands on June 24, 1969, the national "Day of the Indian." On this day, Velasco announced the massive and forceful hand-over of large estates by landowners to their former serfs and employees. Moreover, he prohibited the use of the term *indio*, replacing it with the label of "peasant" (*campesino*). During a televised speech that highlighted the contradictory efforts of a Peruvian state that incorporated Indians by rendering them legally invisible, Velasco stated:

> Today, for the Day of the Indian, the Day of the Peasant, the Revolutionary Government honors them with the best of tributes by giving to the nation a law that will end forever the unjust social order that impoverished and oppressed the millions of landless peasants who have always been forced to work the land of others . . . [T]he Agrarian Reform law gives its support to the great multitude of *peasants who today belong to indigenous communi-*

ties and from this day forward – *abandoning unacceptable racist habits and prejudices* – will be called Peasant Communities (*Comunidades Campesinas*) . . . To the men of the land, we can now say in the immortal and liberating voice of Túpac Amaru: Peasant: the Master will no longer feed off your poverty! (Velasco 1969, emphasis added)

While this move created the category of highland "peasant communities" it was not until 1974 that Velasco legally recognized and organized Amazonian peoples as "native communities," further re-inscribing the distinction between highland and lowland peoples.

In an effort to integrate highland peasants into the national economy, Velasco's plan included the redistribution of all *haciendas* (large landholdings) by 1975.[7] Although the idea was simple – distribute land among those who work it – the reform's implementation was largely unsuccessful.[8] While it effectively ended landowners' control over peasant workers, it also greatly exacerbated tensions between ethnic groups, particularly between highland peasants and lowland "natives" on the one hand, and the *criollo* (American-born Spaniards) middle and upper classes on the other.

An important moment of Velasco's regime came in 1975 when he passed a law making Quechua a national language with equal status to Spanish. Peru thus became the first Latin American country to *officialize* an indigenous language. By placing Quechua next to the dominant language, however, it also raised prejudices against Andeans to the surface, one of the factors leading to the replacement of Velasco with Morales Bermudez, another military leader, in 1975.

With the change in presidents (1975) and in constitutions (1979), the law making Quechua an official language was changed to include Quechua not as an official national language, but rather as "a language of official use in the areas and in the way that the Law mandates." However, the law that would mandate where and how Quechua could be considered an "official" language was never developed (Pozzi-Escot 1981). Known as "Phase Two" of the Revolutionary Government, this and other changes were a systematic dismantling of many Velasco era reforms, including the emphasis that had been placed on rural and indigenous education.

Neoliberalism and Multicultural Reform

With the return to democracy and the economic crises of the 1980s, the state abandoned corporatist forms of government. The decline of corporatism and the subsequent rise of neoliberal policies meant that state social and agricultural programs were dismantled, adversely impacting indigenous populations. When Alberto Fujimori became president of Peru in

1990, neoliberalism became further entrenched despite his populist campaign rhetoric. Moreover, increasing counter-insurgency efforts meant that the military controlled almost two thirds of the national territory. In the capital, the *auto-golpe* (self-coup) of 1992, which closed down the National Congress, signaled the erosion of civil and political rights. A turning point in this adverse political climate came in September 1992 with the capture of Abimael Guzmán, the head of Sendero Luminoso. With the war officially over, by 1993 Peru began a slow transition toward democratic rule. Notably, however, Peru enacted a new constitution that among other things, "recognizes and protects the ethnic and cultural plurality of the nation" by guaranteeing the right of all people to use their own language before the state (Article 2). The constitution also recognizes and "respects the cultural identity of rural and native communities" (Article 89), and protects communal property, though it makes exceptions for land the state deems abandoned (Cited in M. A. Smith 1999).

While there is much skepticism about government commitment to these cultural policies, increasingly, the presence and financial support of international actors, such as NGOs and the World Bank, have helped institutionalize (albeit slowly) a multicultural development agenda. International pressure, for example, forced the Fujimori administration to re-establish what is now the *Dirección Nacional de Educación Bilingüe Intercultural* (DINEBI, National Office of Bilingual Intercultural Education) within the Ministry of Education. Indeed, as we show below, recent efforts at multicultural education reform provide important examples of the spaces that have become available for the re-negotiation of state–indigenous relations.

Mapping Indigenous Politics: Changing Spaces, Models, and Organizations

Peruvian indigenous politics has rarely resembled the flat images of failure that have become so frequent in recent scholarly discussions. In Peru, like in most states that have experienced significant periods of contemporary indigenous organizing, one can identify the main kinds of organizations that Richard Chase Smith (1983) elaborated in his influential typology for indigenous organizing in the central Andean republics. Smith distinguished between peasant labor unions, urban indianist (radical pan-Indian) movements, and ethnic federations.[9]

This typology captured a period of indigenous politics, roughly spanning the turbulent period framed by the populist presidencies of Velasco Alvarado (1968–75) and Alan García (1985–90). During this period, highland campesino unions borrowed from the repertoire of the left in privileging class identification, discouraging ethnic particularity, and emphasized the need for redistribution of land and resources on national levels. Later, ethnic federations emerged – especially but not exclusively in the lowlands – that articulated and confederated more specific local (what Smith called "tribal") identities. For Smith, these two types of organizations differ most radically from the last, *indianista* organizations, in the questionable representativity that urban *indianistas* could claim as they advanced radical ethnic claims. Unlike the rural networks that constituted labor and ethnic federations, *indianista* groups were more often isolated groups of intellectuals or activists that were at best virtual, and not elected, representatives of indigenous communities. While, like R. C. Smith (2002a, 2002b), we see the need to re-think this typology for understanding the most recent period of indigenous politics, it is useful to first review the legacy of early models that current actors are re-defining.

Early Models: Campesino, Ethnic, and Indianist Organizations (1960s–1980s)

During the 1960s, *campesino* union organizing was a central part of rural contention. Between 1960 and 1964, 1,500 unions were organized. Over this time however, class-based organizing was not necessarily in tension with the indigenous structures of local communities; "indeed, one of the union demands was legal recognition of their communities of origin" (Remy 1994: 114). Union and federation membership, then, was a pragmatic means toward achieving a specific end: the "recuperation" of community lands. Between 1958 and 1964, powerful indigenous peasant movements recuperated thousand of hectares (Degregori 1993: 122). While there were various strands of union organizing, the 1950s saw the consolidation of the *Confederación Campesina del Perú* (CCP) led by the Moscow-line Peruvian Communist Party (R. C. Smith 1983, Degregori 1993, Remy 1994).

The subsequent agrarian reform in 1969 and the rule of General Velasco sought to institutionalize peasant identities throughout the countryside and harness peasant movements to an emerging corporatist structure. As stated above, Velasco tried to incorporate rural people officially as "campesino communities," explicitly expunging the term "Indian" from social policy. Additionally, Velasco directly challenged the CCP through the establishment of the official *Confederación Nacional Agraria* (CNA, National Agrarian Confederation). Tensions between the independent CCP and officialist CNA notwithstanding, these confederations continued to be the main national highland rural organizations even after the overthrow of Velasco in 1975.

Even as Velasquista attempts at national integration crumbled, the importance of class-based organizing increased, while indigenous political traditions were in the best cases ignored, and in the worst cases, attacked. Indeed, this hostility toward indigenous practices and traditions is a pervasive theme in twentieth-century Peru, and according to Florencia Mallon (1998) is part of the destructive violence suffered by Quechuas and Aymaras at the hands of Sendero Luminoso guerillas. Echoing the chilling metaphors of Senderistas, Mallon concludes:

> The failure politically to engage indigenous traditions and practices, which emerged in the twentieth century among a variety of oppositional political groups in Peru was reconstructed with the class-based leftist discourses and practices of the 1960s and 1970s, intensified in the Shining Path vision of the 1980s popular war. Indeed, within Senderista strategy, a historically created blindness to Indian-ness, linked to the imperative of total war, transformed communal culture and politics into one more insect to be squashed. (Mallon 1998: 115–16)

Given the early history of organizing, however, there is nothing intrinsically antagonistic between indigenous and class-based forms of protest. One could agree with Marisol de la Cadena (2001: 20) that throughout the 1960s and 1970s, "indigenous utilization of class based rhetoric was a political option that did not represent the loss of indigenous culture, but was rather a strategy toward its empowerment." However, over time state-sponsored reforms and the wave of increasingly radicalized movements they unleashed created a political environment in which, at the national scale, Leftist political projects were pitted against more local "ethnic" alternatives. While ethnicity has always, in various ways, been part of highland protest, it has played a much more visible role in the lowlands.

Ethnic Unions and Federations: AIDESEP and CONAP

Unlike in the highlands, ethnicity has long served as an organizing principle for lowland indigenous protest. "The areas where the ethnic federation has proliferated are precisely those areas which were peripheral to or outside of the integrative horizons which have swept the Andean region over the past several millenia" (R. C. Smith 1983: 18). It is in the Amazon regions where the first indigenous ethnic federations in the Americas emerged in the 1960s. The first is the Shuar federation organized in Ecuador in 1964. The second, the Congress of Amuesha Communities in Peru, was established in 1969. It is significant that this Congress comes together in 1969, the very year when agrarian reform attempted to use a supposedly "empty" Amazon to ease the pressures of land re-distribution in the highlands. In order to better defend their territories from the new Andean colonization, lowland indigenous people began to organize, often with the help of missionaries and NGOs. The Amuesha Congress, along with the Aguaruna and Huambisa Council (founded in 1976) and the Defense Front of the Native Communities (Shipibo), together formed a coordination committee that became the Inter-Ethnic Development Association of the Peruvian Jungle, or AIDESEP (R. C. Smith 1983, Albó 1991: 326, Chirif 1991, Remy 1994).

AIDESEP represents a significant example of how indigenous communities have been able to "jump scales" from local to regional and national levels. As a member of AIDESEP explains,

> As a community group based in one village or river valley, we may have been able to negotiate with the mayor or minor local official. As a regional organization, we might get to see the governor. As a national organization, we soon got to see ministers and even presidents and as an international organization, we have been to see the president of the World Bank and top United Nations people. (Cited in Wearne 1996: 170)

The formation of AIDESEP and the proliferation of regional ethnic federations, however, was not without its problems. Albó (1991) notes that AIDESEP was weakened by division among Amazonian organizations. In 1988, several of them organized a parallel Amazonian confederation called The Confederation of Nationalities of the Peruvian Amazon, or CONAP. Chirif (1991), an anthropologist who has worked closely with AIDESEP, argues that the division reflects not so much a weakness of AIDESEP, but rather the differences in ideology and structure of each confederation. According to Chirif, while AIDESEP is the product of "a rupture between indigenous leaders and independent professionals and NGOs" (Chirif 1991: 354), CONAP reflects instead the now commonplace marriage between indigenous activists and both state and non-governmental supporters. In Chirif's view, while AIDESEP has sought to maintain its autonomy from non-indigenous activists, scholars, and funders, CONAP has instead become dependent on the support of development organizations.

Chirif's praise of AIDESEP and condemnation of CONAP is open to debate as more recent studies (R. C. Smith 1996) have found that AIDESEP and its member organizations have also become increasingly reliant upon foreign financing: "A hundred percent of AIDESEP operations depend upon external funding, the majority of which comes from foreign sources" (R. C. Smith 1996: 100). Despite these difficulties, lowland organizations were extremely important in placing autonomy and protection of territories and resources on national and international agendas. Moreover, their success in attracting international support provided new incentives for organizing along ethnic indigenous lines.[10]

Indianista Organizations: MIP, MITA, and CISA

In the 1970s, *indianista* organizations, organizations that deployed more radical pan-Indian ideologies but usually from urban centers, were successful in attracting national and international attention. These organizations elaborated their political project in line with the angry anti-colonial theorizing of figures like Franz Fanon and Fausto Reinaga, rejecting the occidental impositions of labor unions and calling for a return to the greatness of pre-colonial pasts. In Peru's capital, Lima, the first notable Indianist group emerged under the name the *Movimiento Indio Peruano* (MIP, Peruvian Indian Movement), but lasted only a few years (1977–80) as internal disputes over the use of international funds multiplied. Some members of MIP continued to be active in subsequent organizations like the *Movimiento Indio Tupac Amaru* (MITA, Tupac Amaru Indian Movement) and the transnational *Consejo Indio de Sud America* (CISA, South American Indian Council), both based in Lima (R. C. Smith 1983: 24–5, Albó 1991).

Indianista organizations often proclaimed themselves as the only legitimate voices of indigenous people, especially before international audiences. *Indianistas* accused highland *campesino* federations of betraying indigenous traditions and blindly following white and *mestizo* Leftist leaders. Despite the fact that MIP, MITA, and CISA had few direct links to indigenous communities that were located far outside of Lima, in the early years of the "return of the Indian," many European supporters enthusiastically embraced their ethnic radicalism, which resulted in "a great deal of confusion regarding Indian organizations in Latin America" (R. C. Smith 1983: 28). Among current indigenous activists, *indianista* groups like CISA are seen as shameful examples of political opportunism rather than examples of legitimate struggle. Indeed, over time, in fighting, accusations of rampant corruption, and visibly thin representativity served to undermine the viability of *indianista* organizations. While organizationally, *indianismo* may be a thing of the past, as we will see below, its ideological force can still be felt in the most recent period of indigenous mobilization.

New Political Opportunities: Post-Terrorism, Post-Cold War, Post-Fujimori (1992–2000)

While there are always difficulties in periodizing social and political change, the capture of Sendero Luminoso's leader Abimael Guzmán, in 1992 is a clear landmark for war-weary Peruvians. After a bloodstained decade of insurgency and counter-insurgency, the capture and imprisonment of Guzmán heralded the end of terror and the zenith of Alberto Fujimori's heavy-handed presidency. Without its leader and under the pressure of Fujimori's aggressive military campaigns, Sendero's numbers dwindled and its remaining elements sought refuge in the jungles of Peru. While peace was seemingly at hand, it had come at a high price. According to the recently released report of the Peruvian Truth and Reconciliation Commission (2003), approximately 70,000 people lost their lives, and most of those losses were in the indigenous communities of the Andean highlands.

Indigenous people were not passive in the face of terror, organizing self-defense units in both highland (e.g. *rondas campesinos*, peasant civil patrols*)* and lowland contexts (e.g. *ejército Asháninka*, the Asháninka army). Still, as mentioned earlier, scholars often cite the devastation of war as a prime reason for the lack of national mobilizing structures for indigenous people.[11] Thus, the end of the violence would represent an opening for more explicitly political organizing. Organizational environments certainly do not change overnight, but as the nation began to speak of the times of terrorism in the past tense, the political climate was certainly changing in important ways.

One crucial source of change came from the international sphere and the stunning advances that indigenous people had made in placing indigenous concerns on the agendas of bodies like the United Nations and in the programs of national and multilateral development agencies. The year 1989 saw not only the fall of the Berlin Wall and communism, but also an increasing concern for other issues and identities around which to conceptualize and foment social change. In 1989, the International Labor Organization revised its convention on indigenous peoples and drafted what would be known as ILO Convention 169. Unlike earlier conventions that had emphasized assimilationist goals, ILO 169 recognized the existence and legitimacy of the claims of "tribal and indigenous peoples." Moreover, it stressed the obligation of national governments to work with indigenous peoples to "coordinate and systematize" efforts that "protect the rights of these peoples and guarantee the respect to their integrity" (Article 2, ILO 169, 1989). Soon ILO 169 became recognized as occupying a privileged place in an emerging international regime of norms that legitimated indigenous movement demands. "More than any other international document, the International Labor Organization's Convention 169 represents this shift from an assimilation perspective to one that respects and values Indigenous cultures" (Abya Yala News, cited in Van Cott 2000: 263). The United Nations, with a Working Group on Indigenous Populations since 1982, has become increasingly active in this arena, passing declarations upholding indigenous peoples' right to difference and rejecting all acts of cultural ethnocide or genocide. It also recognized the continuing importance of indigenous issues to international agendas by expanding from the Year of Indigenous People (1993) to the International Decade of the World's Indigenous People, 1995–2005. Additionally, multilateral institutions, including the Inter-

American Development Bank, the World Bank, and the UN Development Program, have institutionalized special programs for indigenous people (Brysk 2000: 130–1).

It is worth emphasizing, however, that transnational politics predate the fall of communism. The 1970s saw several attempts to organize international working groups for the defense of indigenous peoples.[12] Peru was an important site for the formation of these international linkages. In 1980, a group of mestizo university professors of the MIP (the Peruvian Indian Movement), along with European activists affiliated with the New World Council on Indigenous People, hosted an international indigenous conference outside of Cuzco. Out of this meeting emerged the CISA, the South American Indigenous Council, as an international voice for indigenous peoples. However, as we have discussed, it rapidly fell into disrepute due to its secretive nature and accusations of corruption. At a later meeting in Lima, Amazonian indigenous leaders reached the decision that a new organization was needed, but one that would avoid the mistakes of CISA. Thus in 1984, indigenous organizations from all the countries of the Amazon basin,[13] including AIDESEP, founded the *Comisión Coordinadora de Organizaciones Indígenas de la Cuenca Amazónica* (the Coordinating Council of Indigenous Organizations from the Amazon Watershed), known as COICA.

AIDESEP president Evaristo Nugkuag became the first president of COICA. COICA participated actively in the United Nations during the revision of ILO convention 169, which recognized the collective rights of indigenous peoples. Moreover, COICA established links with European green parties, labor movements, and other sectors in international civil society. In 1986, COICA was awarded the Right Livelihood Award, which was accepted by AIDESEP and the Aguaruna-Huambisa Council in COICA's name. This only increased COICA's international visibility. COICA quickly became very successful in articulating indigenous issues with an international, environmental agenda. AIDESEP played a prominent role in COICA's success as Nugkuag was re-elected for a second term (1988–92) as president of COICA.

In addition to earlier examples of transnational activism, notable transnational connections are taking place in the context of intercultural education. In the mid-1990s, a regionally-specific training program for indigenous youths, the *Programa de Formación en Educación Intercultural Bilingüe Para los Países Andinos* (Training Program for Bilingual Intercultural Education for the Andean Countries), or PROEIB, was founded at the Universidad Mayor de San Simón in Cochabamba, Bolivia. It is a master's program for indigenous peoples from five Andean countries including Bolivia, Chile, Colombia, Ecuador, and Peru. To be accepted, a student *must* be a representative of an indigenous organization, and he or she must speak the indigenous language of that group. Supported by the Bolivian and German governments, USAID, UNESCO, and other organizations, this alternative transnational institute is marketed as a program to train indigenous youths as bilingual, intercultural teachers and as a new generation of indigenous intellectuals.

The training of Peruvian indigenous intellectuals in Bolivia has raised hopes about their potential influence on ethnic mobilization in the country.[14] However, the professionalization of indigenous intellectual and activists, through programs like PROEIB or bodies like COICA, is not without its problems and complications. International networks, almost by definition, seem more a part of international fora than extensions of local indigenous peoples. Further, the creation of an international indigenous elite has often reflected the pathologies of criollo politics. In 1992, there was a general recognition among the members of COICA, that the president had administered the body in a very personalistic style. Many saw this as the mirror image of the Latin American *caudillo* (boss). Finally, the distance between local communities and indigenous leaders raises problems not only of representation, but also of accountability: "Unless organizations that represent local indigenous communities can exercise certain authority over the new strategies of Amazonian leaders, COICA will escape the control of its social bases" (R. C. Smith 1996: 117).

Still, it is undeniable that the changing international environment has put pressure on national governments, a phenomenon Keck and Sikkink (1998) have labeled the "boomerang effect." While indigenous affairs have long been marginal to the concerns of national government in Peru, the late 1990s saw even this beginning to change, albeit gradually. "A great part of the indigenous problematic," explained Javier Urrutia, former head of Peru's Secretariat of Indigenous Affairs (SETAI), "was revived and is debated today due to the pressure and financial funding of international organisms" (2001: 70). Yet, in Peru, the boomerang effect was long constrained by the national context of political violence and repression.

The political climate would change dramatically as a remarkable turn of events led to the rapid unraveling of Fujimori's presidency. After ostensibly defeating the electoral challenge of Alejandro Toledo in 2000, the Fujimori administration was rocked by the release of videos which showed Fujimori's spy-chief, Vladimiro Montesinos, bribing an astonishing number of politicians. The "*vladivideos*," as they were dubbed, unleashed a scandal which forced Montesinos and Fujimori out of the country (Montesinos was apprehended in Venezuela and later put in jail, Fujimori took residence and citizenship in Japan, the homeland of his parents and a state from which he cannot be extradited).

The sudden reversal of fortune (from "Fujirambo" to fugitive) meant that new elections had to be called, and that Peru was suddenly in the midst of a transition from a decade of war and authoritarianism to, hopefully, a period of peace and democracy. In the interim, someone had to govern. The task fell to Valentín Paniagua, the president of the Congress, who oversaw the caretaker government that would rule until the 2001 elections. While it only lasted a short time, the Paniagua interim presidency proved to be a crucial period for indigenous politics.

In early February 2001, indigenous delegates from the Asháninka, Nomatsiguenga, and Yanesha peoples of the Central Amazon region made the long journey to Lima. They requested government attention to various urgent problems including those created by concessions given to mining and logging companies, indigenous people's lack of land titles, and the on-going problem of war and violence in their lands. Remarkably, President Paniagua personally received the delegation and promised the formation of a commission that would, in his words, "study each and every one of the complex problems that you are confronting" (quoted in R. C. Smith 2001: 84).

True to his word, the commission was convoked on February 28, 2001 with the participation of delegates from ethnic indigenous federations like AIDESEP and CONAP, as well as social scientists and government functionaries. In several productive days it elaborated policy recommendations concerning native communities and natural resources, indigenous territories and violence, education, and health in indigenous communities. Additionally, Paniagua created spaces for continuing negotiations (*mesas de diálogo*) that would discuss, among other things, the reform of the constitution. To many, the actions of Paniagua represented the opening of a window of opportunity that had been closed for decades. Indeed, the existing government office for indigenous affairs (SETAI) had hardly been a high priority for the government, as suggested by its placement in the Ministry for Women and Human Development, a ministry characterized by such little bureaucratic coherence that former SETAI director Jaime Urrutia called it a "Frankenstein" ministry (Urrutia 2001: 70). The actions of Paniagua suggested that indigenous issues would be taken more seriously. Yet, with elections on the horizon, there existed the real possibility that "the window of opportunity [would] close on July 29, 2001 [the day after the inauguration]," if the next president did not follow through on institutionalizing the recommendations of the commission (R. C. Smith 2001: 86).

Initially, it appeared that Alejandro Toledo, who had made much of his Andean ancestry during the presidential campaign and emerged victorious over former populist president Alan García, would keep that window open. Toledo's highland origins, his self-conscious use of indigenous symbols, and his Quechua-speaking Belgian wife all became important political resources. Additionally, he made a powerful symbolic and diplomatic gesture in expanding his inauguration to include a ceremony at the ancient ruins of Machu Picchu. There, at the heart of the Inca Empire, Toledo – the Stanford-educated, former World Bank employee – seemed to signal his return to a deeper Peru as he addressed the nation in Quechua and Spanish, and, joined by all the presidents of the neighboring Andean states, signed the Declaration of Machu Picchu, a document that pledged the defense of indigenous rights throughout the region.

Moreover, Toledo's party, *Perú Posible*, brought, for the first time, an Aymara woman to the National Congress. Paulina Arpasi, a former secretary general of the CCP, has been vocal in emphasizing her role in representing indigenous people in Congress:

> I think that it is not only necessary that indígenas know that they have a representative in the National Congress, it is also very important that the National Congress knows that it has within it a representative of the *indígenas*. I will change neither my indigenous dress, nor my constant defense (*reivindicación*) of the rights of the indigenous peoples of Peru. (Arpasi 2001)

The election of a Toledo and Arpasi seemed to challenge the lingering racial hierarchies that permeate Peruvian society.[15] However, since these early moments of promise, Toledo's tenure has largely been a disappointment in the eyes of many indigenous rights activists.

To understand the sources of disappointment, it is important to look at the very visible role played by the president's Belgian-born wife Eliane Karp. Karp, who speaks Quechua and studied anthropology as an undergraduate,[16] made indigenous issues part of her official duties as first lady. Paniagua's work was to be taken on by Karp in her controversial role as President of the new National Commission for Andean, Amazonian, and Afro-Peruvian Peoples (CONAPA), a post she recently resigned.[17] Karp has been recognized for giving indigenous issues great visibility. Indeed, some, like OXFAM's Martin Scurrah, note that Karp has "intervened on numerous occasions in support of or in defense of indigenous initiatives." Scurrah points out that she "promoted the proposal for a chapter on indigenous rights in the new constitution" and has provided certain indigenous leaders with access to the presidential palace (Scurrah 2002).

However, other analysts have articulated less positive evaluations of Karp's role as an advocate for indigenous people. Rather than moving the theme of indigenous politics forward, some see CONAPA (sometimes called the "comisión Karp") as a step backwards for institutional, ideological, and political reasons. First, institutionally, CONAPA is a step down in stature. "Rather than being under the charge of a minister, the commission is headed by the first lady [who has no official place in the government hierarchy]. From the negotiation table [under Paniagua], the idea of the commission is downgraded" (Agurto, Interview, 2002). Additionally, SETAI, the office of indigenous affairs, was first made into the technical arm of CONAPA and more recently eliminated. This, critics argue, represents a loss in dynamism and autonomy that indigenous policy issues enjoyed under Paniagua (Benavides 2001: 104–5).

Second, Karp's decision to head the commission herself recalled the uncomfortable paternalism of older populist politics. As Margarita

Benavides, an anthropologist who worked actively with the Paniagua-convoked commission, argues, "the most important thing is that the [indigenous] organizations continue to maintain their autonomy *vis-à-vis* the government." CONAPA, as a governmental, but non-representative body, puts this autonomy somewhat into doubt as its members are hand-picked and new international funds are selectively handed out. In addition, it is difficult to tell where Karp's private NGO, *Fundación Pacha*, ended and where the public work of CONAPA began, as they all seemed to intersect in the office of the First Lady.

In June 2003, Karp resigned her post as President of CONAPA, partly in response to these criticisms. The departure of Karp, however, has not meant the end of criticisms of CONAPA. High-ranking officials like Executive Secretary of CONAPA Hilda Zamalloa and new CONAPA President Miguel Hilario Escobar have been criticized for working "behind the backs" of indigenous organizations and further weakening the institutionalization of indigenous politics in the state (Servindi 2003). Whether one sees Karp and her commission positively as new advocates for indigenous people or negatively as representing the dangers of state co-optation, it is clear that the political context for indigenous movements has changed remarkably in the last few years. As we discuss below, indigenous organizations and communities are negotiating these new opportunities and challenges on a variety of levels.

Responses from Indigenous Civil Society: Local, National, and Transnational Activism

To understand the most recent round of indigenous mobilizing, we depart from R. C. Smith's organizational typology, and focus instead on the scales of indigenous politics. Once we appreciate changes at local, regional, and national levels, it becomes more difficult to characterize indigenous politics as a "failure" as one sees how indigenous people have organized in myriad ways. To illustrate the recent complexities of indigenous organizing, we look at the areas of education, mining, and finally the most recent attempts at pan-regional ethnic organizing. These examples are illustrative and not exhaustive, since indigenous politics has long manifested itself in a variety of dynamic ways, especially on the local level.[18]

Local Ethno-Development Interactions: The Case of Intercultural Education

During the latter half of the 1990s, public struggle for indigenous rights focused on indigenous language rights and higher quality education for indigenous Peruvians.[19] Working simultaneously from within Peruvian state agencies and regional NGOs, and with support from international organizations and indigenous leaders in neighboring Andean countries, activists successfully demanded the incorporation of indigenous languages and cultural practices into national language and education policy. By making the national education system more *intercultural*, activists argued, indigenous people would be better equipped to empower themselves and demand that the state grant them rights as indigenous citizens. According to intercultural activists, promoting indigenous pride in Quechua, Aymara, and other indigenous languages through the implementation of education reform (i.e. the application of bilingual intercultural education) could spark the kind of solidarity necessary for ethnic-based political mobilization in the country.

Paradoxically, efforts at rekindling indigenous identity, language, and culture have been met with tremendous resistance from highland indigenous communities. According to many Quechuas in Cuzco, for example, speaking Quechua means being invisible citizens: existing in the country, but not forming part of it. Pointing to the links between language, identity, and class, an older Quechua man discussed some common concerns about the recent flurry of programs and activists dedicated to improving indigenous education. "If [activists] want to keep our children from learning Spanish," he said, "then they do not want to make things better, they want to keep us at the lower levels of society."

We find a surprising and unexpected example of Peruvian ethnic mobilization in the tensions between indigenous Peruvians and indigenous rights activists. Particularly, Quechua parent challenges to the implementation of education and cultural development policies have led to the (re)construction and mobilization of Peruvian indigenous ethnicity. As indigenous parents have resisted activist efforts, they have created new local spaces for collective action that have resulted in one of the very goals of intercultural activism, greater local participation in development and politics, albeit through means that intercultural activists never expected.

Intercultural activists' attempts to shape the attitudes of indigenous parents according to their own views about the salience of indigenous language and cultural practices has led Quechua parents and community leaders to openly question the rights of others to determine their children's livelihood. Using the same tools activists developed to gain support from indigenous peoples, some Quechua parents have devised strategies to challenge the imposition of education reform in their communities. For instance, the establishment of "parent schools" (*escuelas de padres*), designed by activists to explain their goals, quickly became a forum allowing parents to dispute activist interpretations of concepts such as citizenship, and to contest education reform. For example, during one of these meetings, a Quechua father confronted an activist with an interesting question. "[If teaching our children in Quechua] is so good . . . , why don't you teach your own children in Quechua too? Why do you send them to [foreign language] institutes?" Pointing to the fact that many advocates of indigenous languages do, in fact, send their children to the *Alliance Française* or to the North American Institute, and not to regional Quechua-language programs, this father was delineating the socio-economic and ethnic identities associated with language. In Peru, only upper-middle class or upper-class families can afford to send their children to private language institutes. By emphasizing the real connection in Peru between language, class, and prestige, this father's point was simple: Teach our children Quechua, and they will remain poor. Teach them Spanish, English, or French, and they will get ahead.

By transforming parent schools into spaces of contestation and negotiation, community members have expanded the scope of development efforts, allowing them a greater role in the education of their own children. Women, tackling the new educational changes in a slightly different way, play on the stereotypes perpetuated about them by activists, and use NGO resources for their own, very different, ends. Mothers, aunts, and sisters of Quechua children began organizing (across various communities of the department of Cuzco) in 1998 to demand literacy training from NGOs working in their community schools. Their strategy was to propose to teachers and NGO representatives that if they taught women Spanish by teaching them to read in Quechua (in line with bilingual education pedagogical theory), they would support activist efforts at modifying their children's education. However, their goal was to learn Spanish themselves, and thus be able, in the near future, to teach Spanish to their own daughters and sons. Indigenous women were trying to take control of what their children learned by consciously developing a way to use the NGO for their own purposes. Organizing among themselves to petition NGOs for literacy in both Quechua and Spanish, they look ahead to the possibility of teaching their children basic skills in the nation's official language.

Another important strategy of indigenous leaders has been to promote the establishment of community-controlled schools that are *not* managed by the state, nor by NGOs. While demands for community control over indigenous education in the 1920s came from a movement composed of indigenous leaders and indigenista intellectuals (the *Comité Pro-Derecho Indígena*), in the 1970s, attempts to establish closer links between schools and communities were propelled by the state. In both cases, the motivation for such initiatives was supposed to be the advancement of indigenous peoples through the improvement of highland education. Discussion among Quechua community leaders about their *own* control of education implies a move toward their own self-determination.

The case of intercultural activism in Peru shows how crucial differences between intercultural activists and indigenous ideas about education have turned activists' intentions upside down. Their discussion with indigenous parents and highland teachers about education and indigenous rights has opened up new possibilities for indigenous struggles. Much is at stake in debates over language as they speak to the changing position of indigenous people in the nation-state and, as we show below, in transnational development agendas. In fact, the Peruvian case highlights why, as states and NGOs devote increasing attention to what the World Bank calls "ethno-development," it is important to pay close attention to the complex construction of indigenous identities and the unequal power relations that complicate even the most well-intentioned efforts at advocacy.

Mining and Protest: International Pressures, Local and National Collective Action

International pressures, so clearly at work in the politics of bilingual education, have long been important to the histories of political domination and resistance in Latin America. Indeed, the Spanish "discovery" of Inca and Aztec silver and gold set in motion dynamics in the sixteenth century whose force can still be felt today. While the role of mining and other extractive industries have certainly been complex and varied – often encouraging the penetration of foreign capital and other times funding nationalist and populist reforms – there can be no question that they have profoundly affected indigenous livelihoods. So it should perhaps be of little surprise that recent indigenous mobilization has centered on the effects that mining has had on indigenous communities.

While one could look for roots of this resistance deep in the colonial past, for our purposes, it is more instructive to begin closer to the present. In 1993, as mentioned earlier, the government of Alberto Fujimori oversaw the drafting of a constitution that finally contained some encouraging language for indigenous people, including articles that spoke of respect for "the cultural identity of rural and native communities" and protection of communal property. Yet, in the fine print of the constitution and of later investor-friendly legislation, exceptions were carved out from those protections that facilitated the expansion of mining activities on community lands.

A "before and after" statistical snapshot illustrates the point. In 1992, before the legal changes, approximately 4 million hectares had been claimed by mining industries. In the years after Fujimori's legal reform, mining claims skyrocketed to cover over 25 million hectares. "Of the 5660 [legally recognized] communities in all of Perú, there exist mining claims (*denuncios*) in 3200 of them."[20] Miguel Palacín, the president of an important new indigenous organization, the National Coordinator of Communities Adversely Affected by Mining (CONACAMI), listed these figures with the ease of someone who has recited them many times to many audiences as we spoke with him in the Lima offices of his organization. Concessions have been granted mostly to transnational mining companies, Palacín noted in an earlier interview, mostly from Canada (Palacín 2001).

This increase in foreign investment may have pleased the economic planners in the government, but for many communities the effects continue to be disastrous. Populations have been displaced, productive agricultural lands have been dramatically reduced in size, and water sources have been taken over by mining interests. In addition, environmental contamination has provoked the outcry of communities like Choropampa where a mercury spill resulted in widespread reports of sickness and inaction by the company and the state (Caballo and Boyd 2002). To add further insult to injury, none of the profits or rents generated from the mining activities benefited the affected communities. Extractive industry, remarks Palacín, is part of the "ficticious development" that has trapped Peru. "Before mining, [the northern department of] Cajamaca was the fourth poorest department in Peru, now it is the second poorest."

In the mid-1990s, Palacín and others began to organize protests against this unequal exchange in which state and industry profited while highland communities suffered. Mining companies however used the legal system, already tilted in their favor, to denounce Palacín and accuse him of criminal activity. In Latin America, criminal charges can often result in a situation in which the accused is effectively presumed guilty and often detained indefinitely if he or she lacks adequate legal or financial resources. Palacín was forced to leave the highlands and go into hiding on the coast. Emblematic of the double-edged nature of globalization, however, Palacín received unexpected aid from the north.

News of the trouble Palacín was causing Canadian companies reached indigenous organizations in Canada through Internet sources. With their own histories of conflicts with extractive industries, Canadian First Nations formally requested that the charges against Palacín be investigated by the state. The state attorney looked into the Palacín case and found that there was no base to any of the charges, which were subsequently dropped. With this brush with the law, Palacín realized that "the only weapon is organization." Thus, in 1998 he led organizing efforts throughout the central and Southern sierra to bring communities together. In October 1999, the first congress of a new national organization, CONACAMI, was convened and Palacín was elected president (Palacín 2002).

But is this struggle against mining an "indigenous" struggle? After all, CONACAMI does not fit in any of R. C. Smith's (1983) ideal-typic categories (it is not an *indianist*, peasant, or ethnic federation, at least not in the sense of his original typology). And while most of the communities represented by CONACAMI were Quechua communities, the new organization did not initially fashion itself as a Quechua organization. Palacín acknowledges some of the difficulties that arose around identity – a theme, he says "which was not taken up by the organization's leadership, but was present in the base communities, the majority of which are Quechua-speakers of the sierra." More recently, the organization has begun placing greater emphasis on the question of indigenous culture, locating its struggles within the broader framework of "human rights and the rights of indigenous peoples." Culture, argues Palacín, "cannot be bought, it is the only mechanism of resistance." As Palacín spoke of the upcoming national march planned for June, he warned that if President Toledo did not heed their protests, they would have soon call for a "*levantamiento*," the word for "uprising" used to describe the Indian revolts of the colonial period and a term forcefully deployed by CONAIE, the powerful indigenous confederation in Ecuador.

CONACAMI's increasingly visible role as an indigenous actor, however, is not only about what its pragmatic leadership says or even what the organization does. As identity formation is always relational and representational, it is important to understand how other actors in the state and civil society shape this new organization's collective identity. While there are certainly different opinions over CONACAMI and its leadership, there seems to be an emerging consensus that it is the most coherent and influential indigenous highland organization to come along in a while. Eliane Karp, in recognition of the importance of CONACAMI, named Palacín to her new commission CONAPA. While Palacín has registered discomfort over this selection process and has recently severed ties between his organization and the state commision, his presence provided a critical voice and increased the new organization's visibility (Palacín 2002). From the side of civil society, CONACAMI is also gaining support and recognition. Oxfam America, one of the key international funders of indigenous organizations in the Andean republics, has funded CONACAMI since its founding, and provides support for exchange programs so that its leaders can share experiences with indigenous organizations in Ecuador (CONAIE) and Bolivia (CONAMAQ) (Naveda 2002). A recent evaluation prepared by a lowland organization recognized the need to bring Amazonian and Andean organizations together, making special mention of CONACAMI as "the most representative expression of the highland movement (CINA 2002: 4). CONACAMI, along with the lowland organization, AIDESEP, is playing an important role in the strentghening of COPPIP, a new organization that may be the start of what scholars have said was long absent in Peru: a national organization that links indigenous peoples from coastal, highland, and lowland regions.

A National Organization at Last? COPPIP

COPPIP, the last organization that we will discuss in this brief panoramic survey, is different from the other organizations we have discussed in two important ways. First, it is a pan-ethnic and pan-regional national body. Unlike most organizations that center on the highlands, lowlands, or represent a specific ethnic group, COPPIP (the Permanent Coordinator of the Indigenous People of Peru) is a nationwide organization. In this respect, it is the mirror image in civil society of what Karp has tried to construct in her state commission, CONAPA. Second, and also like Karp's commission, it is not an "organization" in the sense that this term is usually used to describe the autonomous local, regional, or national federations and confederations of indigenous people that constitute social movement fields. As a "coordinator," COPPIP, as currently constituted, is a space in which various organizations come together and debate and discuss common issues and strategies, without losing their individual autonomy.[21] Less hierarchical and structured than confederations, it is also less of an "actor" in the traditional sociological sense. This should not be read, however, as a polite description of political marginality. To the contrary; in our view, COPPIP represents a truly unprecedented space for the articulation of an indigenous political project and subject, and a potentially crucial counterweight to the co-optive powers of the state.

While there are differing views on the history of COPPIP, it seems to have emerged in part as a result of a long struggle for the creation of a space for indigenous discussion and organization. As part of this struggle, a forum on indigenous rights was held in Cuzco in December 1997. At that meeting, various NGOs and organizations agreed to form a "permanent conference" for dialogue and debate. Most notably it brought the ethnic federation from the lowlands (e.g. AIDESEP and CONAP) together with the more class-based organizations of the highlands (i.e. CNA and CCP). It also included many other local indigenous groups of various ideological and ethnic stripes. In 1998, the inaugural event of COPPIP was convoked to bring the various dimensions of indigenous politics together.[22] With the support of a Canadian NGO, the Institute of Democratic Rights, COPPIP held subsequent workshops to elaborate legislative proposals and put together a technical team to support its projects (Agurto 2002).

However, the constitution of COPPIP was not without its problems. First, its open membership allowed in a variety of different kinds of organizations that could claim varying degrees of representativity; some COPPIP member organizations were sent by communities, others were more free-floating indianista groups. Debate and discussions, then, could become a bit unruly (Agurto 2002).

Second, instability in the staffing and leadership of COPPIP created some problems for the organization in acquiring funds from external sources. A former staff member of COPPIP criticized external sources as dividing the movement and weakening the autonomy of indigenous actors (Lajo n.d.). Others signaled the importance of maintaining strong transnational alliances. Recently, COPPIP has seen the renewal of support from international sources including Oxfam America and the Japanese Development Agency, with which a series of workshops and meetings have been held to evaluate the state of the indigenous movement in Peru and to integrate COPPIP into international networks of indigenous politics.

The new flurry of activity coming from COPPIP has been registered in a new on-line newsletter, *SERVINDI: Servicio de Información Indígena* (Indigenous Information Service).[23] Recently, SERVINDI published the summary of an evaluation of indigenous-state relations (based on a meeting convoked by Guillermo Ñaco, head of the National Amazonian Indigenous Commission or CINA) which was critical of Toledo and Karp. The document, however, did not stop short of criticizing the movement, asking "Is the problem Eliane or the indigenous organization?" In that vein, it called for the strengthening of COPPIP so that indigenous peoples would have an independent "space, agenda, and strategy of their own" (CINA 2002: 3). While there are still acrimonious debates over the representativity of COPPIP and the selection process of its leaders (Lajo n.d.), COPPIP seems to be recovering its role as a new space of articulation and contestation.

Re-situating Peruvian Exceptionalism

While acknowledging important differences in the patterning of indigenous politics, we have argued in this chapter that news of the death of Peruvian indigenous politics has been exaggerated. In this concluding section, we would like to emphasize the dynamic, if uneven, contributions of indigenous people to national and international politics, mention some recent developments that raise intriguing new possibilities, and finally, suggest how the Peruvian case may raise important questions for indigenous movements throughout the continent.

First, as we have seen, indigenous people in Peru have experienced *and gone beyond* the full range of indigenous organizational models that have been identified by scholars of Latin American indigenous movements. Peasant organizations, indigenous intellectual movements, non-governmental organizations, and ethnic federations have been among the many important elements of indigenous contention in ways similar to neighboring republics. While Leftist movements in the highlands, especially the nightmarish Maoism of Sendero Luminoso, had an adverse impact on indigenous peoples and their communal organization, "Indianness" never disappeared from highland Peru. In a long history of indigenous resistance (Stern 1987), strategic adaptation has often been mistaken for silence or absence.

In the Amazon, indigenous resistance has been more visible and perhaps more influential, especially in terms of shaping indigenous movements throughout the region. The Amuesha Congress of the Peruvian Amazon can claim to be among the pioneers of the ethnic federation models that have shaped later-day indigenous organizing in Ecuador and Bolivia. As indigenous organizing "goes global," Peru has hardly been on the sidelines. Amazonian and (more recently) highland peoples have contributed significantly to the internationalization of indigenous politics through the creation of transnational alliances (like COICA) and participation in transnational networks (like PROEIB).

Second, as "development with identity" has become a watchword for recent state and international policies, indigenous people continue to negotiate notions of Indianness and citizenship in ways states and NGO activists have not expected. The case of IBE activism has been especially illustrative of the ability of indigenous communities to shape the kind of policies that – as has often been the case – were designed for them, but not designed with them. Moreover, as the Fujimori regime came to a close with the farce of *Vladivideos*, new possibilities began to emerge on the horizon. CONACAMI has shown its ability to create a powerful highland movement around the urgent environmental and cultural questions raised by mining, an "indigenous" issue since the sixteenth century. Additionally, it and other organizations in COPPIP have challenged First Lady Eliane Karp's perhaps well-intentioned, but problematic, efforts to structure indigenous representation from above.[24] While the Toledo administration has hardly been the indigenous opening he promised during the campaign, indigenous actors have emerged in an unprecedented way during a critical juncture in Peru's political history.

Finally, the actions of indigenous people at local, national, and transnational scales all raise questions that can usefully be asked of indigenous movements throughout the region. Why do people choose or reject Indianness? Who is speaking for indigenous people? How are local communities responding to NGO and state initiatives ostensibly meant to help indigenous people? How have multicultural education and the politics of culture, language, and development become terrains of dispute in Latin America? What should "indigenous movements" look like? In short, we come back to the questions of identity, representation, and social movements that some scholars seemed to suggest were out of place in the Peruvian context.

Notes

The authors would like to thank Javier Lajo, Luis Maldonado, Brígida Peraza [sp], Marin Scurrah, Richard Chase Smith, and the volume editors for their helpful comments. Research for this chapter was generously supported by summer research funds from Temple University.

1 All translations, unless otherwise noted, are our own.

Un País Sin Indígenas?

2 For excellent "state of the field" discussions about indigenous political and ethnic mobilization, see the editors introduction and the chapters of our fellow contributors in this volume. Some earlier and notable works include Stephen (2002) for Mexico; K. Warren (1998) on the pan-Maya movement in Guatemala; Ramos (1998), Turner (1995), and J. Warren (2001) on Brazil; Rappaport (1994, 1996) and Van Cott (2000) on Colombia; Albó (1994) and Van Cott (2000) on Bolivia; León (2002) and Lucero (2003) on Ecuador; Van Cott (2003) on Venezuela; and Albó (1991), Stavenhagen (1992), Van Cott, ed. (1994) and Yashar (1998) on Latin America generally.

3 The designation of "national" is somewhat problematic as many organizations that analysts tend to label as regional, like the Amazonian confederation AIDESEP, explicitly see themselves as a national level organization. At the same time, as we discuss below, new bodies like the National Commision for Andean, Amazonian, and Afro-Peruvian Peoples (CONAPA) are of questionable "national" representativity.

4 The Movimiento Revolucionario Túpac Amaru or MRTA, like Sendero Luminoso, was a revolutionary guerrilla movement operating in the country between 1985 and 1997. Unlike Sendero, the MRTA was less fanatical, urban-based, and more likely to negotiate with official political forces. They received international attention when they held prominent politicians and diplomats hostage at the Japanese Embassy in Lima between December 1996 and April 1997, an act widely acknowledged to have led to their dissolution after government forces re-took the Embassy.

5 For a discussion of recent socio-political history in Peru, and particularly of political violence during the 1980s and 1990s, see Poole and Rénique 1992. For examinations of the origins, organization, and "defeat" of Sendero Luminoso, see Degregori 1990, 1998a, and 1998b; Degregori, ed. 1996; Gorriti 1999; Palmer, ed. 1992; and for detailed explorations of social relations during this time, as well as meticulous case studies of the political, cultural and social upheaval created by Sendero, see Stern, ed. 1998.

6 For in-depth discussions of the Velasco Government, see Cotler 1983; McClintock and Lowenthal 1983; and Turino 1991.

7 Throughout the colonial period and into the late 1960s, *haciendas* were estates owned by European land-holders and maintained (worked on) primarily by Indian laborers. The hacienda became a hallmark of colonial Peru (and Mexico), though it only developed into a powerful economic institution after the 1600s.

8 Much of the agrarian reform did not achieve the goals set by Velasco and his government. In the Andes, less than half of landless peasants actually received land, and on the coast and jungle regions, cooperatives established from expropriated plantations were plagued by mismanagement. For diverse perspectives on the limitations of the economic and agrarian reform goals of the Velasco government, see Eckstein 1983 and Lowenthal 1983.

9 Recently, R. C. Smith (2002) re-visited his typology to note the decline of indianista organizations and the emergence of two additional ideal-types for the Andean countries: the indigenous non-governmental organization, which does exist in Peru, and the indigenous political party, a form still foreign to Peru.

10 The only example in the highlands similar to the lowland ethnic federations

is the *Unión Nacional de Comunidades Aymaras* or UNCA. For additional information on this organization, see the website: <www.rcp.net. pe/ashaninka/coppip/unca1.html>. Also see Montoya 1993.

11 Violence certainly shaped political possibilities. However, as we discuss below, the violence itself provided a motivation and cause around which to organize, thus creating conditions for later periods of indigenous politics even in the places like the Central Jungle region, where violence is very much part of the region's present.

12 A brief list of these meetings include the First and Second Encounter of Indigenous People in Barbados (1971 and 1977), the UN World Conference to Combat Racism and Discrimination (1978), and the foundation of the International Working Group for Indigenous Affairs in the late 1960s.

13 COICA is made up of organizations from Bolivia (CIDOB), Brazil (COIAB), Colombia (OPIAC), Ecuador (CONFENIAE), French Guyana (FOAG), Guyana (APA), Peru (AIDESEP), Surinam (OIS), and Venezuela (CONIVE).

14 See García forthcoming for a more detailed discussion of the PROEIB.

15 For an example of these lingering racial hierarchies, see Vargas Llosa 1990.

16 Though she is often referred to as an anthropologist, Dr. Karp's graduate studies at Stanford, where she and Toledo met, were not in anthropology but in French literature.

17 Karp resigned in June 2003. The presidency of CONAPA was assumed by Miguel Hilario, though most decision-making authority resided with Executive Secretary Hilda Zamalloa. For more on recent shake-ups in CONAPA see Rios 2004.

18 The two most notable omissions in this discussion involve the coca growers' protests and the rondas campesinas. *Cocaleros* have become increasingly visible actors in Peru and Bolivia. Attempting to reclaim coca as an ancestral and sacred Andean staple, cocaleros have been labeled terrorist and subversives by governments participating in the US-funded "wars" on drugs and terror. For more on coca politics in Peru see Rojas 2003. The rondas campesinas have represented a response not only to the political violence associated with Sendero Luminoso but also to the failure of the Peruvian state to protect rural communities from theft and other crimes. For more on the rondas see Degregori 1998b and Starn 1998, 1999. Conflict over the management of vital resources like water has also been an important area for local indigenous political contestation, see Gelles 1999.

19 The observations about intercultural activism and community responses to education policies in Peru are based on 17 months (1997–99) of ethnographic research in the Southern Peruvian highlands, and form part of a larger project on indigenous activism, development, and citizenship in Peru (See García 2003, and García Forthcoming).

20 Unless otherwise noted, all quotations from Miguel Palacín are taken from an interview conducted by the authors in Lima on June 4, 2002.

21 COPPIP was founded not as a coordinator of indigenous organizations, but as a "permanent conference." The name only changed from "*conferencia*" to "*coordinadora*" at the end of 2002.

22 CONACAMI, constituted only in 1999, would later join COPPIP and be regarded, in the words of COPPIP's Technical Secretary as "one of the more critical organizations, and one that deals with matters that are usually more concrete and urgent" than many of the other organiations (Agurto 2002).

23 Serivindi can be obtained by writing servindi@hotmail.com. The newsletter is edited by Agurto, though unlike the previous secretary, his name does not accompany many COPPIP related items.
24 It is worth noting that CONACAMI, AIDESEP, and COPPIP have all formally broken ties with CONAPA.

References

Agurto, Jorge. 2002. Interview, 6/6/02. COPPIP. Lima, Peru.
Albó, Xavier. 1991. El Retorno del Indio. *Revista Andina*, 9(2): 299–345.
——. 1994. And from Kataristas to MNRistas? The Surprising and Bold Alliance between Aymaras and Neoliberals in Bolivia. *Indigenous Peoples and Democracy in Latin America*, Donna Lee Van Cott, ed. New York: St. Martin's Press.
Arpasi, Paulina. 2001. Entrevista por Juan Pina. *Perfiles del Siglo XXI*, No. 101, December 2001, Online <www.revistaperfiles.com>.
Benavides, Margarita. 2001. Estea Mesa Nadie la Instala: Entrevista por Martin Paredes. *Quehacer*, 132 September–November: 102–7.
Brysk, Alison. 1996. Turning Weakness into Strength: the Internationalization of Indian Rights. *Latin American Perspectives*, 23(2): 38–57.
——. 2000. *From Tribal Village to Global Village: Indian Rights and International Relations in Latin America*. Stanford: Stanford University Press.
Caballo, Tito, and Stephainie Boyd. 2002. *Choropampa: The Price of Gold*. Video. Lima: Guarango Productions.
Chirif, Alberto. 1991. Comentario. *Revista Andina*, 9(2): 353–7.
CINA (Comisión Indígena Nacional de la Amazonia). 2002. Evaluación y Perspectivas del Movimiento Indígena Peruano: Conclusiones de una Reunión de Trabajo. Unpublished document. July 18.
Cotler, Julio. 1983. Democracy and National Integration in Peru. *The Peruvian Experiment Reconsidered*, Cynthia McClintock and Abraham Lowenthal, eds. Princeton: Princeton University Press.
Degregori, Carlos Ivan. 1990. *Ayacucho 1969–1979. El Surgimiento de Sendero Luminoso*. Lima: IEP.
——. 1993. Identidad Étnica: Movimientos Sociales y Participación en el Perú. *Democracias, Etnicidad,y Violencia Política en los Paises Andinos*, Alberto Adrianzén *et al.*, eds. Lima: IEP/IFEA.
——. 1998a. Ethnicity and Democratic Governability in Latin America: Reflections from Two Central Andean Countries. *Faultlines of Democracy in Post-Transition Latin America*, Felipe Aguero and Jeffrey Stark, eds. Miami: North-South Center Press.
——. 1998b. Harvesting Storms: Peasant Rondas and the Defeat of Sendero Luminoso in Ayacucho. *Shining and Other Paths: War and Society in Peru, 1980–1995*, Steve Stern ed. Durham: Duke University Press.
——, ed. 1996. *Las Rondas Campesinas y la Derrota de Sendero Luminoso*. Lima: IEP.
De la Cadena, Marisol. 2000. *Indigenous Mestizos: the Politics of Race and Culture in Cuzco, 1919–1991*. Durham: Duke University Press.
——. 2001. Reconstructing Race: Racism, Culture, and Mestizaje in Latin America. *NACLA, Report on the Americas*, 34(6): 16–23.
Eckstein, Susan. 1983. Revolution and Redistribution in Latin America. *The*

Peruvian Experiment Reconsidered, Cynthia McClintock and Abraham Lowenthal, eds. Princeton: Princeton University Press.

García, María Elena. Forthcoming. *Making Indigenous Citizens: Identities, Education, and Multicultural Development in Peru.* Stanford: Stanford University Press.

——. 2003. The Politics of Community: Education, Indigenous Rights, and Ethnic Mobilization in Peru. *Latin American Perspectives* 30(1) Issue 128: 70–95.

Gelles, Paul. 1999. *Water and Power in Highland Peru: The Cultural Politics of Irrigation and Development.* New Brunswick: Rutgers University Press.

——. 2002. Andean Culture, Indigenous Identity, and the State in Peru. *The Politics of Ethnicity: Indigenous Peoples and Latin American States,* David Maybury-Lewis, ed. Cambridge, MA: Harvard University Press.

Gorriti Ellenbogen, Gustavo. 1999. *Shining Path: A History of the Millenarian War in Peru.* Translated by Robin Kirk. Chapel Hill: University of North Carolina Press.

Keck, Margaret and Kathryn Sikkink. 1998. *Activists Beyond Borders.* Ithaca: Cornell University Press.

Lajo, Javier. n.d. La Invisibilidad Indígena en el Perú: comentarios a Un País Sin Indígenas. Unpublished manuscript.

León, Jorge. 2002. "La Política y los Indígenas en América Latina: la Redefinición de las Relaciones entre el Estado y los Pueblos Indígenas." Paper presented to OXFAM-Ford Workshop, Avisorando los Retos para Los Pueblos Indígenas de América Latina en el Nuevo Milenio: Territorio, Economía, Política, e Identidad y Cultura. Lima.

Lowenthal, Abraham. 1983. The Peruvian Experiment Reconsidered. *The Peruvian Experiment Reconsidered,* Cynthia McClintock and Abraham Lowenthal, eds. Princeton: Princeton University Press.

Lucero, José Antonio. 2003. Locating the 'Indian Problem': Community, Nationality and Contradiction in Ecuadorian Indigenous Politics. *Latin American Perspectives* 30(1): 23–48.

Mallon, Florencia. 1998. Chronicle of a Path Foretold? *Shining and Other Paths,* Steve Stern, ed. Durham: Duke University Press.

McClintock, Cynthia and Abraham Lowenthal. 1983. *The Peruvian Experiment Reconsidered.* Princeton: Princeton University Press.

Milliones, Luis. 1999. Hay un País sin Indígenas entre Ecuador y Bolivia. *Conversaciones para la convivencia,* Marta Bulmes, ed. Lima: GTZ.

Montoya, Rodrigo. 1993. Libertad, Democracia, y Problema Étnico en el Perú. *Democracia, Etnicidad, y Violencia Política en los Países Andinos,* Alberto Adrianzén *et al.,* eds. Lima: IEP/IFEA.

Naveda, Igidio. 2002. Interview. 6/6/02. Oxfam America. Lima, Peru.

Palacín, Miguel. 2001. El Problema de la Tierra, Otra Vez. Una Entrevista con Miguel Palacín. *Quehacer,* 130 (May–June): 110–14.

——. 2002. Interview. 6/4/02. CONACAMI. Lima, Peru.

Palmer, David Scott, ed. 1992. *Shining Path of Peru.* New York: St. Martin's Press.

Poole, Deborah and Gerardo Rénique. 1992. *Peru: Time of Fear.* London: Latin American Bureau.

Pozzi-Escot, Inés. 1981. La Educación Bilingüe en el Marco Legal de la Reforma Educativa Peruana. *Acerca de la Historia y el universo Aymara.* Lima: CIED.

Un País Sin Indígenas?

Ramos, Alcida. 1998. *Indigenism: Ethnic Politics in Brazil*. Madison: University of Wisconsin Press.

Rappaport, Joanne. 1994. *Cumbe Reborn: An Andean Ethnography of History*. Chicago: The University of Chicago Press.

——. 1996. Introduction, Ethnicity Reconfigured: Indigenous Legislators and the Colombian Constitution of 1991. *Journal of Latin American Anthropology*, 1(2) spring: 2–17.

Remy, María. 1994. The Indigenous Population and the Construction of Democracy in Peru. *Indigenous Peoples and Democracy in Latin America*, Donna Lee Van Cott, ed. New York: St. Martin's Press.

Rios, Adan. 2004. Algo Camina Mal en la Conapa. *Perú 21*. January 7: 8–9.

Rojas, Isaías. 2003. The push for Zero Coca: Democratic Transition and Counternarcotics Policy in Peru. *WOLA, Drug War Monitor*, February 2003.

Scurrah, Martin. 2002. Personal communication.

SERVINDI-Servicio de Información Indígena. 2003. Los Pueblos Indígenas y su relación con el Estado – El Caso Peruano. SERVINDI – Servicio de Información Indígena, No. 30.

Smith, Michael Addison. 1999. "Indigenous Law and the Nation-States of the Latin American Region." Unpublished Ms., University of Texas School of Law.

Smith, Richard Chase. 1983. Search for Unity Within Diversity: Peasant Unions, Ethnic Federations, and Indianist Movements in the Andean Republics. Paper presented at Cultural Survival Symposium, Iniciativas Indias y Autodenominación Económica. Cambridge, Massachusetts.

——. 1996. Política de la Diversidad. COICA y las Federaciones Étnicas de la Amazonía. *Pueblo Indios, Soberanía, y Globalismo*, Stefano Varese, ed. Quito: Abya Yala.

——. 2001. Pueblos Indígenas y el Estado Plurinacional en el Perú. *Quehacer*, 129: 82–6.

——. 2002a. Tejido Forjado por las Viscisitudes de la Historia, el Lugar y la Vida Cotidiana: Un Marco para Visualizar los Desafíos para los Pueblos Indígenas de América Latina en el Nuevo Mileno: Territorio, Economía, Gobernabilidad e Identidad. Unpublished manuscript/CD Rom.

——. 2002b. Interview. 6/6/02. Instituto del Bien Comun. Lima, Peru.

Spalding, Karen. 1984. *Huarochirí: An Andean Society under Inca and Spanish Rule*. Stanford: Stanford University Press.

Stavenhagen, Rodolfo. 1992. Challenging the Nation-State in Latin America. *Journal of International Affairs*, 45(2): 421–40.

Starn, Orin. 1998. Villagers at Arms: War and Counterrevolution in the Central-South Andes. *Shining and Other Paths: War and Society in Peru, 1980–1995*, Stern, Steve, ed. Durham: Duke University Press.

——. 1999. *Nightwatch*. Durham: Duke University Press.

Stephen, Lynn. 2002. *Zapata Lives!: Histories and Cultural Politics in Southern Mexico*. Berkeley: University of California Press.

Stern, Steve. 1987. The Age of Andean Insurrection, 1742–1782: A Reappraisal. *Resistance, Rebellion, and Consciousness in the Andean Peassant World, 18th to 20th Centuries*, S. Stern, ed. Madison: The University of Wisconsin Press.

——, ed. 1998. *Shining and Other Paths: War and Society in Peru, 1980–1995*. Durham: Duke University Press.

Turino, Thomas. 1991. The State and Andean Musical Production in Peru.

Nation-States and Indians in Latin America, Greg Urban and Joel Sherzer, eds. Austin: University of Texas Press.

Turner, Terence. 1995. Indigenous People's Struggle for Socially Equitable and Ecologically Sustainable Production. *Journal of Latin American Anthropology*, 1(1) Fall: 98–121.

Urrutia, Jaime. 2001. Indios o Ciudadanos: Una Entrevista por Luis Olivera y Martin Paredes. *Quehacer*, 128 January–February: 69–78.

Van Cott, Donna Lee, ed. 1994. *Peoples and Democracy in Latin America*. New York: St. Martin's Press.

——. 2000. *The Friendly Liquidation of the Past*. Pittsburgh: University of Pittsburgh Press.

——. 2003. Andean Indigenous Movements and Constitutional Transformation: Venezuela in Comparative Perspective. *Latin American Perspectives*, 30(1) Issue 128: 49–69.

Vargas Llosa, Mario. 1990. Questions of Conquest: What Columbus Wrought and What He Did Not. *Harper's Magazine*, December 1990: 45–51.

Velasco Alvarado, Juan. 1969. The Master Will No Longer Feed Off Your Poverty. *The Peru Reader*, Carlos Ivan Degregori, Orin Starn, and Robin Kirk, eds. Durham: Duke University Press.

Warren, Jonathan. 1995. *Racial Revolutions: Anti-Racism and Indian Resistance in Brazil*. Durham: Duke University Press.

Warren, Kay. 1998. Indigenous Movements as a Challenge to the Unified Social Movement Paradigm for Guatemala. *Cultures of Politics, Politics of Cultures: Re-visioning Latin American Social Movements*, Alvarez, Sonia, Evelina Dagnino and Arturo Escobar, eds. Boulder: Westview Press.

Wearne, Phillip. 1996. *The Return of the Indian*. Philadelphia: Temple University Press.

Yashar, Deborah. 1998. Contesting Citizenship: Indigenous Movements and Democracy in Latin America. *Comparative Politics*: 23–42.

Articulation and Fragmentation

Indigenous Politics in Bolivia

Nancy Grey Postero

In the mid-1990s, after a decade of organizing and massive public demonstrations calling for recognition and territory, Bolivia's indigenous peoples gained substantial new legal and political rights by allying with dominant political parties. Under the administration of President Gonzalo Sánchez de Lozada (1993–7) and his Aymara Indian Vice-President Victor Hugo Cárdenas, Bolivia amended its constitution to declare itself to be "multi-ethnic" and pluri-cultural," and instituted a series of "multicultural" reforms intended to transform the traditional relationship between the state and indigenous peoples. Lauded across the continent, these state-led reforms were to construct a new form of indigenous citizenship, based on indigenous participation in local politics, collective ownership of territories, and bilingual-bicultural education. This was seen as a long-needed step toward social justice, as the indigenous people who make up approximately 60 percent of Bolivia's population have traditionally been excluded from political participation.[1] The reforms were also held up as evidence of a maturing civil society, in which indigenous groups, characterized by scholars as a "new social movement" (Escobar and Alvarez 1992), played critical roles in the ongoing process of democratization (Van Cott 1994).

In 2004, however, the situation looks very different. Over the last four years, there have been frequent blockades of the country's highways by indigenous and peasant groups protesting the neoliberal government's failure to live up to its promises. In 2001, highland farmers mounted and won a battle against a water privatization scheme in Cochabamba. Evo Morales, an Aymara Indian who heads the embattled *cocalero* (coca growers) union, captured the sense of disillusionment expressed by indigenous and poor people across the country. He said,

> We all know that there are two Bolivias. One Bolivia of "charlatans" who always make promises and sign agreements that they never fulfill; and the other Bolivia which is always tricked, subjugated (*sometida*), humiliated, and exploited. I denounce before the Bolivian people that this is a cultural confrontation: the culture of death against us, the indigenous peoples. (Morales 2003)

In 2001 Morales formed a new political party, MAS (*Movimiento al Socialismo*, Movement Toward Socialism), campaigned in the national elections, and then won second place in the June 2002 presidential election, thanks to an outpouring of indigenous and popular support. His party won 20 percent of the votes, just one percent behind Sánchez de Lozada's MNR (*Movimiento Nacional Revolucionario*) party. In August 2002, Bolivians watched in awe as thirty-five MAS congress-people – highland Indians, lowland indigenous people, and peasants – took their places in the national congress, vowing to change the way the Bolivian state governs its people.

An even more surprising event happened in October of 2003. When President Sánchez de Lozada revealed his plans for the development of newly found natural gas resources, and the export of the gas through a pipeline through Chile to the US and Mexico, popular sectors exploded against what they saw as the sale of their patrimony. After six weeks of massive demonstrations lead by indigenous leaders Evo Morales and Felipe Quispe, mainly in the cities of La Paz, El Alto, and Cochabamba, and many dead and wounded, the president resigned and fled the country. The media celebrated an indigenous victory over neoliberalism and racism.

What happened? The 2002 election and the events of "Black October" are, in many senses, verdicts: the state-led multicultural reforms did not bring the promised benefits for Bolivia's indigenous and *campesino* (peasant) population. It thus represents an end to the articulations between indigenous groups and the political parties that claimed to represent their interests through state-led reforms. Now indigenous groups have chosen another strategy, direct political challenge, on the one hand through elections and on the other, through massive protests. Why did these multicultural reforms "fail" in the eyes of their supposed beneficiaries? How would success be measured when evaluating multiculturalism? Successful for whom? What, ultimately, does it mean for Bolivia to be "pluri-cultural" and "multi-ethnic"?

These are not just rhetorical questions. Rather, they are at the heart of some of the most important social and political issues currently affecting today's multi-ethnic societies. As we argue in the introduction, indigenous peoples across Latin America are pushing for political inclusion, on the one hand, and autonomy, on the other. In response, two important changes are taking place. First, countries are experimenting with forms of state-led multiculturalism – government efforts to embrace and manage ethnic difference. Second, as the other chapters in this collection attest, indigenous peoples formerly marginalized are entering state bureaucracies with the intention of changing the model of the state and the ways their citizens are represented. The history of Bolivia's particular "multiculturalism" offers an illustration of both of these responses.

Multiculturalism: Articulations on the Terrain of the Conjuncture

"Multiculturalism" can be used in many ways. It can refer to the multi-ethnic makeup of a place or a society – that is, the "shybrid co-existence of diverse cultural life-worlds" (Žižek 1997: 46). More often it refers to the efforts of liberal democratic governments to accept and embrace these ethnic differences. There are various terms for it: "Multicultural consti-tutionalism" (Van Cott 2000), "state-sponsored multiculturalism," "liberal multiculturalism," "pluralism," or the term widely used in Latin America, "interculturality." I use "state-led multiculturalism."[2] These policies specifically recognize formerly marginalized groups, ensuring their individual rights as citizens, and, in some cases, granting collective rights as groups. Both the meanings and the produced effects of "multi-culturalism" vary widely from country to country, and are the subject of continuing debates. At issue is the question of whether minority cultures or ways of life can be sufficiently protected by ensuring individual rights, or whether special group protection or rights are required (Bennett 1998, Goldberg 1994, Okin 1999).

What state-led multiculturalism means depends upon the historical and political particularities of the country and the form citizenship takes in that context. That is because the construction of citizenship is a key part of state formation – as people are interpellated as citizens, they become subjects of the nation-state (Corrigan and Sayer 1985). The laws, discourses, and practices which make up Bolivia's multiculturalism have arisen in part through contestations between indigenous peoples,[3] who assert cultural and political autonomy through these reforms, and the ruling elite classes, which have used these reforms to fashion new forms of domination and incorporation. Thus, citizenship is not just a politically or morally neutral status with uncategorical benefits for its new bearers, but a "term of belonging" ultimately enforced by the state (Schild 1998:98). This enforcement is not strictly a top-down process of assimilation. Rather, that sense of belonging is created, communicated, and incorporated through a constant political and cultural process of contestation.

It is important to emphasize that this contestation is both *processual* and *conjunctural*. Indigenous groups, like all social actors, struggle against dominant political forces at some times and ally themselves with them at others, depending upon the historical and political contexts. Such a perspective is lacking in many studies of indigenous politics, which have focused primarily on indigenous groups' resistance to hegemonic, assimilating, and often violent, states and/or capital flows (Maybury-Lewis 2002, Rappaport 1990, 1994, Varese 1996). Resistance has been the key trope for the analysis of indigenous struggles since the early 1970s, when scholars explored indigenous reactions to structural inequalities or internal colonialism (Isbell 1978, Whitten 1975). Similarly, in the 1980s historians began to re-examine previous characterizations of Indian and peasant rebellions. Rather than seeing them as momentary reactions to exploitation, the new studies explored the ways Indians acted as "continuous initiators" of rebellions and resistance, thus focusing on the agency of subaltern groups and their intellectuals (Mallon 1995). In the 1990s, attention to resistance was refocused to forms of "everyday" and "popular" resistance (Scott 1985, Alonso 1995, Joseph and Nugent 1994), and the discursive and symbolic forms of struggle indigenous social movements employ to maintain and defend cultural identities in light of globalizing discourses of modernity and development (Escobar and Alvarez 1992, Garfield 2001).

A second approach has been those studies which focus on the democratizing role indigenous groups can play as actors in civil society. This has come mainly from two groups. The first is political scientists influenced by the neo-Toquevillean arguments of such theorists as Robert Putnam and Francis Fukuyama who argue that civil society associations are essential to making democracy work (Putnam 1993). The second is the next generation of New Social Movement scholars, who focus on the alternative models of citizenship these movements can provide (Alvarez, Dagnino, and Escobar 1998.) Scholars with this approach have pointed out the importance of indigenous challenges to the newly consolidating democracies of Latin America. Partly because of their historical marginalization from state power, indigenous groups may have alternative visions for the state and society (Varese 1996). Their disagreements with the ideologies of homogenizing nationalism have found new transnational platforms, where they can contest the "foundations and contours of contemporary democratic and liberal institutions," which have failed to provide universal participation or political autonomy (Yashar 1999). In this view, indigenous organizations' pressure "to truly democratize Latin American governments, by expanding political participation to excluded groups . . . represents the process of democratization itself, as well as an indication that this process is working" (Van Cott 1994: 22).

Several synthetic analyses that show how indigenous organizations often combine overt political resistance and strategic accommodation to state policies (Garfield 2001, K. Warren 1998). For instance, several scholars have demonstrated that, as indigenous people rework dominant ideologies about the nation through narratives of resistance or political practices, their resistance may ultimately reshape the prevailing visions of the nation (Alonso 1995, Rappaport 1994, Stephen 2002). These works, along with recent studies of the limited effectiveness of social movements after democratization (Berman 1997, Oxhorn 1995, Uggla 2002), urge a more nuanced and contextual analysis of indigenous social movements.

In this chapter, I show that Bolivian indigenous social movements have acted *both* as forces of resistance *and* as forces of consolidation and alliance with other classes and political parties. Gramsci (1971) pointed out that diverse groups or classes can unite under particular historical circumstances, in particular moments, to form a collective will which might allow them to dominate other groups, enforce their interests, or take control of the state. Social movements often come together when points of rupture link the interests of antagonistic groups. Thus, the meaning of social movements cannot be understood outside their "articulations" with other struggles and demands. Following Stuart Hall, I use the term "articulation" to mean the way "ideological elements come, under certain conditions, to cohere together within a discourse, and a way of asking how they do or do not become articulated, at specific conjunctures, to certain political subjects" (Hall 1996: 141–2). Consequently, to understand the articulations that produced and are producing the particular practices and discourses of multiculturalism in Bolivia, we must look at the history of the contentious relations between the state and the indigenous peoples at critical moments of conjuncture.

The Eternal Other

In Bolivia, indigenous subjects have been a crucial element of the formation of a "modern" Bolivian nation-state. Since colonial times, Indians have served as the "Other." The Spaniards established separate and dual republics for Spaniards and Indians, characterized by colonial relations of domination and economic exploitation. These colonial dualities continued after independence in 1825 when elites created the new republic of Bolivia, in part by contrasting the new *ciudadanos*, or citizens, with the *indiada desestructurada y no reconocida* (unrecognized and destructured Indians) (Albó 1996, Unzueta 2000).[4] The elite, echoing the ideological themes of nineteenth-century European imperialism, argued that for the good of the nation, *nuestros bárbaros* (our savages) had to be either civilized and assimilated, or encouraged to disappear (Unzueta 2000: 44, Rivera Cusicanqui 1987: 17). This was helped along by the reforms the new republic adopted, especially the codification of the liberal concept of private property as the only legal form of land tenure, which served as an excuse for widespread expropriation of indigenous lands (Rivera Cusicanqui 1987, Platt 1991).[5]

During the following years, highland Indians fought the forms of economic and political domination brought by the new republic. In a cycle of rebellions from 1910–30, which were ultimately put down, leaders articulated a series of political demands including restitution of lands and access to markets being taken over by large-scale agricultural production (Rivera Cusicanqui 1987). These demands were at odds with oligarchs who wanted control, as well as modernizers who saw the future of Bolivia as a unified nation of small-holders contributing to the national market. In the heady years after the Chaco War in the 1930s, however, the oligarchy was replaced by new political actors, who saw the Indian peasantry and the workers' unions, especially the miners, as allies for political change. Although their ethnic demands for autonomy and collective land were ultimately ignored by the reformers, Indians went along with the MNR (*Movimiento Nacionalista Revolucionario*, National Revolutionary Movement) party's promises to make a place for Indians in the new revolutionary state.

After the 1952 revolution, the governing MNR party reorganized Indians into state-sponsored peasant unions, thus integrating them into the state as producers, and not as Indians *per se* (Larson 1988, Stroëbele-Gregor 1996). This was part of a unifying nationalist program in which highland Indians were called *campesinos* (peasants), and their organizations were converted to *sindicatos* (peasant unions or leagues). As the chapters on Mexico, Peru, and Ecuador show, this move to a corporate model of state–indigenous relations was widely adopted in Latin America. Ethnicity was seen as a form of racism, which had to be replaced by a vision of class, or simply be seen as a "primitive form condemned to disappear with the rapid processes of modernization" (Albó 1996: 8).

Rivera Cusicanqui (1987) points out that the *sindicato* movement had very different effects in different areas of the highlands. In the Cochabamba area, the union model fit in fairly well with already established Quechua small-holder models. There, Indian peasant unions exercised some power, and were rewarded with agricultural credit and government attention (see also Ströbele-Gregor 1996, Yashar 1998). In the Aymara areas of the *altiplano* (highlands), where people maintained strong cultural ties to collective land-holding and strong traditional social organizations, however, the unions were perceived as externally imposed. In those areas Indians continued to feel excluded from the nation and struggled against the state, allying with radical worker's unions during the years of the military dictatorships. This sense of exclusion also gave rise to an Aymara political and cultural movement, the Katarista movement, which linked rural and urban Aymaras, and pushed their demands for cultural difference, special education, and political inclusion (Van Cott 2000).

In the 1970s and '80s, highland Indians were among the most vocal opponents of the government through the *campesino* federation, the CSUTCB (Bolivian Unitary Syndical Peasant Workers Confederation), and through miners' organizations and uprisings (Barrios de Chungara 1978). Moreover, highland groups began to push for political and cultural recognition of Indian peoples through various means. The 1973 Manifesto of Tiwanaku by Aymara intellectuals denounced the economic and cultural oppression of indigenous peoples; the mid-1980s political agenda of the CSUTCB advocated "unity in diversity"; and in the 1990s the urban populist party CONDEPA (Conscience of the Fatherland) championed the rights of *cholos* (urban Indian migrants) in the La Paz area (see generally Van Cott 2000).

The Push from Below

The 1990s brought new indigenous social forces to the national scene. Over the last thirty years, the *Oriente,* the eastern lowlands, home to many indigenous groups, had become the focus of government develop-ment strategies in Bolivia. Businesses, lumber companies, cattle ranchers, and highland migrants streamed into the Oriente, and Santa Cruz, the capital of the department. But the Oriente was not empty – it was the home of native peoples who had to be recognized and incorporated into the new national scheme. Old models of state–indigenous relations, based on highland peoples, were not appropriate for indigenous people of the Oriente with limited historical relations to the patron state.

As in many countries in Latin America, the Bolivian indigenous move-ment grew throughout the 1980s and '90s (Brysk 2000), thanks to NGO and church funding, continent-wide organizing, and the impetus of the 1992 *Quincentenario,* the 500 year anniversary of Colombus' arrival in the Americas. In the early 1980s, lowland indigenous peoples began to organize and in 1982, founded a regional federation of indigenous groups called CIDOB (*Confederación de Indígenas del Oriente de Bolivia,* Confederation of Indigenous Peoples of Eastern Bolivia).[6] While the historical hostility between groups was an initial obstacle to organizing, one central issue unified them: the need to defend and control their land from the increased settlement in lowland areas (Riester 1985). In 1990, lowland indigenous peoples took this demand for territory public. They staged a massive (and well publicized) march from the lowlands up the Andes to La Paz in what was called the *Marcha por Territorio y Dignidad,* the March for Territory and Dignity. Andean groups met the lowland groups at the summit, and together they marched into La Paz. The march changed the face of Bolivia forever.[7] Then-President Paz Zamora met with the indigenous leaders, negotiated with them on their demands, and created seven indigenous territories by presidential decree. *Territorio* (territory) became an icon of indigenous–state relations.

So, when Gonzalo Sánchez de Lozada (called "Goni") ran for president two years later in 1992, issues of indigenous rights were very much present in the political agenda of the country. His strategic choice of Aymara leader Victor Hugo Cárdenas as vice-president gained support from both highland indigenous groups allied with labor organizations, and lowland groups who saw this as a benefit for all indigenous peoples (Albó 1994). Once again, the MNR elite, this time with Aymara elite by its side, promised to incorporate indigenous demands into the new state. Once again, as they had after the 1952 revolution, indigenous peoples joined forces with an MNR party in the process of reorganizing the state.

Multiculturalism in the Nineties

When Goni was elected, the new government created a Secretary of Ethnic, Gender, and Generational Affairs (SNAEGG) which included the Sub-Secretary of Ethnic Affairs, (SAE), run to begin with by Cárdenas' Katarista party. In April of 1994, the SAE signed an agreement with CIDOB, the national indigenous federation, in which they agreed to work together on the SAE's projects and legislation.[8] This radically altered government–indigenous relations, because for the first time, indigenous leaders were participating in decisions rather than just being the "beneficiaries" of policies. Prior to this, most indigenous people lived outside the national legal framework without documentation or recognition, collective indigenous land holding was illegal, and tribes or other traditional socio-political organizations had no place in the Bolivian juridical system (Rivera Cusicanqui 1987). Although the control of the SAE shifted over time to other parties, and the dedication to these revolutionary alliances diminished, the articulation between indigenous peoples and the MNR was critical to the legal changes that occurred under the Goni administration.

Goni's decisive victory gave him the political power to make wide-ranging reforms to both the economic and political systems in Bolivia (Van Cott 2000). As part of the neoliberal push, Goni and his team of technocrats began by privatizing five of the largest state firms.[9] The Law of Popular Participation (LPP), Bolivia's version of decentralization[10] shifted 20 percent of the federal budget money to the 311 municipalities throughout the country and established a new system for local participation in the development decisions at the municipal level. These reforms were part of a larger plan to streamline the state, make the government more efficient at the local level, liberalize the internal market, and make Bolivia more competitive on the world market, all classic strategies of neoliberal governments (Bierstecker 1990, Mosley, Harrigan, and Toye 1991).

The Goni administration also revolutionized the position of Bolivia's indigenous peoples. Article One of the Reformed Constitution of the State declares Bolivia to be a "multi-ethnic and pluri-cultural" nation. More specifically, Article 171 declared that "the social, economic, and cultural rights of the indigenous peoples *(pueblos indígenas)* who inhabit the national territory are recognized, respected, and protected." These articles were the foundational language for Bolivia's state-instituted multiculturalism, and they were followed by legislative acts that gave specific rights to indigenous peoples in all sorts of areas, from a bilingual-bicultural education program to a new framework for recognizing and titling indigenous forms of collective land tenure.[11]

Perhaps the most important of all the reforms in terms of citizenship is the Law of Popular Participation, which specifically names indigenous people as popular representatives able to participate in government administration at the municipal level. The law establishes vigilance committees, made up of representatives of constituent population groups called *Organizaciones Territoriales de Base* (OTBs), or Territorial Grassroots Organizations, who have input into municipal budget decisions. The regulations specifically recognize traditional indigenous leaders as representatives of the OTBs, chosen by their own groups according to their uses and customs. For the first time, the law gave some measure of political power to indigenous social organizations and their customary leaders and acknowledged this was an expression of collective identities.

Thus, through these reforms, the MNR and indigenous peoples linked their interests. This alliance, like all articulations of differing groups, was provisional, depending upon the political moment. Also, as these groups are not homogenous, this articulation served the interests of some, but not all, members of the groups. It was embedded in a new discourse that stitched together potentially competing histories and goals: the discourse of multiculturalism. The multicultural reforms did not abolish the historic contradictions between Bolivia's ruling elite and indigenous groups. What multiculturalism provided, instead, was a new framework for contingent alliances between the MNR and indigenous groups as it was constituted in the early 1990s. As William Roseberry suggests, what hegemony constructs is not a shared ideology but a "common material and meaningful framework for living through, talking about, and acting upon social orders characterized by domination" (Roseberry 1996: 80).

What was the basis of the articulation between the Goni administration and the indigenous movement? That is, what was in it for the state and for the MNR party? And what was in it for indigenous groups?

Healing a Rift

First, we must look at the context of state-building in Bolivia in recent years. After the 1952 revolution, the MNR's control was continuously contested by more radical sectors, particularly the workers federation, *Central Obrera de Bolivia* (COB, Bolivian Workers Central), with whom it originally collaborated after the revolution. In 1964, the military over-threw the MNR government, retaining power until 1982, when popular discontent over military brutality and the collapse of the economy brought the dictatorship to an end. In 1982, a leftist democratic party took power, only to fall into economic and political chaos shortly thereafter. The political goal of the governments and political elite since that time has been to bring stability to the fractured political scene in order to engage Bolivia with international capital markets (Van Cott 2000).

From 1985 to 1989, the MNR, in an alliance with former dictator General Hugo Banzer Suárez's ADN party (*Acción Democrática Nacional*, National Democratic Action), sought to do this by instituting a neoliberal economic program, which combined structural adjustment programs with massive closings of the state-owned mines. Since then, historian Harry Sanabria suggests, the MNR party has used neoliberalism to "reconstitute the state and capitalism" (Sanabria 2000:62). By developing a corps of well-trained bureaucrats and by making alliances with other political parties, the MNR created a new stronger state, brought in more revenues to the state coffers, and increased the stream of international capital (Sanabria 2000).

This period also brought a crisis to the traditional Left. On the one hand, the government crippled the most vocal opponents of the government, the labor movement (Gill 2000). On the other, many of the intellectual elite who had worked against the military from their positions in NGOs, found themselves working with the government Social Emergency Fund to combat the excesses of structural adjustment (Arellano-López and Petras 1994; Kruse 1994). Meanwhile, many Bolivian intellectuals began to articulate a growing concern: a "lack of a pact between society and the state" (Van Cott 2000: 134). By the early 1990s, the country was abuzz with proposals for new state models to overcome Bolivia's chronic instability, give marginalized groups autonomy and power, and reorganize political power by altering the model of the state.

It was in this context that Goni came to power. Goni's 1993 campaign allied the MNR with the Indian MRTKL (Katarista) party and presented a plan for constitutional reform as the *Plan de Todos* (Plan For All) (Kohl 2003b). It called for a transformation of the nation through a democratic revolution at the municipal level, intended to please local elites. It called for the modernization of the state and a continuation of neoliberal economic policies, intended to please the business community. Finally, it called for an opening of political space for civil society organizations, intended to please indigenous, peasant, and some labor groups (Van Cott 2000).

Embracing Multiculturalism

The MNR's new reforms were received by the Bolivian public in a period of great public debate and activity. There were frequent and noisy demonstrations about the social costs of neoliberal policies, the changes in the Education Law, and especially the privatization project (Gill 2000). There was also a palpable sense of pride in the new multicultural nature of the state. Through the discourse of a "pluri-cultural and multi-ethnic" Bolivia, the Goni government was able to re-fashion Bolivia's own image and assert a particular and new kind of modernity, based on democracy and participation (Gupta 1998). This was accompanied by a newly articulated understanding of indigenousness as an essential component of Bolivian modernity. Thus, as in many other Latin American countries, Bolivians' national self-image (which is, of course, multiple and heterogeneous) reflects an ambivalent combination of cosmopolitan modernity and self-conscious reference to the traditions of the past, most often represented by the icons of indigenousness.[12]

This can be seen in the example of Bolivian indigenous folklore and *artesania* (craftswork). They are marketed to international tourists, but they also form a reference for internal identity consolidation. Bolivians are fiercely protective of their "traditional" highland dances. Oruru, in the *altiplano*, is considered the most "traditional" site for *Carnaval* celebrations. Every year, hundreds of musical and dance groups participate in three days and nights of "indigenous" highland dances and processions, while thousands of visitors watch, drink, and revel. The event is broadcast by television to the rest of the country, where similar but smaller events are occurring. Oruru's *Carnaval* has become an icon of Bolivian identity, freezing the "traditional" indigenous past into the "modern" Bolivian present (Abercrombie 1991).

The state also uses indigenousness and indigenous values to stake a claim to cultural uniqueness in the globalizing market (Comaroff 1996, and Hall 1991). For instance, I heard a non-indigenous official of the VAIPO, the Ministry for Indigenous Affairs, talking to a group of indigenous leaders about the ethnic tourism which the VAIPO was promoting. "Why do these rich *gringos* want to come see Bolivia?" he asked. "Because they can see here the things they have lost in their cultures: generosity, goodness, communalism, participatory democracy, and strong values."[13] It can be in the interest of the state, then, to include its indigenous people as citizens, and to embrace (or appropriate) their values into the discourse of Bolivia's particular modernity.[14] This is all the more true when doing so leads to increased money from foreign tourists, or to more international aid for indigenous development programs.[15]

This "modern" image is not merely for export. An interesting example of this is the effects of the reforms upon government workers. During the Goni administration, many progressive social scientists who had long been outsiders, fighting against the military dictatorships, came to work for the new government to take advantage of the opening to work for political change. They were part of the interpellating force of the state, but they themselves were also answering the call of the "pluri-cultural, multi-ethnic" nation. Many were quite torn about being in this dual position, but they were responding to and internalizing the rationalities of this form of government, which proposes a particular model of common good. That is, their genuinely felt hopes for the new reforms were born from years of anti-state activism and also shaped by the neoliberal logic of civil society and citizenship.

This emphasizes one of the appeals of liberal state-sponsored multiculturalism. As Povinelli (1998) argues, by seeming to erase the racism of the past and embracing formerly marginalized peoples, the institutions of the state appear vindicated and legitimated. Cleansed, they offer the hope of a democratic society, even to people like the workers who had been outside the state apparatus all their lives. Thus, the state is re-constituted, but the changes do not threaten liberal democratic institutions or values.

Indigenous Responses – Answering the Hail

If government workers embraced the possibility of a more participatory society, so did many indigenous people. The Goni years were a very exciting time for indigenous groups. CIDOB, the national federation in Santa Cruz, buzzed with consultants and indigenous leaders found themselves in frequent meetings with government officials. The new agrarian reform law, called INRA, revolutionized the indigenous movement, as groups across the country filed their claims for recognition of their territories. International aid money poured in to help the process, and a huge infrastructure of technicians, anthropologists, and lawyers went to work to implement the new law. At the same time, the LPP (Popular Participation Law) began to offer some opportunities for participation in local government. Government agencies and NGOs organized workshops to teach peasants and indigenous people their rights and obligations as citizens under the new laws. Even from the beginning, there were grave problems with the implementation of the LPP, which will be discussed below. However, the initial effect of the reforms, and of the discourse of participation that accompanied it, was to encourage many indigenous people.

The Guaraní people[16] with whom I worked in Santa Cruz were very excited. One afternoon, I sat with a Guaraní family in the patio of their home in one of the villages outside Santa Cruz. Samuel[17] saw the reforms in terms of power: "There has always been a strong marginalization in Bolivia, and so we Guaranís have never been accepted as a people (*pueblo*). We need sovereignty, we need land, but mostly, we need to be able to govern ourselves as Guaranís (*gobernarse por si mismo como Guaraní*)." With the reforms, he said, they felt accepted as fellow Bolivians, with rights to their own culture and language. His father, Don Jesús, a linguist, agreed. "Before, we often denied our identity, but now, I feel more Guaraní than before! Since the new educational reforms, our language is an official language, not just a dialect." Another friend told me that government recognition of indigenous people in the new reforms was extremely important to their sense of dignity. "Maybe," he speculated, "some of the people who have been living as *karai* (non-indigenous, or white) will come back to being indigenous . . . "

Things Fall Apart

The excitement of the Goni years did not last. The alliances between the MNR and the other parties fell apart, and public support fell as the neoliberal economic reforms, especially privatization, took their toll. In the 1997 elections, former dictator General Hugo Suárez Banzer and his conservative ADN party won the presidency. The ADN's main constituency has traditionally been the landed elite of the *Oriente*, and the agri-businesses associated with them.

When the Banzer government took over in 1997, it had little choice but to continue to operate through the framework established by the Goni administration, given the overwhelming support the reforms received nationally. Bolivian anthropologist Ricardo Calla points out, however, that laws are made up of two dimensions, the formal, and the discursive (Calla 2000: 81). When Banzer took over, the formal nucleus of the indigenous reforms – the legal and political reorganization of the government – was carried forward, but the discursive nucleus – the meanings that surrounded the actual legal changes – were radically altered. Taking a more traditional business approach, the Banzer government looked to the market to resolve what it designated as the most important goal for the country: the fight against poverty (see Calla 2000). The discourse about indigenous rights and multiculturalism was almost entirely absent. Instead, indigenous people and peasants were lumped together in a new group: the poor, who needed to be incorporated into a modern labor force necessary for Bolivia to go forward into the global marketplace. Some government programs attempted this. As Lema notes, however, "*no hay muchos hechos*" (nothing much has happened) (Lema 2001: 8).

The most significant problem from the indigenous perspective, however, was the lack of progress on the INRA territorial titling reforms. Despite an enormous amount of money and time invested in the process, by 2001, only 8 percent of the total hectares for which indigenous groups have filed claims under the law had been titled, leaving over 21 million hectares to be investigated and litigated (Flores 2001). The Banzer government was inefficient and, many said, corrupt. Certainly, in the areas where landowners have political power, the titling process was often thwarted by government officials (Tamburini and Betancur 2001). While the process dawdled on, third parties, called *terceros*, consolidated their holds on the land, continuing to exploit lumber and other resources (Stocks 1999). These incursions form the basis for rights of possession, so that when the clearing of title is finally carried out, the areas granted to indigenous groups are greatly reduced.

To make things worse, the Banzer government threatened to introduce changes in the INRA law to allow for individual, as opposed to collective, titling of lands. This change is part of the general neoliberal push toward opening up the land to market forces, with an accompanying weakening of collective rights. Such changes would eviscerate the laws for which a generation of indigenous people struggled. These challenges and the lack of progress in INRA implementation caused enormous frustration among indigenous people, as well as conflicts over what strategy was appropriate to combat it. As a result, the lowland indigenous organizations, which had been such strong social actors in the 1990s, began to fight among themselves and to have less and less political power at the national level.

Popular Participation: The Limits of the Reforms

Meanwhile, the Banzer/Quiroga administration continued to implement the rest of the reforms, albeit in a half-hearted manner. While the reforms were very meaningful in terms of creating an expectation of citizenship among the newly interpellated indigenous citizens, the actual practices of the reforms, particularly the Law of Popular Participation, did not result in a substantial change in economic or political power in most indigenous communities. This varied widely, of course, depending upon the community, the demographics, and the interactions between indigenous communities, political parties, and NGOs facilitating indigenous participation (Kohl 20003a, 2003c, 1999). There were three main problems with the Law of Popular Participation, as it was implemented (see Postero 2001).

First, there were significant structural obstacles to indigenous participation. The LPP changed the rules of the game of politics, switching the power struggles to a much more local level. Suddenly, municipal governments became the site of fights over money and intense public scrutiny.

For some communities with strong local leaders and large numbers of indigenous people, the LPP opened a new space of indigenous political action. In the case of the Guaranís of the Izozog region, for example, the federation formed what is called an Indigenous Municipal District and won the sub-mayor position, which allowed them to manage a substantial amount of funds for the benefit of the Guaraní people.

For the majority of indigenous communities, however, the new laws did not result in a change in elected officials. In the Guaraní communities where I worked in the lowlands, for instance, the Guaraní do not make up a majority, they have few connections to political parties, and they did not put forward any political candidates. So, what the LPP did was to greatly increase the political power of already existing politicians, the local elites, who have had traditional racist relations with the Guaraní. Popular participation had obviously not changed these attitudes or their effects.

For good or for bad, though, since more money is at stake, political parties are now involved in municipal and even community concerns. Indigenous villages are more important now, because local voting patterns have financial consequences. Guaranís in several outlying villages told me that previously, they only saw politicians once a year, if then, when they brought T-shirts and cases of beer before election time. Now, political parties have begun to meddle in internal community politics, often trying to get their party members installed as leaders, or bribing indigenous leaders. This is one important way in which the state apparatus has reached into the farthest village in Bolivia.

Second, the practices of participation tended to diminish ethnic difference. One of the highly touted features of the LPP was its recognition of indigenous organizations. Through the OTB system, difference was supposed to be brought together in a participatory process of democracy – civil society in action. Investigation has shown, however, that, rather than supporting difference, the LPP can result in the fragmentation of indigenous organizations and the over-riding of traditional forms of socio-political organization. One problem is that the law imposes a generic requirement for representation in municipal meetings that is based upon western cultural models. This "New England town meeting" model, as one USAID official described it, with its clearly defined roles of president, vice-president, etc., does not match indigenous forms of authority or representation, either the collective assembly (*asamblea*) model of most lowland indigenous groups or the dual, complimentary, and couple-based structure of the highland *ayllus* (Calla 2000:83). Another problem is that the law allows only one OTB organization to represent each community. In mixed-ethnicity villages, this means that the minority ethnicity usually is not represented.

Third, even when indigenous people do find their way into the municipal government process, the institutionalized form of participation offered by the LPP did not allow for real participatory debates about what development should be. Instead, inclusion in municipal politics has effectively limited the range of questions indigenous people should ask. Instead of making demands about autonomy or cultural rights, these new citizens were forced to work within prescribed, scripted processes to gain access to limited co-participation funds. In some municipalities, the struggles over these issues were empowering, and brought to light the cultural inequalities underlying the poverty of indigenous citizens. This was particularly true in the large urban areas with large numbers of indigenous people, such as El Alto, the large satellite city outside La Paz with a majority Aymara population (Kohl 2002, 1999). In others, particularly where indigenous populations were small, indigenous demands were fragmented and refocused to the immediate decisions of local governing, precluding more critical responses to existing inequalities.

These problems reflect the unresolved tensions of state-led multiculturalism. The Law of Popular Participation sought to include all people into a western democratic notion of participation, and, at first, indigenous organizations seemed pleased to be invited to the table. In practice, however, it became clear that ethnicity posed a continued thorn in this liberal vision. Indigenous people were not free to participate because the basic institutions of power, racism, and traditional political parties had not been sufficiently challenged by the reforms.

Understandably, this generated great disappointment and frustration among the indigenous and peasant sectors that were supposed to have been the great beneficiaries of the LPP. Among the Guaraní of Santa Cruz, with whom I have worked most closely, optimism gave way to resignation. "Why" they asked, "would those rich people want to give us anything anyway? No, that is not the way to power in this country."

To the Streets!

Indigenous people were not the only people who felt this way. The social convulsion and conflict that has overtaken Bolivia since 2000 shows that a broad swath of the popular sectors agreed.

The year 2000 began with what was called *la guerra del agua*, the water war, when a raise in water rates caused department-wide strikes and demonstrations in Cochabamba. Then, throughout that year, strikes spread throughout the country as several years of economic crisis took its toll. Angry peasants and workers, disgruntled teachers and transport workers, and *cocaleros* (the coca growers) mounted their protests and blockaded the highways, cutting off La Paz. In the highlands, the CSUTCB, the farmer's union, mounted particularly vehement demonstrations, in which several farmers were killed and many wounded in struggles with the police. These strikes were resolved through the mediation of the Catholic Church and the government ombudsman. This compounded the already widely held view that political parties were not the means to achieving social justice or political participation (Uggla 2002).

In this period of near constant confrontation, the struggles of the *cocaleros* became particularly important in the eyes of the popular sectors. Since the late 1980s, when relocated Quechua and Aymara miners fled to the Chapare to colonize, Evo Morales and the coca-growers have been fighting a low intensity war with the anti-narcotics forces lead by US DEA agents and the US embassy. This struggle has erupted several times in violence, as the narcotics agents brutally put down the demonstrations and highway blockades staged by the *cocaleros*. Decrying US imperialism in the coca eradication program, "Evo," as he is called, was elected to Congress in 1997. When the *cocaleros* staged a new round of highway blockades in 2001, supported by Evo, Congress finally rose against him, and he was impeached for treason. This "setback" allowed Evo to begin to campaign for President, and also gave him reason to broaden his platform beyond the *cocalero* issue. As his campaign progressed, Evo brought together the old Left, an influential leftist lawyers' group, current leaders of *campesino* and workers unions, members of the new *Movimiento Sin Tierra* (Movement of the Landless), and some lowland indigenous leaders, presenting a varied popular front. While still strongly weighted toward the highland peoples, this new political party declared itself to be the representative of all the popular and indigenous peoples of Bolivia who had suffered indignities and oppression by the white elite.

Evo's party was not the only voice of the highlands to be raised in the recent social convulsions. At the same time, the charismatic Aymara, Felipe Quispe, a veteran political activist and former *Katarista* guerrilla, began to urge a sort of separatist Aymara power movement. Quispe uses a strong language of cultural nationalism, and has a pugnacious negotiating style – in 2003 he was able to extract a promise for 800 tractors from the government for his union. While some see the rise of Aymara activism as a positive sign, others worry that Quispe's leadership, with its machismo and violence, is not a progressive turn. He has certainly antagonized lowland groups by declaring his support for individual land titling. Although he asserts a strident anti-government policy, Quispe also ran for Congress and was elected on the MIP (*Movimiento Indígena Pachakuti)* ticket. The MIP managed to win almost 9 percent of the national vote (Van Cott 2003).

Within the lowland indigenous movement, the last four years have also been extremely important. Longtime divisions within CIDOB, the national indigenous federation, increased as the presidential elections neared. Many of the CIDOB leaders allied themselves with the MIR party, several of them running for Congress on this ticket. Others allied with Evo Morales' MAS party and leftist lawyers pushing a Marxist-influenced politics of class unity between highland and lowland Indians. Lowland indigenous groups have been very wary of such alliances, because of their continued fears that landless and poor highland peoples will invade the lands the lowlands peoples have struggled so hard to protect.

This tension became more salient in early 2002, when indigenous leaders disagreed over strategies in organizing a national march for a constituent assembly to reform the constitution again, to give indigenous people more real representation. One sector began a march from Santa Cruz to La Paz, while another hung back, debating. Eventually, both groups marched, but the groups remained separate during most of the march, making a divided and confusing public representation. Nevertheless, the march received a great deal of public and media attention, especially the symbolic co-ordinations with highland groups of Aymara and Quechua peasants. The march was not successful in forcing the government to hold the assembly, but it was very important in reasserting the lowland indigenous peoples as political actors in 2002. The issues brought up by the march – the need to reform the constitution to allow the indigenous and peasants to have a voice in government – expressed what many at the bottom of Bolivian society had been feeling and expressing throughout the conflictive previous years: that the rich white politicians and the constitutions and reforms they had instituted in the past just did not represent them or their interests.

Conclusion: *Octubre Negro*

These sentiments were at the crux of the uprising that brought down Goni's second administration in October 2003. While indigenous and poor people organized this revolution because they objected to the gas exports, especially in the context of a globalization based on unequal power relations, it is clear that the deeper reasons underlying the events reflect a wide-spread frustration with systemic exclusion from political decision-making. Bolivia's poor want a say in the way the state is composed and how its resources are used. This is a matter of citizenship, and it is a matter of urgency not only for indigenous people, because all of Bolivia's poor have felt the effects of neoliberal restructuring. Whatever the long-term results of the uprising, it has put the issues of citizenship and participation on the public agenda.

The October uprising also marks two important shifts in indigenous politics. First, it clearly demonstrates that the articulations of the 1990s are over. Indigenous groups gained power in the 1980s and '90s by political resistance to the structured inequalities in which they lived, what Oxhorn (1995) calls "coerced marginalization." From this outsider position, they staged marches and demonstrations, and made alliances with international NGOs. This put them into a position of allying with the dominant political parties, and reaching some sorts of mutually bene-ficial articulations with them. Once the alliance was in full swing, however, indigenous power began to be absorbed by the greater power of the elite, through the continued influence of political parties and long-term racism. As the articulations began to fail, the alliances fragmented, and resistance – either via electoral politics or massive uprisings – returned as the strategic choice.

That is not to say that the alliances were a complete loss. Many see the reforms as a first step to power, a sort of apprenticeship in political processes. Although they did not produce a system of viable participation, they produced a new category of subject: indigenous citizens, with new hopes and a notion of their rights. This was not purely symbolic; in some communities, popular participation has meant the management of resources, indigenous leaderships, and community organization. Even where the material effects were limited, however, the reforms signal the importance of state recognition. Interpellated as citizens, indigenous Bolivians now claim real representation in a system which listens to them.[18]

Second, the October revolution was only possible because of new artic-ulations with new allies. Indigenous activism since the 1970s has been focused around indigenous identity and interests. In 2003, however, indigenous leaders made strategic alliances with other non-indigenous popular sectors to contest Goni's neoliberal policies. It is not surprising that the media has called this an indigenous uprising. It was lead by indige-nous leaders (the two most important were Evo Morales, the MAS leader, and Felipe Quispe, the Aymara campesino leader from the La Paz region,) and the faces on the frontlines of the demonstrations were overwhelm-ingly Indian, especially in El Alto, where most of the violence occurred. The leaders of the protests used ethnic tropes and metaphors to make their arguments, referring to the strength of the Andean warrior people, etc. Even when accepting the new president's request for a treaty, Felipe Quispe said that blood would run in the streets if their demands were not met, evoking the white/mestizo Paceños centuries-old fear of Indian insur-rection and vengeance.

Yet the political demands were more general, for "the people." Besides a resolution of the gas issue, the protesters demanded clarity in coca erad-ication laws, rejection of the ALCA free trade agreement, rejection of harsh national security laws, and a raise in basic wages. Here we see what has also occurred in Ecuador: an articulation between the interests of indigenous people and the rest of the poor and popular sectors (see Leon Zamosc's chapter in this volume). Thus, in the process of the contests over gas and neoliberalism, indigenous leaders are forming a new public which is demanding political participation. Moreover, indigenous leaders are claiming that it is through their experience as indigenous people that they have the right to make these demands for the people. Evo Morales put it this way:

This uprising of the Bolivian people has resulted not only from the issue of natural gas, of hydrocarbons, but from a collection of many issues: ffom discrimination and from marginalization, but fundamentally from the exhaustion of neoliberalism. The culprit responsible for so many deeds, and also responsible for the uprising of Bolivian people, has a name: it is called neoliberalism. Now, with the recent events in Bolivia, I have realized that what matters is the power of an entire people, of an entire nation. For those of us who are convinced that it is important to defend humanity, the best support we can offer is *to create the power of the people.* (Morales 2003, emphasis added)

If indigenous leaders are suggesting they are creating a new power of the people, it is a public entirely different from that imagined by the neoliberal state-led multiculturalism.[19] It is a public that is demanding real changes to the existing political and economic structures that have maintained relations of inequality to date.

This can be seen by the response of the new president (former vice-president), Carlos Mesa Quisbert, an independent historian and journalist. His main goal is to try to keep Bolivia from fragmenting further, but it is also clear that he is trying to come to grips with the new articulated public to which he is now responsible. In his inaugural speech, he promised two immediate responses to the demands of the protesters: to hold a public referendum about the uses of natural gas, and to convene a constituent assembly to rewrite the constitution and reform the state. He ended his speech calling for a Bolivia in which there is "unity in diversity." We will design a nation, he said, with "more equity, more justice, and with the security that comes from making that which we have not made in centuries" (Mesa Quisbert 2003). Here he evokes a multicultural democracy in which there will be equitable participation, which none of the constitutional reforms or state-lead multicultural reforms to date have accomplished.

After the successful alliances between the MAS, Aymara peasant organizations, and other popular sectors in the 2003 uprising, Bolivian indigenous groups have greatly increased their political power. What will come of this new power will depend upon the ability of Indian leaders to consolidate power in the transition government and offer a political platform acceptable to a large cross-section of the population. If indigenous organizations can articulate this new idiom of Bolivian indigenous nationalism, they may be able to win a sufficient majority at the ballot box to gain control of the state. What that would mean is not yet known, but it would certainly mean a refiguring of the status of indigenous people in Bolivia, coming to some resolution of the Indian Question. Would this amount to new form of bottom-up multiculturalism? Or is this a recognition that Bolivia is moving past multiculturalism to a period where citizenship is not a matter of identity politics? Whichever they choose, I suggest that Bolivians will find that new cultural and political forms – which will be both indigenous and popular – are necessary to remake the nation.

Notes

The author would like to thank Susana Wappenstein, Elizabeth Dougherty, Donald Moore, and Joel Robbins for suggestions on previous versions of this chapter. In Bolivia, my work has been greatly helped by Enrique Herrera, Wendy Townsend, Juan Leon, Tom Kruse, Pamela Calla, Ricardo Calla, and Julio Calla. I am particularly grateful to the Guaraní of the *Capitanía Zona Cruz* with whom I have worked and studied since 1995. This chapter received helpful suggestions from the participants, commentators, and audience members of the May 2003 conference in Cochabamba, and especially from anthropologist Sarela Paz, whose critical comments on the relation between neoliberalism and multiculturalism proved particularly relevant.

1   This figure depends, of course, upon how "indigenous" is defined. Terms used to describe the native Amer-Indian peoples have a long history in Bolivia, as elsewhere. The word "indigenous" came into popular use in Bolivia the 1970s and '80s, mainly in reference to lowland and Amazonian Indian peoples. Originally, both highland and lowland native peoples were called *indios,* or Indians. Then, as is described in the text, highland peoples came to be referred to by the term *campesinos,* or peasants. In the 1990s, *campesino* began to be replaced by the term *pueblos originarios* (original peoples) to refer to highland folk who self-identified as Indian. The government Indian ministry, for example, was renamed the *Vice Ministro de Asuntos Indígenas y Pueblos Originarios* (VAIPO, the Vice Ministry of Indigenous and Original Peoples Affairs) to reflect this change in usage. *Campesino* is still widely used, however, to refer to highland farmers, who may or may not consider themselves to be Indian. Only in the last few years has the term indigenous come to be used in some circles to refer to both highland and lowland peoples. The secondary question of how people are identified for the purposes of population statistics is equally complicated. Is the category of "indigenous" the result of self-reporting? A measure of language spoken? These issues make the widely reported 60 percent figure somewhat vague.

2   In this chapter, I have opted to use the term *multiculturalism* in a specific way to describe the constitutional and legislative reforms directed by the state with the intention of granting cultural and political rights to Bolivia's indigenous populations. This term is not used much in Bolivia. Although the constitution declares the country to be "pluri-cultural" and "multi-ethnic," the preferred term these days is *interculturality*. While multiculturalism implies numerous cultures, each deserving equal treatment, interculturality signals a more interactive process of mutual recognition of diversity, cultural difference, and especially linguistic difference (personal communication Pablo Regalsky, Cochabamba, May 2003). This term is used to describe the programs of bilingual bicultural .education that accompanied the other

reforms described in this chapter. It is used more widely now to describe other kinds of recognition of cultural difference. Although it might have been better to use here the term commonly used by Bolivians, NGOs, and indigenous people, I find the term interculturality too vague. I prefer to use the more precise term state sponsored multiculturalism, which calls attention to the fact that this is a legislative project promulgated by the government. Hale 2002 uses similar terms, *state-endorsed multiculturalism* and *dominant bloc-endorsed multiculturalism*. Nevertheless, it is important to emphasize that when I use the term multiculturalism, I am not referring to the type of multi-culturalism that exists in the United States.

3 The widely perceived opposition between indigenous groups and the elite, to which I refer here, is fraught with the dangers of dualisms, which I do not mean to reproduce. First, it makes the two groups appear polarized on both ethnic and class terms. That is, the opposition is posed between poor, ethnic Indians and rich, white elite. This monolithic characterization is not accurate: neither group is homogenous in makeup or in interests. The lowland indige-nous movement is made up of varying groups with widely different experiences, contact with national society, and economic interests (see Herrera Sarmiento 1998). Highland peoples may not represent themselves as indigenous, and are often prosperous farmers or merchants. There is large middle class of highland Indians, many of whom are educated and cosmopolitan. The elite class is equally diverse. There is a wide spectrum of ethnic backgrounds, and many consider themselves *mestizos,* with proud connections to their Indian heritage. Second, neither group is unified in their political perspectives and interests. In fact, in each sector, there is substantial contestation over strategy and power.

4 This echoes Mamdani's (1996) duality of colonial African indirect rule: citizen and subject. Thurner (1997) describes a similar duality in Peru, between the tributary subject (those Indians who paid tribute to the Spanish crown in exchange for their autonomy and their lands), and the citizen taxpayer.

5 Until 1945, all Bolivian constitutions made a distinction between being a Bolivian – a person born in the country or married to a Bolivian – and being a citizen – a status restricted to the literate. The 1952 revolution extended suffrage to all Bolivians over 21, but these rights were not incorporated into the constitution until 1961. See Tiro (1958), and Kohl (2000).

6 In the late 1970s an NGO called APCOB, run by German anthropologist Jürgen Riester, sponsored meetings between several lowland indigenous groups, (Chiquitanos and Ayoreos), and slowly these meetings grew to include other groups (Guaranís, Guarayos, and Matacos).

7 This was not the first such meeting of indigenous leaders in La Paz, however. Rivera Cusicanqui describes the first national Indigenous Congress sponsored by the MNR party in May of 1945, in which hundreds of highland Indian leaders arrived in La Paz, and for the first time were allowed to walk freely in Plaza Murillo (the plaza where the government buildings stand). Before this time, Indians were not admitted in the city. According to Rivera, the citi-zens of La Paz were upset and frightened by the sight. She says that "the ideological impact of this Indian conclave, held at the seat of the government and in the presence of its highest authorities was perhaps more important that any of the measures it adopted" (see Rivera Cusicanqui 1987: 50).

8   The SAE published a four point statement of its ethnic policies: (1) formal recognition of indigenous peoples by the State and the recognition of their collective rights; (2) the promotion of the participation of indigenous organizations' representatives in the decisions regarding their development; (3) respect for and strengthening of indigenous organizations and cultural systems, based on their own development, and the strengthening of their own capabilities for determining and managing (*gestión*) their own development; and (4) active state support for bettering the conditions of indigenous peoples' lives (see Lema 2001: 7). I thank Luz Maria Calvo and Ana Maria Lema for the first hand accounts of this period in SAE's history.

9   They were oil and gas, telecommunications, airlines, power generation, and the railroads. Instead of selling the enterprises outright, the government sold 50 percent of the businesses to "strategic partners" who agreed to invest money into the businesses to make them more efficient and profitable. The remaining equity in the firms was divided 49 percent to fund a national pension system and one percent to employees of the former state owned firms. See Kohl (1998) for a critical analysis of Bolivia's capitalization and popular participation projects.

10   Decentralization is the term used for programs to divest the national government of its overarching financial and political control over the hinterlands, often calling for more power to be given to municipal or regional governments. Decentralization is part of the neoliberal package which has been encouraged by international finance and development institutions, as it is supposed to modernize government, making administration more efficient. For a history of Bolivia's long debates about decentralization, see Molina Monasterios in SNPP (1996) and Laserna 1994. See also Kohl (1998), Van Cott (2000). For a discussion of decentralization generally, see Morris and Lowder (1992) and McCullough and Johnson (1989).

11   Other laws included a new forestry law which grants indigenous peoples some collective rights of commercial forestry laws protecting indigenous peoples' customary rights (*derechos consuetudinarios*) and access to water resources; and new administrative systems which establish indigenous municipal districts. See generally Marinissen (1998), Van Cott (2000).

12   Bhabha reminds us that national identities will always be ambivalent because they are built on Janus-faced notions of modernity and cultural contestations (1990). See also Friedlander (1975), Garcia Canclini (1989, 1993), and Chatterjee (1990) for descriptions of the ambiguities of national representations.

13   Pedro Avejera, official of VAIPO, Santa Cruz, Bolivia, March 3, 1998.

14   This appropriation of indigenous values is reminiscent of the double bind that Friedlander pointed out so many years ago in Hueyapan, Mexico (1975). She showed how indigenous people were seen as backwards obstacles to modernity, and at the same time valued for the benefits their anachronistic dances and crafts provided to the Mexican tourism industry.

15   Favorable treatment of indigenous minorities is not only important for a good international image; it is now a requirement for much international aid. See Hale (2002).

16   The Guaraní of Santa Cruz are migrants from the southwest part of Bolivia, coming mostly to the boom town of Santa Cruz in the 1960s following the

sugar cane harvest. They now form a federation of over twenty communities, called the *Capitanía Zona Cruz.* I have been working with them since 1995. See Postero 2001.

17 The names of all the indigenous people in this essay are pseudonyms.

18 I thank Ricardo Calla for his comments about the importance of the reforms. He believes that without this first phase, the second phase would never have taken place. Comments during the International Seminar in Cochabamba, Bolivia, May 23, 2003.

19 I am grateful to Rob Albro and Jeff Himpele for discussions about the relation between the popular and the public. See Albro and Himpele, forthcoming.

References

Abercrombie, Thomas. 1991. To Be Indian, To Be Bolivian: "Ethnic" and "National" Discourses of Identity. *Nation-States and Indians in Latin America,* Greg Urban and Joel Sherzer, eds. Austin: University of Texas Press.

Albó, Xavier. 1994. And from Kataristas to MNRistas? The Surprising and Bold Alliance between Aymaras and Neoliberals in Bolivia. *Indigenous Peoples and Democracy in Latin America,* Donna Lee Van Cott, ed. New York: St. Martin's Press.

——. 1996. La Búsqueda Desde Adentro, Calidoscopio de Auto-Imagenes en el Debate Étnico Boliviano. *Artículo Primero,* 1 (1). Santa Cruz, Bolivia: CEJIS.

Albro, Robert and Jeff Himpele. Forthcoming. Introduction: Popularizing the Public and Publicizing the Popular in Latin America. *New Public Appearances of the Popular in Latin America: Regional Variations from North and South,* Robert Albro and Jeff Himpele, eds.

Alonso, Ana María. 1995. *Thread of Blood, Colonialism, Revolution, and Gender on Mexico's Northern Frontier.* Tucson: University of Arizona Press.

Alvarez, Sonia, Evelina Dagnino, and Arturo Escobar. 1998. *Cultures of Politics, Politics of Culture.* Boulder: Westview Press.

Arellano-López, Sonia, and James Petras. 1994. Nongovernmental Organizations and Poverty Alleviation in Bolivia. *Development and Change,* 25: 555–68.

Barrios de Chungara, Domitila. 1978. *Let Me Speak, Testimony of Domitila, A Woman of the Bolivian Mines,* Moema Viezzer, ed. Victoria Ortiz, trans. New York: Monthly Review Press.

Bennett, David. 1998. *Multicultural States, Rethinking Difference and Identity.* London: Routledge.

Berman, Sheri. 1997 Civil Society and the Collapse of the Weimar Republic. *World Politics,* 49: 401–29.

Bhaba, Homi. 1990. Introduction: Narrating the Nation. *Nation and Narration.* London: Routledge.

Biersteker, Thomas. 1990. Reducing the Role of the State in the Economy: A Conceptual Exploration of IMF and World Bank Prescriptions. *International Studies Quarterly,* 34(4): 477– 92.

Brysk, Alison. 2000. *From Tribal Village to Global Village, Indian Rights and International Relations in Latin America.* Stanford: Stanford University Press.

Calla, Ricardo. 2000. Indigenous Peoples, the law of popular participation, and changes in government: Bolivia, 1994–1998. *The Challenge of Diversity,* Willem Assies, Gemma van der Haar, and Andre Hoekema, eds. Amsterdam, the Netherlands: Thela Thesis.

Chatterjee, Partha. 1990. *The Nation and Its Fragments, Colonial and Postcolonial Histories.* Princeton: Princeton University Press.

Comaroff, John. 1996. Ethnicity, Nationalism, and the Politics of Difference in an Age of Revolution. *The Politics of Difference, Ethnic Premises in a World of Power*, Edwin Wilmsen and Patrick Macallister, eds. Chicago: University of Chicago Press.

Corrigan, Philip and Derek Sayer. 1985. *The Great Arch: English State Formation as Cultural Revolution.* Oxford: Basil Blackwell.

Escobar, Arturo and Sonia Alvarez. 1992. *The Making of Social Movements in Latin America, Identity, Strategy and Democracy.* Boulder: Westview Press.

Flores, Elba. 2001. La TCO de las Tierras Bajas de Bolivia. *Artículo Primero*, August–December 2001. Santa Cruz, Bolivia: CEJIS.

Friedlander, Judith. 1975. *Being Indian in Hueyapan: A Study of Forced Identity in Contemporary Mexico.* New York: St. Martin's Press.

García Canclini, Nestor. 1989. *Hybrid Cultures: Strategies for Entering and Leaving Modernity.* Minneapolis: University of Minnesota Press.

———. 1993. Transforming Modernity: Popular Culture in Mexico. Austin: University of Texas Press.

Garfield, Seth. 2001. *The Indigenous Struggle at the Heart of Brazil.* Durham: Duke University Press.

Gill, Lesley. 2000. *Teetering on the Rim, Global Restructuring, Daily Life, and the Armed Retreat of the Bolivian State.* New York: Columbia University Press.

Goldberg, David Theo. 1994. *Multiculturalism: A Critical Reader.* Oxford: Blackwell.

Gramsci, Antonio. 1971. *Selections from the Prison Notebooks*, Q. Hoare and G. N. Smith, eds. New York: International Publishers.

Gupta, Akhil. 1998. *Postcolonial Developments: Agriculture in the Making of Modern India.* Durham: Duke University Press.

Hale, Charles. 2002. Does Multiculturalism Menace? Governance, Cultural Rights, and the Eclipse of Official Mestizaje in Central America. *Journal of Latin America Studies*, 34: 485.

Hall, Stuart. 1996. On Postmodernism and Articulation: An Interview with Stuart Hall, ed. Lawrence Grossberg. *Stuart Hall, Critical Dialogues in Cultural Studies,* David Morley and Kuan-Hsing Chen, eds. London: Routledge.

———. 1991. The Local and the Global: Globalization and Ethnicity, and Old and New Identities, Old and New Ethnicities. *Culture, Globalization, and the World-System: Contemporary Conditions for the Representation of Identity.* Binghamton: SUNY Press.

Herrera Sarmiento, Enrique. 1998. Informe de Caracterización Preliminar de la Demanda TCO Ese Eja, Tacana, y Cavineño. La Paz, Bolivia: SAE/VAIPO.

Isbell, Billie Jean. 1978. *To Defend Ourselves: Ecology and Ritual in an Andean Village.* Austin: Institute of Latin American Studies, University of Texas.

Joseph, Gilbert and Daniel Nugent. 1994. *Everyday Forms of State Formation, Revolution and the Negotiation of Rule in Modern Mexico.* Durham: Duke University Press

Kohl, Benjamín. 2002. Stabilizing Neoliberalism in Bolivia: Popular Participation and Privatization. *Political Geography*, 21: 449–72.

———. 2003a. Nongovernmental Organizations as Intermediaries for Decentralization in Bolivia. *Environment and Planning C: Government and Policy*, 21: 317–31.

———. 2003b. Restructuring Citizenship in Bolivia: El Plan de Todos. *International Journal of Urban and Regional Research*, 27(2): 337–51.

———. 2003c. Democratizing Decentralization in Bolivia: The Law of Popular Participation. *Journal of Planning Education and Research*, 23 (2): 153–64.

———. 2000. Restructuring Citizenship in Bolivia at the End of the Millennium: El Plan de Todos. Paper presented at the Meeting of the Latin American Studies Association, Miami, March 2000.

———. 1999. The Role of NGOs in the Implementation of Political and Administrative Decentralization in Bolivia. Paper presented to the American Colleges and Schools of Planning Meetings, Chicago, October 1999.

———. 1998. Market and Government Reform in Bolivia: Global Trends and Local Responses. Paper presented at American Colleges and Schools of Planning Meetings, Pasadena, California, November 5–8, 1998.

Kruse, Thomas A. 1994. *The Politics of Structural Adjustment and the NGOs: a Look at the Bolivian Case.* Master's Thesis, Cornell University Department of Regional Planning.

Larson, Brooke. 1988. *Colonialism and Agrarian Transformation in Bolivia, Cochabamba, 1550–1900.* Princeton, New Jersey: Princeton University Press.

Laserna, Roberto. 1994. Movimientos Regionales y Descentralización en Bolivia, una Experiencia de Concertación. *Reflexiones sobre la Descentralización.* La Paz: ILDIS/PROADE.

Lema, Ana María. 2001. *De la Huella al Impacto.* La Paz, Bolivia: PIEB.

Mallon, Florencia. 1995. *Peasant and Nation, The Making of Postcolonial Mexico and Peru.* Berkeley: University of California Press.

Mamdani, Mahmood. 1996. *Citizen and Subject, Contemporary Africa and the Legacy of Late Colonialism.* Princeton: Princeton University Press.

Marinissen, Judith. 1998. *Legislación Boliviana y Pueblos Indígenas, Inventario y Análisis en la Perspectiva de las Demandas Indígenas.* Santa Cruz, Bolivia: SNV-CEJIS.

Mesa Quisbert, Carlos. 2003. *La Razon,* 10/18/03. La Paz, Bolivia.

Maybury-Lewis, David. 2002. *Indigenous Peoples, Ethnic Groups, and the State.* Boston: Allyn and Bacon.

McCullough, James, and Ronald Johnson. 1989. Analyzing Decentralization Policies in Developing Countries: A Political-Economy Framework. *Development and Change,* 20(1): 57–87.

Morales, Evo. 2003. Bolivia, the Power of the People. Speech delivered at a conference entitled "En Defensa de la Humanidad (In Defense of Humanity)", October 24, 2003, Mexico City. Translated by Bruce Campbell. Online <http://www.americas.org>.

———. 2002. *Juguete Rabioso,* February 3, 2002. Santa Cruz, Bolivia.

Morris, Arthur and Stella Lowder. 1992. *Decentralization in Latin America, An Evaluation.* New York: Praeger.

Mosley, Samuel, Jane Harrigan, and John Toye. 1991. *Aid and Power: The World Bank and Policy-Based Lending.* London: Routledge.

Okin, Susan Moller. 1999. *Is Multiculturalism Bad for Women?* Princeton: Princeton University Press.

Oxhorn, Philip. 1995. From Controlled Inclusion to Coerced Marginalization: The Struggle for Civil Society in Latin America. *Civil Society, Theory, History, Comparison,* John A. Hall, ed. Cambridge: Polity Press.

Platt, Tristan. 1991. Liberalismo y etnocidio en los Andes del Sur. *Autodeterminación*, 9: 7–29.

Postero, Nancy. 2001. *Suburban Indians: Constructing Indigenous Identity and Citizenship in Lowland Bolivia*. Ph.D Dissertation, University of California, Berkeley, UMI No. 30444632.

Povinelli, Elizabeth A. 1998. The State of Shame: Australian Multiculturalism and the Crisis of Indigenous Citizenship. *Critical Inquiry*, 24: 575 (Winter 1998).

Putnam, Robert. 1993. *Making Democracy Work: Civic Traditions in Modern Italy*. Princeton: Princeton University Press.

Rappaport, Joanne. 1994. *Cumbe Reborn: an Andean Ethnography of History*. Chicago: University of Chicago Press.

——. 1990. *The Politics of Memory: Native Historical Interpretation in the Colombian Andes*. Cambridge: Cambridge University Press.

Riester, Jürgen. 1985. CIDOB's Role in the Self-Determination of the Eastern Bolivian Indians. Cultural Survival, Occasional Papers, N.16: 55–74. Cambridge, MA.

Rivera Cusicanqui, Silvia. 1987. *Oppressed but Not Defeated, Peasant Struggles among the Aymara and Qhechwa in Bolivia, 1900–1980* (English translation). Geneva, Switzerland: United Nations Research Institute for Social Development.

Roseberry, William. 1996. Hegemony, Power, and Languages of Contention. *The Politics of Difference*, Edwin Wilmsen and Patrick McAllister, eds. Chicago: University of Chicago Press.

Sanabria, Harry. 2000. Resistance and the Arts of Domination, Miners and the Bolivian State. *Latin American Perspectives*, 27 (1): 56–81.

Schild, Verónica. 1998. New Subjects of Rights? Women's Movements and the Construction of Citizenship in the "New Democracies". *Cultures of Politics, Politics of Culture*, Alvarez, Sonia, Evelina Dagnino, and Arturo Escobar, eds. Boulder: Westview Press.

Scott, James. 1985. *Weapons of the Weak: Everyday Forms of Peasant Resistance*. New Haven: Yale University Press.

SNPP (Secretaría Nacional de Participación Popular). 1996. *El Pulso de la Democracia, Participación Ciudadana y Descentralización en Bolivia*. La Paz: Editorial Nueva Sociedad.

Stern, Steve. 1987. *Resistance, Rebellion, and Consciousness in the Andean peasant World, 18th to 20th Centuries*. Madison: University of Wisconsin Press.

Stocks, Anthony. 1999. *Iniciativas Forestales en el Trópico Boliviano, Realidades y Opciones*. Technical report for BOLFOR. Santa Cruz: BOLFOR.

Stephen, Lynn. 2002. *Zapata Lives! Histories and Cultural Politics in Southern Mexico*. Berkeley: University of California Press.

Ströbele-Gregor, Juliana. 1996. Culture and Political Practice of the Aymara and Quechua in Bolivia: Autonomous Forms of Modernity in the Andes. *Latin American Perspectives*, 23(2): 72.

Tamburini, Leonardo, and Ana Cecilia Betancur. 2001. El Proceso para la Titulación de la TCO Monteverde, La Realidad del Saneamiento de la Propiedad Agraria. *Artículo Primero*, August–December 2001. Santa Cruz, Bolivia: CEJIS.

Thurner, Mark.1997. *From Two Republics to One Divided, Contradictions of*

Postcolonial Nationmaking in Andean Peru. Durham: Duke University Press.

Tiro, Felix. 1958. *Constituciones.* La Paz, Bolivia.

Uggla, Fredrik. 2002. Protest Politics, Civil Society, and Political Parties. Paper presented to CEISAL Congress, Amsterdam, July 2002.

Unzueta, Fernando. 2000. Periódicos y Formación Nacional: Bolivia en sus Primeros Años. *Latin American Research Review,* 35(2): 35–72.

Van Cott, Donna Lee. 2003. From Exclusion to Inclusion: Bolivia's 2002 Elections. *Journal of Latin American Studies,* 35: 751.

——. 2000. *The Friendly Liquidation of the Past, The Politics of Diversity in Latin America.* Pittsburgh: University of Pittsburgh Press.

——. 1994. *Indigenous Peoples and Democracy in Latin America.* New York: St. Martin's Press.

Varese, Stefano. 1996. Parroquialismo y Globalización, las Etnicidades Indígenas ante el Tercer Milenio. *Pueblos Indios, Soberanía, y Globalismo.* Quito, Ecuador: Ediciones Abya-Yala.

Warren, Kay B. 1998. *Indigenous Movements and Their Critics, Pan-Maya Activism in Guatemala.* Princeton: Princeton University Press.

Whitten, Norman. 1975. Jungle Quechua Ethnicity: an Ecuadorian Case Study. *Ethnicity and Resource Competition in Plural Societies,* Leo Despres, ed. The Hague: Mouton.

Yashar, Deborah. 1999. Democracy, Indigenous Movements, and the Postliberal Challenge in Latin America. *World Politics,* 52: 76–104.

——. 1998. Contesting Citizenship: Indigenous Movements and Democracy in Latin America. *Comparative Politics,* 1998: 23–42.

Žižek, Slavoj. 1997. Multiculturalism, Or, the Cultural Logic of Multinationalism. *New Left Review* 225: 28–51.

Socialist *Saudades*

Lula's Victory, Indigenous Movements, and the Latin American Left

Jonathan W. Warren

For those of us who have been opponents of the Washington Consensus and struggled for more democratic and transparent societies, land and tax reform, environmental protection, and greater social justice in Latin America, the landslide victory in 2002 by the Workers' Party presidential candidate, Luiz Inácio Lula da Silva, has generated a new sense of hope, excitement, and possibility. Against this sanguine backdrop, I offer a cautionary tale. In this chapter I discuss how Lula's electoral victory could help to enliven an anti-race narrative of liberation among the left, or at least large segments of the Latin American left. However before delineating the perils of socialist *saudades* (nostaligic longings) and other Marxist hauntings, I consider the impact that the Workers' Party administration will likely have on the Indian Question in Brazil.

The Brazilian Indigenous Question Under Lula's Administration

The indigenous question was of most salience to the Brazilian left, including the Workers' Party, in the late 1970s and 1980s. Ironically it was the military dictatorship (1964–85) that brought Indian matters to the forefront of political concern. To enhance its legitimacy the military regime publicized the previous government's maltreatment of Indians "as a symbol of all that was rotten in the state of Brazil before the coup"

Jonathan W. Warren

(Garfield, 1999: 268). A twenty volume, 5,115-page government report was released in 1968 which documented ethnocide, human rights violations, and other atrocities committed against Indians by the military regime's predecessors. One problem with this strategy, as Seth Garfield observes, was that "few believed that long-neglected Indian rights were suddenly being safeguarded by the most unlikely of heroes – a regime set on the rapid development of the Amazon" (1999: 270).

Not only did the report do little to bolster its image, but also it offered a political opportunity to those opposed to the dictatorship. Pro-democracy activists quickly appreciated that by attacking the military regime's own maltreatment of indigenous people they could inflict political damage and even put the government on the defensive regarding its development initiatives. As a result, the indigenous cause was adopted as a symbol and *cause célèbre* of the democratization movement in the late 1970s and 1980s. Large segments of the Brazilian population, who might otherwise have been disinterested or ignorant of the Indian question, became aware of the indigenous struggle and were sympathetic toward many of the indigenous movement's goals.

The Indian movement was and continues to be a loose alliance of scores of indigenous communities and organizations, a handful of charismatic indigenous leaders, anthropologists, non-governmental organizations, and the Brazilian Catholic Church. Despite its cacophony of opinions and interests, the movement has at moments harmonized around particular issues such as opposition to official "celebrations" of Brazil's Quincentennial in 2000. The movement was also able to unify during the drafting of the 1988 Constitution and thus take full advantage of the political opening created by the particularities of the pro-democracy movement for which the Indian Question held great symbolic and tactical significance. The resulting constitution recognized the rights of indigenous people to "their social organizations, customs, languages, beliefs, traditions, and the original rights to the lands they traditionally occupy, it being incumbent on the Union to demarcate them, to protect and ensure respect for their goods" (Schwartzman *et al.* 1996: 39). The constitution represented a radical departure for the Brazilian state from the policies it had pursued for almost five hundred years. The idea of a multicultural nation-state was officially sanctioned, and for the first time in Brazilian history, government policy was not directed toward civilizing, Christianizing, evolving, nationalizing, integrating, and whitening – in short, exorcising – Indians.

The hard-won "right to be different," a catch phrase that continues to be uttered frequently at Indian meetings and political rallies, shields indigenous communities from universalistic articulations of liberalism that have been so successful in other parts of the Americas in undercutting or containing antiracist movements and policies. Subaltern racial groups in Brazil, in particular Indian and maroon societies, have the constitutional right to their own institutions, territories, and cultural traditions. Moreover, the state is required to help finance these distinctions and their production. In the United States, to take a counter example, such practices have in the post-apartheid era increasingly been defined as unfair, racist, and unconstitutional (see Lubiano 1997).

A lasting legacy of the particularities of the Brazilian democratization movement, in which the Indian question figured so centrally, is that the Workers' Party continues to espouse support for the indigenous cause. This consideration, however, is largely rhetorical. This is due in part, if not primarily, to the indigenous movement's lack of political clout. First, indigenous identified Brazilians constitute a small proportion (at most one percent) of the electorate (Kennedy and Perz 1999). Second, the more leftist faction of the indigenous base is highly concentrated in a few marginal sectors: the indigenous base communities affiliated with the Indigenous Missionary Council (CIMI), anthropologists associated with the Brazilian Anthropological Association (ABA), a handful of non-governmental organizations concerned with indigenous matters, and a few government functionaries involved in Indian affairs. Third, the large indigenous organizations with some political power at the regional level – such as the Coordination of Amazonian Indigenous Organizations (COIAB) or the Articulation of Indigenous People and Organizations from the Northeast, Minas Gerais, and Espiríto Santo (APOINME) – have been unable to build national-level organizations.

Many in the indigenous movement have long recognized that a national organization would help to advance their agenda. Nonetheless, the genesis of a more centrally coordinated and unified movement has been stymied by a number of logistical and substantive issues. For instance, most indigenous communities are relatively small, poor, and widely dispersed, sometimes separated by hundreds, if not thousands, of miles. Moreover, in the southeast and northeast the majority of indigenous communities speak Portuguese, are attempting to create or recuperate cultural distinctions, and are struggling over land often of little monetary value; whereas in the Amazon, Indians are dealing with Portuguese as a second language, sharp cultural distinctions, a frontier context of violence and exploitation, and struggles over vast tracks of land rich in natural resources.

Not surprisingly the relative weakness of the indigenous movement in Brazil (coupled with the Workers' Party's lingering old left view of ethnic matters being of secondary importance) figure much more importantly than sympathies that have their moorings in the democratization movement of decades past. Hence the current government will likely be, at best, a slight improvement over the previous center-left Fernando Henrique Cardoso government. This is a particularly bitter pill for many in indigenous movement to swallow given that Lula was to represent a new political era for *les misérables* of Brazil rather than the status quo or a mere incremental improvement. This frustration and sense of betrayal has

Jonathan W. Warren

prompted the Brazilian Catholic Church to publicly declare that, "For the Lula administration, indigenous people have acquired a political invisibility and insignificance" (Bugge 2003).

The Lula government will probably continue, or at least not reverse, the increasingly favorable climate that evolved during the Cardoso administration for antiracism and Indian resurgence. Fernando Henrique Cardoso helped to soften an important foundation of the racial status quo by officially acknowledging the existence of racism in Brazil. The result has been the slow but steady erosion of the widely held belief that Brazil is a racial democracy. This has prompted an increasingly vibrant public debate on racism as well as several anti-racist policy initiatives such as a federal law against white-only ads for employment, the establishment of slave archives in the state of Rio de Janeiro, and the institutionalization of affirmative action policies in a few of the most prestigious universities. Moreover, the various problems that indigenous peoples historically encountered in Brazil when seeking federal recognition, such as an anti-Indian judiciary and bureaucratic obstructionism, eased under the Cardoso administration. This facilitated the doubling of the number of communities and Indian identified Brazilians during Cardoso's tenure. Indications are that this trend will continue under Lula's stewardship.

Initially there were hopes that the Lula administration would succeed in government reform where the more neoliberally oriented Cardoso administration failed. Expectations were high that the new government would attempt to root out or at least lessen the corruption, clientelism, and intimidation endemic in the National Foundation for the Indian (FUNAI).[1] In fact, the Indian movement continues to protest and lobby aggressively for the creation of a Superior Council of Indigenous Politics as a means for transforming the corporatist federal Indian agency. The Superior Council would be administered by Indians elected by indigenous people, usurping many of the responsibilities of FUNAI. Current government indigenistas – such as the bureaucrats in FUNAI – would be reduced to a consulting and accounting function. For reasons that are yet unclear, and despite pre-election promises, it appears that the Workers' Party will not support change. To the chagrin of the Indian movement, Lula recently appointed Mércio Pereira Gomes as the 33rd president of FUNAI. Professor Gomes, an anthropologist at the Fluminese Federal University, is a supporter of the institutional status quo and represents anthropological thinking on Indianness and race that many argue harks back to the salvage anthropology of the 1940s and '50s (see Warren 2001).

Given the Lula administration's response to the Indian movement's proposal for the reform of FUNAI, it seems unlikely that the government will side with Indians on the even more contentious and politically sensitive issue of land demarcation and regularization – still the most important issue in Indian country. At present it appears that the new government will support the return of some federal lands, such as a few national parks, to indigenous communities. The new president of the federal agency responsible for the environment, the Brazilian Institute of the Environment and Renewable Natural Resources (IBAMA), has stated that certain areas should be the exclusive dominion of indigenous people. However, with respect to those lands that threaten the interests of the regional elite the outcome will likely be much less favorable for Indians. The most contentious case is probably the Raposa/Serra do Sol lands in Roraima. The political and economic elite in the Amazon region – including a few who belatedly joined the Lula coalition such as the governor of Roraima – are staunchly against the regularization of demarcated Indian lands. To date Lula and his administration have not given any signal as to whether they will regularize these lands and remove the non-Indian settlers who occupy them. Clearly they are worried about alienating the regional elite and thus jeopardizing much-needed support on other policy fronts (the Workers' Party, one must remember, is not in the majority in Congress[2]). How the government responds to the Raposa/Serra do Sol conflict as well as few other bitter land disputes such as the Yanomami in Roraima, Cinta-Larga lands in Mato Grosso, the Xucuru in Pernambuco, the Pataxó Hã Hã Hãe in Bahia, and the Guaraní territories in Mato Grosso do Sul will be an excellent indicator of both the degree of support within the Workers' Party administration for the indigenous people of Brazil and the effectiveness of the Indian movement under Lula's tutelage.

Anti-Race Reincarnations

This political victory may go beyond immediate policy impacts on the Brazilian indigenous movement to affect the Latin American left's broader vision such as its understandings of power, social inequalities, liberatory subjectivities and critical consciousness. Although the Workers' Party has made significant steps away from a conventional leftist political project – class reductive, state-centric and elitist (if not authoritarian) – there is the danger that its electoral success could harden or rejuvenate elements of such a leftist project throughout the hemisphere.

For decades a Marxist analysis of power was so foundational to the left in Latin America that many still cannot imagine a liberatory political project absent socialism. For example, Martin Hopenhayn (2002) writes that with the death of the socialist God there are "no prospects of revolution" and thus "present life loses its epic potential." He audaciously asserts that without the socialist dream there is an incapability of even imaging radical change. "Great Projects" and "redeeming utopias" are no longer possible. "All that remains is individualism and a capitulation to the market." Remarkably, Hopenhayn – and I believe he is fairly typical of many on the Latin American left – cannot even imagine a progressive political project, a revolutionary utopia, that is not grounded in socialism.

From a more liberal perspective, Forrest Colburn (2002) reaches a similar conclusion. He considers the collapse of the socialist project as the demise of any kind of ideological contestation and competition. He writes, "Arguably, the strength of the 'left' as a political force – or at least the threat – compelled Latin American states to be as humane – or benign – as they were in the last century. [Given the collapse of a socialist project,] what will now elicit compassion from the state and society?"

It is startling, and indeed rather pathetic, how limited their definition of the "left" is. In their minds, the exclusive path to social justice, the realization of more equitable, democratic and prosperous societies, is a socialist one. It is believed to be the only possibility for contestation, competition, and justice. With this project closed off, the only putative option is laissez-faire capitalism, capitulation to the market, alienation, and inhumane societies.

One can easily imagine, then, that for such opinion makers and activists the death of socialism is not without its ghosts. There is a lingering and deep nostalgia amongst many leftist activist and intellectuals for a socialist utopia that leaves them unable to imagine or appreciate alternative paths to social justice. Moreover, iterations of the anti-race assumptions of Marxism still haunt the left. Fernando Coronil, for one, characterizes Indian and other ethnic movements as, at best, symptoms of and, at worst, allies of an emerging "imperial cartography of modernity" (2001: 66). Rather than seeing antiracist politics as a means for strengthening the nation-states of Latin America by making them less racist and therefore more cohesive, he implies that ethnic politics leave nation-states even more vulnerable to the neoliberal onslaught because they facilitate the erosion of collective attachments to nation. Neoliberalism, he writes, "has led . . . to the demise of projects of national integration and the erosion or at least the redefinition of collective attachments to the nation. The social tensions resulting from these processes often lead to a racialization of social conflict and the rise of ethnicities" (2000: 73). Echoes of the old left's anti-race tradition are not very faint: the economy is the principal engine behind social formations. Ethnic movements are the offspring of the polarizing dynamics of neoliberal globalizations.

García Canclini also portrays ethnic politics as fragmenting and weakening communal bonds. With Mexico City as his referent, he asserts that "Large cities torn by erratic growth and multicultural conflicts are the sites where we can best observe the decline of meta-narratives, of utopias that projected an ascendant and cohesive human development throughout time" (2001: 84). Indeed he doubts whether "we will ever be able to narrate the city again," thanks in part to ethnic politics that have left postmodern cities "dominated by disconnectedness, atomization and insignificance" (2001: 85). It is troubling how multiculturalism, rather than racism, is blamed for the inability to tell unifying stories about the city or nation.

García Canclini goes further in his criticisms of multiculturalism. He argues that ethnic movements and identities are typically rooted in archaic if not reactionary assumptions, which are ontologically antagonistic. "The demands on behalf of [ethnic] identity," he argues quoting Paul Ricoeur's critique of multiculturalism favorably, "always contain violence toward the other" (2001: 13). It is important to add that García Canclini, unlike Coronil, does not regard the emergence of ethnic politics as a by-product of the material alone. In his opinion, multiculturalism is a consequence of the "postmodern disorder" with its dispersion of signs, dissemination of meaning, dislodging of shared and stable codes, and concomitant dispersion of subjects (2001).

Thus at socialism's wake its anti-race spirit is reborn in the body of the left's latest theoretical tastes. White supremacy is still not regarded as foundational to the social fabric of the hemisphere. Race matters are not considered central to the endemic violence, erosion of public space, extreme social inequalities, "striptease" of the state, stagnant economies, and fragmentation of community that characterize the Americas. The Latin American left is dominated by the belief that these phenomena are grounded in neoliberal capitalisms or postmodernities. Yet colonial, modern, and postmodern American cities and nations do not figure any better *vis-à-vis* the above social problems. In the past, violence was common, social inequalities acute, subalterns excluded from public spaces, and societies were built upon liberal ideals that applied only to the elite or meta-narratives that could be more easily imposed upon the non-elite. The continuities across developmental projects, moments of modernization, and political regimes suggest that racism is equally, if not more, foundational to American social formations than neoliberal glob-alizations and postmodernities. Unfortunately, few, if any, within the Latin American left have yet to seriously consider such a possibility given its anti-race predilections. Hence movements and identities, which may offer solutions to the hemisphere's ills, are either derided as divisive or regarded as a sideshow to more fundamental issues and struggles.

Liberatory Possibilities

During the past two decades, throughout most of Latin America, there has been a revolutionary shift in the direction of identity formations. As Nancy Postero and Leon Zamosc note in the introductory chapter, across the region the historical direction of identity formations has turned away from whitening toward Indianning.[3] Individuals whose parents or who themselves once identified as non-Indians are increasingly assuming indigenous identities.

Due much less to neoliberal capitalisms than to the death of socialism and the continent-wide trend toward democratization, growing numbers of non-Indian intellectuals and activists have been encouraging the production of Indian-centered activism. One sees this with individuals such as Sub-commandante Marcos. A generation earlier a leftist, *mestizo*, urban philosopher like Marcos would not have struggled to build an Indian movement but rather would have channeled his energies into encouraging Indians to shed their tribal identities and mobilize for social justice as peasants or workers.

This shift has been so profound that nations where Indian resurgence is less present are increasingly seen as backward, if not racist. To take one example, Marisol de la Cadena notes that "Some analysts have interpreted the absence of 'ethnic social movements' in present-day Peru to reflect indigenous 'assimilation' and cultural loss. According to this perspective, Peruvian Indians are either behind in terms of ethnic consciousness or have yielded to dominant mestizaje projects" (2000: 20). Ironically, then, racial identities that were until recently considered archaic and anti-modern, have come to represent, at least in some quarters, cosmopolitan-ness. The change in subjectivities and idioms of political mobilization is significant not only because it represents a reversal of the flow of racial formations but also, and more importantly, these emerging identifications offer liberatory possibilities. This is because only by taking seriously the issues of race can social inequalities be addressed.

Latin America is infamously one of the most socially unequal regions of the world. One of the principal reasons that such inequalities exist has to do with race. Racism underpins their economic and social marginal-ization. Latin Americans of all political persuasions typically do not appreciate the veracity of this tenet because they understand power in class reductive terms. Observe how Helena, a twenty-two year-old black tutor in Belo Horizonte has no sense of how her class subordination may be connected to racism:

> If I were to rank my problems from one to twenty, with one being the worst of all my problems, racism would be number eighteen or nineteen. Racism just isn't something I'm greatly concerned about. I have bigger problems, such as putting food on the table, getting into a university, or getting a decent job. (Warren, 2001, 270)

Many racial subalterns in Brazil and elsewhere in Latin America, who are overwhelmingly concentrated in the poorer sectors of the economy, rarely grasp how their capacity to get a job and put food on the table are intimately entwined with race. There is scant understanding of how racism, both its contemporary and historical forms, is directly linked to the particular configurations of the labor market, social welfare, taxation policies, housing, educational opportunities, and so forth, which make meeting even basic economic needs extremely precarious for most racial subalterns. Subsequently, without an anti-racist movement to forge a race–class analysis of power, economic and cultural democratization are not likely to be forthcoming. Or as Antonio Sérgio Guimaraes aptly puts it, "Where material and cultural privileges associated with race, color and class subsist, the first step to an effective democratization consists precisely in naming the bases of these privileges: race, color, class" (2002: 39).

Importantly Brazilian Indians – much like Indians in other parts of Latin America – have been found to be an exception to the above rule. Compared to *mestizo*, black or white identified Latin Americans, Indians tend to consistently and aggressively challenge racist ideologies such as whitening, mobilize for representation in various institutions including government, and demonstrate high levels of racial literacy (see Warren 2001). Significantly the progressive potential of the Indian politic is also elaborated around questions in which the racial content is less obvious such as notions of private property, working conditions, the environment, and the structure and practice of the state. To take one example, in Guatemala ethnicity has been used to leverage land reform in communities where the idiom of class failed. Daniel Wilkinson writes,

> During the liberal era at the end of the nineteenth century, [the people of Cajolá] had appealed to the beneficence of the dictator-presidents, couching their appeals in the liberals' own rhetoric of property rights and national progress. During the Arbenz years, they had formed a "peasant union" and briefly acquired land through a petition under Decree 900, only to lose it after the 1954 coup. And during the war years, they had joined the guerillas, who promised the possibility of another agrarian reform. Each time they had told a different story about who they were and why they deserved the land. But only in 1992 did they hit upon one that worked.
>
> They changed the name of their movement from "Pro-Land" to "Pro-Ethnicity," and began to talk about themselves as "Mayans." The community soon became the poster child for the cause of "indigenous rights" in Guatemala. A photo of them facing off against the riot police appeared on a postcard, with the caption "The Clash of Two Worlds, 1492–1992" and was sold in tourist shops throughout the country to foreigners who, in turn, sent it to their homes around the world. Joined now by the voices of these strangers, the sound of their protests grew louder and louder until, several months later, they were able to wrest from the government one of the largest land grants in Guatemala since the Agrarian Reform. (2001: 357–8)

The liberatory possibilities of the Indian politic also extend from the fact that Indianness is a category that could encompass large segments if not majorities in many Latin American countries. The obvious examples are countries like Bolivia and Guatemala where Indian populations are already in the majority. Important, too, are those countries where Indians do not presently constitute majorities but could become majorities as the racial terrain changes. To take an analogous situation, Stuart Hall wrote that he and most of the rest of his countrymen were not black when he was a young man. It was only with the rise of black power in the 1960s that he and the majority of Jamaicans began to identify as black (Lubiano 1997).

Similar outcomes are possible in several Latin American countries as anti-racist movements mature and begin to affect the imaginings of citizens throughout the region. In Brazil, for instance, the number of indigenous-identified citizens doubled in the 1990s from 350,000 to 700,000 due in large measures to racial identity shifts. This trend is likely to continue given the present material and cultural context in which, among other factors, the legal and social scientific boundaries of Indianness have been redrawn so that any Brazilian of indigenous descent – which includes more than half of the population – could be legally recognized as Indian (Warren 2001: 231–2). Despite the fact that more than 50 percent of the population could, if individuals so chose to identify, the likelihood of this occurring is remote at present. Yet how might the idea of what is probable change radically if, for instance, several of the neighboring Andean countries were to become "Indian"?

Another reason that Indianness may prove an increasingly popular and effective site for political mobilization stems from the fact that there are not, at least as of yet, many effective counter-discourses. Most attacks against these emergent identities rest on outdated and therefore not very effective notions of race. At present the most common counter-offensive is to suggest that such Indians are racial charlatans based on biological or colonial notions of Indianness that have little or no support in academic or legal discourses. For instance, García Canclini characterizes these arguments as the musings of "racist elites, who still see indigenous cultures as antiquated remnants or mere survivals that are of interest only to folklorists and tourists" (2001: 125–6).

Many of the more credible criticisms that could be invoked to sustain the racial status quo – such as arguments based on constructionist ideas of race or universalistic notions of liberalism – will likely not find much traction in Latin America. For example, the principal argument used by those in the United States who are opposed to race-cognizant social movements and policies is that racial justice can only be achieved via color-blind practices and a greater emphasis on national, hybrid, or individual, rather than ethnic, identities. It will be difficult to pitch these ideas and policy recommendations in Latin America, no matter how well they are repackaged. These have been, of course, the hegemonic practices in the region for decades. The outcome, unfortunately, has not been less racist societies. Consequently the region is well inoculated against many of the more successful "against race" arguments currently circulating in the North.

A final reason Indianness may prove an especially significant basis for political mobilization is because the imperial power in the region, the

United States, will be much less likely to militarily intervene against progressive movements anchored in ethnicity. Due to the European Holocaust and anti-racist movements within the United States, it is much less politically tenable to support a military solution, even a covert one, to political challenges to the status quo that are ethnic centered. It is much easier to sustain brutal counter-insurgency measures against Marxist rebels than against indigenous rebels who can frame their struggle as one against genocide, ethnic cleansing, and racism.

Missed Opportunities

Despite its potential for being a powerful site for building a progressive political project, Indians and their social movements continue to be ignored if not snubbed by many on the left.[4] As we have seen it is not uncommon to read about the end of liberatory politics given that the socialist project is dead. It is telling that that these authors would probably not be lamenting the absence of alternative ideologies or unifying utopias, if the people of Ecuador, Mexico, Bolivia, Guatemala, and Brazil were experiencing the same degree of political mobilization around a class-articulated project that has been occurring on racial terrain. It is important to underscore that these have not been narrow, sectarian movements but ones calling for an end or modification of neoliberal, macro-economic policies and agreements, governments that are more democratic, transparent, and ethical, land and taxation reform, greater investments in health and education, decriminalization of drugs, and so forth.

A principal reason that an Indian politic has been overlooked or dismissed by many on the Latin American left has to do with its anti-race predilections. I have emphasized how Marxism and the persistence of some its ontological assumptions have helped to promote this bias. It would be, however, inaccurate to suggest that Marxism and its hauntings are solely responsible for what the sociologist Florestan Fernández once called Brazil's most deeply held prejudice: "the prejudice of not being prejudiced" (1989) In the essay "Masters in the Field" (Warren 2000), I explain how "white talk" (the race-evasive, color-blind language of race) and an emotional investment in white privilege have caused many scholars either to avoid the issue of racism altogether and thus effectively communicate that it is a non-issue or to seemingly bend over backward to reinterpret and reframe evidence that could disrupt the racial democracy imagining. For example, in her 1992 *Death without Weeping*, Nancy Scheper-Hughes

> failed to examine how racist attitudes may have impacted parents' perceptions in northeastern Brazil of whether a baby was "already wanting to die"

and thus "given-up-on." This is especially perplexing since she had no alternative or competing explanations. "And so after all is said and done," she concedes, "I still do not know what exactly prompts a mother or father to conclude that a baby is a victim of child sickness or child attack and is therefore under a death sentence." In avoiding a discussion of racism in this context, Scheper-Hughes took what might have been an excellent opportunity to illuminate "this traditional practice of letting go" and turned it into yet one more affirmation of the putative insignificance of race. (Warren 2000: 139–40)

Thus there is more behind the anti-race tendencies of the left in Latin America than Marxism and its spiritual iterations. More research is required to adequately dissect the genealogy of racial denials and dismissals. Nonetheless the influence of Marxism on the Latin American left should not be underestimated. As we have learned, at socialism's wake many cannot even imagine a liberatory project absent the death of the socialist God. Were it not for this paradigm, a class reductive, anti-race understanding of power and liberation surely would not have become so ubiquitous and lasting. Even from the grave Marxism's anti-race spirit continues to influence the avant-guard of the academic left rendering subjectivities and movements grounded in the idiom of race invisible, irrelevant, or problematic.

It is precisely this leftist tradition, or at least elements of it, that could be extended with Lula's victory. The significance of Lula's electoral success for how the region, including the left, imagines politics has been extensive. Even the editors of the *Herald Tribune*, who are likely not suffering from socialist *saudades*, view Lula's wide-ranging impact on Latin American politics through the lens of a conventional leftist trope.

A year after assuming Brazil's presidency, Luiz Inácio Lula da Silva, a long time labor activist, has displaced Vicente Fox of Mexico as the most influential Latin American leader and is an increasingly powerful presence on the global stage. His growing clout reflects a broader shift in Latin America's center of political gravity in the last three years. (. . .) From Hugo Chavez in Venezuela to Néstor Kirchner of Argentina, Latin leaders are looking less to Mexico and more to Brazil to provide regional leadership. Brasília is more interested in cementing a close-knit South American bloc than in buying into a Washington dominated hemispheric arrangement. Brazil led the entire developing world last year in opposing further global trade liberalization absent the removal of agricultural subsidies for the United States and Europe. (2004: 6)

Lula's principal contribution, in the editors' opinion, is not the forging of a new political project that appreciates the centrality of racism to American modernities but rather one (led, no less, by a long-time labor activist) that challenges Washington hegemony and neoliberal globalizations via Latin American and Southern solidarity. Lula is likely to have a similar meaning for the Latin American left given how seamlessly such a reading of his political project connects with the comfort narratives of the old and new left. Lula's victory, then, could very easily prolong, rather than unsettle, the leftist tradition of avoiding and dismissing race matters, including Indigenous movements. In the context of socialist *saudades* and postmodern understandings of ethnic movements as "consistent with the cultural logic of multinational capitalism" (García Canclini, 2001: xxxiii), the Workers' Party success could easily reinvigorate fantasies of class redemptions, denials of the significance of white supremacy, and the concomitant failure to engage adequately, if at all, the Indigenous movements presently transforming the hemisphere.

Conclusion

Ironically, given the above discussion, the Brazilian Workers' Party has made important strides toward recognizing the centrality of race to class inequalities and social problems. Currently it is common to hear political speeches by party members underscoring how the poor in Brazil are primarily women and racial subalterns. In much of its literature the party stresses that fundamental societal changes in Brazil will be impossible without taking into account "the race question." According to Martvs das Chagas, the party's National Antiracist Secretary, "within Lula's administration, the issue of race is always present in the formulation of political strategy and policy" (2002). This appreciation of how race and racism are relevant to a range of social and political issues in Brazil – even if it is an appreciation that is still rather superficial and primarily confined to the level of discourse – is testament to the degree to which antiracist activists and intellectuals have influenced thinking on the left.

One hopes that the Workers' Party's electoral success coupled with its evolving understanding of how race and class are intersected will push the Latin American left to finally turn a corner and transcend a narrative of liberation and utopias overly determined by class. The threat, as we have learned, is that it could have precisely the opposite impact. As long as the left's anti-race bias persists, the progressive potential that indigenous movements and anti-racism more generally offer will likely remain unrealized. Even more disturbing is the very real danger that the detached, if not dismissive, posture of many on the left to indigenous movements increases the odds that these movements and subjectivities will be articulated in the service of an anti-democratic, militaristic, authoritarian, patriarchal, and clientelistic political project.

In closing, let me stress that I am not suggesting that the meta-narrative of socialism be replaced with a new god of Indian or anti-racist politics. Nor am I arguing that anti-racist politics, including Indian movements, are a panacea for various social ills. My point is simply that transforming the racist foundations of the hemisphere is required if we are to realize more democratic, less violent, and more prosperous societies. In general, Indian actors, organizations, and movements understand the primacy of race to American social formations. The sooner the left can also come to such a realization, the quicker it can stop mourning the death of its god and become a much more effective force for the actualization of the humane, healthy, fulfilling, and just hemisphere for which we will struggle.

Notes

1   FUNAI was established in 1967 to replace the previous federal Indian agency, the Indian Protection Service (SPI).
2   The Workers' Party holds 14 out of 81 seats in the senate and 80 seats out of 513 in the chamber of deputies.
3   The change in the direction of racial formations highlights why it is inaccurate to refer to the current moment, as many do, as one of increased ethnicization. Ethnicization has occurred for centuries in the Americas. What has changed is the direction of ethnicization.
4   This, of course, varies widely. In some countries, the Left supports indigenous organizing and electoral policies. See the chapters in this volume on Bolivia, Ecuador, and Colombia.

References

Bugge, Axel. 2003. Novo presidente da Funai promete dar 12% do Brasil aos índios. Online <Yahoo Notícias, Sept. 9, br.news.yahoo. com/030909/16/eOft.html>.
de la Cadena, Marisol. 2000. *Indigenous Mestizos*. Durham: Duke University Press.
Colburn, Forrest. 2002. *Latin America at the End of Politics*. Princeton: Princeton University Press.
Coronil, Fernando. 2001. Toward a Critique of Globalcentrism: Speculations on Capitalism's Nature. *Millennial Capitalism and the Culture of Neoliberalism*, Jean and John L. Comaroff, eds. Durham, NC: Duke University Press.
Da Chagas, Martvs. 2002. O combate ao racismo e as eleicoes de 2002. July 7. Online <http://www.pt.org.br/site/secretarias/openmat.asp?IDNews=7046&id-secr=8>.
Fernández, Florestan. 1989. *Significado do Protesto Negro (Colecao Polemicas do Nosso Tempo)*. São Paulo: Editora Autores Associados.
García Canclini, Néstor. 2001. *Consumers and Citizens: Globalization and Multicultural Conflicts*. Minneapolis, MN: University of Minnesota Press.
Garfield, Seth.1999. The "Greatest Administrative Scandal." *The Brazil Reader: History, Culture, Politics*, Robert M. Levine and John J. Corcitti, eds. Durham, NC: Duke University Press.
Guimarães, Antonio Sérgio. 2002. *Classes, Racas e Democracia*. São Paulo: Editora 34.
Herald Tribune. 2004. The Powerful Role of Brazil, January 26: 6.
Hopenhayn, Martin. 2002. *No Apocalypse, No Integration: Modernism and*

Postmodernism in Latin America (Post-Contemporary Interventions), translated by Cynthia Tompkins and Elisabeth Rosa Hora.
Kennedy, David P. and Stephen G. Perz. 1999. *Who Are Brazil's Indígenas? Contributions of Census Data Analysis to an Anthropological Demography of Indigenous Populations.* Unpublished Manuscript.
Lubiano, Wannema, ed. 1997. *The House the Race Built: Black Americans, US Terrain.* New York: Pantheon Books.
Scheper-Hughes, Nancy. 1992. *Death without Weeping: The Violence of Everyday Life in Brazil.* Berkeley, CA: University of California Press.
Schwartzman, Stephan, Ana Valeria Araujo, and Paulo Pankararu. 1996. Brazil: The Legal Battle over Indigenous Rights. *NACLA Report on the Americas*, 24, no. 5: 36–43.
Warren, Jonathan W. 2000. Masters in the Field: White Talk, White Privilege, White Bias. *Racing Research, Researching Race: Methodological Dilemmas in Critical Race Studies*, France Winddance Twine and Jonathan W. Warren, eds. New York: New York University Press.
——. 2001 *Racial Revolutions: Antiracism and Indian Resurgence in Brazil.* Durham, NC: Duke University Press.
Wilkinson, Daniel. 2001. *Silence on the Mountain: Stories of Terror, Betrayal and Forgetting in Guatemala.* Boston: Houghton Mifflin.

Contributors

Nancy Postero is Assistant Professor in the Anthropology Department at the University of California, San Diego. Her work examines the relations between neoliberalism, multiculturalism, and citizenship in Bolivia. Her former work as a human rights lawyer and public radio journalist informs her anthropological research on political economy and indigenous identity in Latin America.

Leon Zamosc is Associate Professor of Sociology and Academic Director of Latin American Studies at the University of California, San Diego. He is the author of books and articles in Spanish and English on rural development, peasant political participation, and indigenous movements in Colombia and Ecuador. His current endeavors include the launching of a new academic journal, Latin American and Caribbean Ethnic Studies, which will be published by Taylor and Francis starting in 2006.

Gunther Dietz is Professor of Social Anthropology at the University of Granada (Spain). He has conducted ethnographic work on indigenismo policy, intercultural education, indigenous communities and ethnic movements in Mexico. He is the author of *Teoría y Práctica del Indigenismo* (1995), *La Comunidad Purhépecha es Nuestra Fuerza: Etnicidad, Cultura y Región en un Movimiento Indígena en Michoacán* (1999) and *Multiculturalismo, Interculturalidad y Educación: una Aproximación Antropológica* (2003).

Edward F. Fischer is Associate Professor of Anthropology and Director of the Center for Latin American and Iberian Studies at Vanderbilt University. His ethnographic work has focused on the Kaqchikel Maya of highland Guatemala. His publications include *Cultural Logics and Global Economies: Maya Identity in Thought and Practice* (2001), *Maya Cultural Activism in Guatemala* (co-edited with R. McKenna Brown, 1996), *Tecpan Guatemala: A Modern Maya Town in Global and Local Context* (with Carol Hendrickson, 2002), and *Pluralizing Ethnography* (co-edited with John Watanabe, 2004).

Contributors

Theodor Rathgeber is Associate Professor of Political and Applied Social Sciences at Kassel University (Germany). He also works as a free lance consultant on international law, human rights, minorities, indigenous peoples and development policies. He has published numerous articles on these topics and is currently investigating models of 'indigenous economy'.

María Elena García is Assistant Professor of Anthropology at Sarah Lawrence College. She has published on the politics of ethnography, community, development and education in the Andes. Her book, *Making Indigenous Citizens: Identities, Education, and Multicultural Development in Peru* (forthcoming, Stanford University Press) is a multi-sited ethnographic exploration of the local and transnational articulations of indigenous movements, multicultural development policies and indigenous citizenship in Peru.

José Antonio Lucero is Assistant Professor of Political Science at Temple University. His research interests include social movements, democracy, and the politics of race and ethnicity. His work has been published in *Comparative Politics, The Journal of Democracy*, and *Latin American Perspectives*. He is completing a book manuscript on indigenous movements and political representation in Ecuador and Bolivia.

Jonathan Warren is the Director of Latin American Studies in The Henry M. Jackson School of International Studies at the University of Washington in Seattle. He is the co-producer of the film *Just Black* (Filmmakers Library), co-editor of *Racing Research, Researching Race* (2000), and author of *Racial Revolutions* (2001). His current research explores race, modernization and development in Vietnam, Germany and the Americas.

Index

ABA (Brazilian Anthropological Association), 219
Abercrombie, Thomas, 199
Academia de las Lenguas Mayas de Guatemala (ALMG), 89–90, 91
Acción Democrática Nacional (ADN), 198, 201
acculturation, Mexico, 41–2, 44–5
ADN (*Acción Democrática Nacional*), 198, 201
affirmative action
Brazil, 220
Guatemala, 19, 87, 96, 97
AGAFA (*Asociación de Generales y Almirantes de las Fuerzas Armadas*), 133
agrarian counter-reform, Mexico, 57
Agrarian League, 40
agrarian reform, Bolivia, 200, 202
agrarian reform, Colombia, 110, 118
agrarian reform, Ecuador, 134
agrarian reform, Guatemala, 225
agrarian reform, Mexico
dotación (land grant), 35–6, 38, 40–1
educational campaigns, 38
ideological penetration, 36–7
lack of implementation, 41
limits of, 35
opposition to, 38
peasant organizations, 21, 43
restitución (restitution), 36, 38, 41, 47
retreat from, 49, 52
agrarian reform, Peru, 21, 162–3, 165, 166, 183*n*
agrarismo, 33, 37–41
agrarista teachers, 38
agricultural industrialization, Mexico, 34, 35, 42
Aguablanca indigenous reserve, 117
Aguado López, Eduardo, 41
Aguaruna and Huambisa Council, 166–7, 170

Aguirre Beltrán, Gonzalo, 34, 43
Agurto, Jorge, 173, 180
AIDESEP *see* Inter-Ethnic Development Association of the Peruvian Jungle (AIDESEP)
ALAI, 53
Albó, Xavier
AIDESEP, 167
Cárdenas as vice-president, 196
colonial dualities, 193
ethnicity, 194
Katarista (MRTKL) movement, 15
Peruvian indigenous movements, 159, 160, 168
"return of the Indian", 2, 158
Alianza Cívica, 51
Alianza Nacional de Profesionales Indígenas Bilingües (ANPIBAC), 43, 44, 45, 46, 47, 49, 53
ALMG (*Academia de las Lenguas Mayas de Guatemala*), 89–90, 91
Alonso, Ana María, 38, 192, 193
Alto Sinú area, 123
Alvarez, Sonia, 7, 189, 192
Amuesha Congress, 166–7, 181–2
Anderson, Benedict, 37
Andolina, Robert, 7, 137
ANIPA (*Asamblea Nacional Indígena Plural por la Autonomía*), 65, 66
ANPIBAC *see Alianza Nacional de Profesionales Indígenas Bilingües* (ANPIBAC)
anti-globalization movement, 102
anti-racism, Brazil, 218–19, 220, 221–3, 225, 226, 227–8, 229–30
Antioquia region, 113, 120
APCOB, 210*n*
APOINME, 219
Arauca, 116, 117
Arellano-López, Sonia, 198
ARIC (*Asociaciones Rurales de Interés Colectivo*), 48

Index

Index

Index

237

Index

colonialism *(continued)*
Colombia, 111, 117
Guatemala, 81, 84, 85
Mexico, 33–4
Peru, 179, 183*n*, 210*n*
colonos, 41
Columbus Quincentennial debate, 52–3,
105, 195
Comalapa, 88
Comaroff, Jean, 20
Comaroff, John, 20, 199
El Comercio (EC), 147, 148, 149, 150
COMG (*Consejo de Organizaciones
Mayas de Guatemala*), 90, 91
comisariado ejidal, 38, 40
*Comisión Coordinadora de
Organizaciones Indígenas de la
Cuenca Amazónica* (COICA), 106,
170, 171, 182, 184*n*
*Comisión Indígena Nacional de la
Amazonia* (CINA), 179, 181
*Comision Parlamentaria de Concordia y
Pacificación* (COCOPA), 67
*Comisión Permanente del Seguro Social
Campesino* (CPSSC), 135
*Comité Clandestino Revolucionario
Indígena* (CCRI), 60
Comité de Unidad Campesino (CUC), 14,
91
Comité Pro-Derecho Indígena, 176
*Comité Proformación del Partido Político
Sociedad Ixim*, 88, 91
comités de solidaridad, 50
Committee of Campesino Unity (CUC),
14, 91
communal assemblies
Bolivia, 203
Mexico, 54–6, 59–60, 63
communal statutes, 54
*Communidades de Población en
Resistencia* (CPR), 91
community and communalism, Mexico,
53–6
comuneros, 35, 52, 54, 55
CONACAMI (National Coordinator of
Communities Adversely Affected by
Mining), 177, 178–9, 182, 184*n*,
185*n*
Conaghan, C., 132
CONAIE *see Confederación de
Nacionalidades Indígenas del
Ecuador* (CONAIE)
CONAMAQ, 179
CONAP (Confederation of Nationalities of
the Peruvian Amazon), 167, 172, 180
CONAPA (National Commission for
Andean, Amazonian, and Afro-
Peruvian Peoples), 173–4, 179, 180,
183*n*, 185*n*

CONAVIGUA, 91
Concha Malo, Miguel, 66
Concheiro Bórquez, Luciano, 57
CONDEPA (Conscience of the
Fatherland), 195
Confederación Campesina del Perú (CCP),
165, 180
*Confederación de Indígenas del Oriente de
Bolivia* (CIDOB), 12, 195, 196, 200,
205
*Confederación de Nacionalidades
Indígenas del Ecuador* (CONAIE),
8–9, 12, 145–7, 179
Bucaram's presidency, 137
Durán's presidency, 134–5
Gutiérrez's presidency, 147, 148–50,
152
Mahuad's presidency, 138, 140, 147
neoliberal protests, 1–2, 24, 144, 145
Pachakutik Movement, 11, 136, 147,
148, 149, 152
Confederación Nacional Agraria (CNA),
165, 180
Confederación Nacional Campesina
(CNC), 38–40, 41, 46, 48
Confederation of Indigenous Peoples of
Eastern Bolivia (CIDOB), 12, 195,
196, 200, 205
Confederation of Nationalities of the
Peruvian Amazon (CONAP), 167,
172, 180
Congress of Amuesha Communities,
166–7, 181–2
Conscience of the Fatherland
(CONDEPA), 195
*Consejo de Nacionalidades y Pueblos
Indígenas Ecuador* (CODENPE), 137,
146, 149
*Consejo de Organizaciones Mayas de
Guatemala* (COMG), 90, 91
*Consejo de Pueblos Nuahuas del Alto
Balsas*, 62
*Consejo Estatal de Organizaciones
Indígenas y Campesinas de Chiapas*
(CEOIC), 65
*Consejo Guerrerense 500 Años de
Resistencia Indígena*, 66, 68
Consejo Indio de Sud America (CISA),
168, 170
*Consejo Mexicano 500 Años de
Resistencia Indígena*, 53
Consejo Nacional de Pueblos Indígenas
(CNPI), 43, 44, 45–6, 47, 53
Consejo Supremo (Supreme Council), 44
consensus, principle of, 55–6
consociational systems, 18
Convención Nacional Democrática
(CND), 59
Convención Nacional Indígena (CNI), 65,
66, 67

238

Index

Index

Index

Index

Index

Index

Index

Movimiento Nacional Revolucionario
(MNR), 22–3, 190, 194, 196, 197,
198, 199, 201
Movimiento Revolucionario Túpac Amaru
(MRTA), 160, 183n
Movimiento Sin Tierra, 205
Moya, R.A., 134
MRTA (Movimiento Revolucionario
Túpac Amaru), 160, 183n
MRTKL see Katarista (MRTKL) move-
ment
Mueller-Plantenberg, C., 120, 122
multiculturalism, 7, 86, 222
Bolivia, 17, 189–93, 196–7, 199–200,
208, 209–10n
Peru, 164
Münzel, M., 107
Muratorio, Blanca, 13
Muyuy Jacanamejoy, G., 114

Nación Purhépecha, 57, 62, 68
Ñaco, Guillermo, 181
NAFTA (North American Free Trade
Association), 57, 58
Ñahñu community, 47
Nasa (Páez) community, 106, 114, 115
Nash, June, 58
National Action Party (PAN), 67
National Agrarian Confederation (CNA),
165, 180
National Alliance of Bilingual Indigenous
Professionals see Alianza Nacional de
Profesionales Indígenas Bilingües
(ANPIBAC)
National Amazonian Indigenous
Commission (CINA), 179, 181
National Assembly of Indigenous
Pluralities for Autonomy (ANIPA),
65, 66
National Commission for Andean,
Amazonian, and Afro-Peruvian
Peoples (CONAPA), 173–4, 179,
180, 183n, 185n
National Commission for Indigenous
Territories, 115
National Confederation of Indian
Nationalities (CONAIE) see
Confederación de Nacionalidades
Indígenas del Ecuador (CONAIE)
National Coordinator of Communities
Adversely Affected by Mining
(CONACAMI), 177, 178–9, 182,
184n, 185n
National Council of Indian Peoples, 46
National Council of Indigenous Peoples
(CNPI), 43, 44, 45–6, 47, 49, 53
National Democratic Action (ADN), 198,
201
National Democratic Convention (CND),
59

National Foundation for the Indian
(FUNAI), 220, 230n
National Front, 108
National Indigenist Institute (INI), 42, 44,
46, 66
National Indigenist Institution, 99
National Indigenous Convention (CNI),
65, 66, 67
National Institute for Agrarian Reform
(INCORA), 117
National Office of Bilingual Intercultural
Education (DINEBI), 164
National Peasant Federation (CNC),
38–40, 41, 46, 48
National Revolutionary Movement
(MNR), 22–3, 190, 194, 196, 197,
198, 199, 201
National Revolutionary Unity of
Guatemala (URNG), 83
natural resources
Colombia, 23, 107, 110, 116, 117–19,
124–7
Mexico, 34
Peru, 23, 177–9
Naveda, Igidio, 179
Negri, T., 116
neocardenistas, 50
neoliberalism, 2, 5, 21–5
Bolivia, 20, 22–3, 24–5, 189–90, 196–7,
198, 199, 201, 202, 208
Brazil, 222, 224
Colombia, 107, 110, 126, 127
Ecuador, 1–2, 22, 24, 131–2, 133–45,
150–1
Mexico, 21–2, 33, 34–5, 52, 53–4, 58
Peru, 22, 163–4
see also decentralization; privatization
Nicaragua, 1
Nilo hacienda, 115
Noboa, Alvaro, 147
Noboa, Gustavo, 140
Nolte, D., 110
Nomatsiguenga community, 172
Norman, Wayne, 7
North American Free Trade Association
(NAFTA), 57, 58
North Santander department, 116
Notisur
Bucaram's presidency, 137
Durán's presidency, 133, 135
Gutiérrez's presidency, 147, 148, 149,
150
Mahuad's presidency, 138, 139, 140
Nugent, Daniel, 38, 192
Nugkuag, Evaristo, 170
Nukak territory, 177

Oaxaca, 54, 61, 62
Obregón, General Alvaro, 37

Index

Index

Index

república de indios, 33, 37
resguardo único, 119
resguardos, 111, 117, 118, 120, 124–7
restitució de tierras (restitution), 36, 38, 41, 47
Restrepo, L.A., 109
Revolutionary Party (PR), 88
Richards, Michael, 88
Riester, Jürgen, 195, 210n
rights see human rights; indigenous rights
Rivera Cusicanqui, Silvia, 22, 194, 196, 210n
Roldocista Party, 136, 150
rondas campesinas, 169, 184n
Roosens, Eugeen E., 68
Roper, J. Montgomery, 2, 3, 5, 24
Roquel Calí, Edwin Domingo, 88
Roraima, 221
Ros Romero, María del Consuelo, 43
Roseberry, William, 197
Rosset, Peter, 58
Rubio, Blanca, 59
Ruiz, Bishop, 10
Rujunamil ri Mayab' Amaq', 90
Rural Associations of Collective Interest (ARIC), 48
rural corporatism, 21–2, 33, 37–41

Salazar Peralta, Ana María, 48, 57
Salgado, W., 143
Salinas de Gortari, Carlos, 49, 50, 52, 53, 57, 58
Saltos, N., 134
Samper, Ernesto, 114, 117
San Andrés Chicahuaxtla, 54
San Andrés Peace Accords, 10, 67
San Juan Ostuncalco, 87
Sanabria, Harry, 24, 198
Sánchez de Lozada, Gonzalo (Goni), 24, 189, 190, 196–7, 198–201, 206
Sánchez, G., 109
Sánchez Gómez, G., 109
Santana, Roberto, 32
Santiago Indigenous Institute, 99
Saqb'ichil, 91
Sarmiento Silva, Sergio, 43, 46, 47, 53
Sawyer, S., 134
Sayer, Derek, 191
Schele, Linda, 93
Scheper-Hughes, Nancy, 227–8
Schild, Verónica, 6, 191
Schuldt, J., 132
Schwartzman, Stephan, 218
Scott, James, 192
Scurrah, Martin, 173
Secretaría de Educación Pública (SEP), 37, 42, 44, 45, 46
Secretaría de Reforma Agraria, 47
Segundo Congreso Lingüístico Nacional, 89

Seguro Campesino, 135
self, Maya perspective on, 103
Selva Lacandona, 58, 59
Sendero Luminoso, 11, 160, 166, 168, 181, 183n
SEP (Secretaría de Educación Pública), 37, 42, 44, 45, 46
Servicio de Información Indígena (SERVINDI), 174, 181, 184–5n
SETAI, 171, 172, 173
Shell, 118
Sherzer, Joel, 3, 6, 13, 32
Shipibo (Defense Front of the Native Communities), 166–7
Shuar federation, 166
Shugart, M.S., 132
Sierra Leone, 87
SIISE (Sistema Integrado de Indicadores Sociales del Ecuador), 142
Sikkink, Kathryn, 171
SIL (Instituto de Lingüístico del Verano), 89, 99, 100
sindicato movement, 194
Singer, P., 127
Sinú River, 121, 122
Sistema Integrado de Indicadores Sociales del Ecuador (SIISE), 142
Smith, A.D., 32
Smith, Carol, 12
Smith, M.A., 164
Smith, Richard Chase, 172, 174
  AIDESEP, 167
  COICA, 171
  ethnic federations, 165, 166, 167
  indianista organizations, 165, 168
  indigenous organizations typology, 164, 165, 178
Social Indigenous Alliance (ASI), 106
socialism, 221–2, 223, 224, 228
Sociedad Económica, 86
Sociedad Ixim, 88, 91
Softestad, Lars T., 66
solidarity committees, 50
Sonnleitner, Willibald, 51
South American Indian Council (CISA), 168, 170
Spalding, Karen, 162
Specific Rights of the Maya People, 90
Spenser, Daniela, 38
Stanford, Lois, 57
State Council of Indigenous and Peasant Organizations of Chiapas (CEOIC), 65
Stavenhagen, Rodolfo, 159
Stephen, Lynn, 2, 193
Stern, Steve, 162, 181, 192
Stocks, Anthony, 202
Stoll, Davis, 84
Ströebele-Gregor, Juliana, 116, 194

Index

Suma community, 1
Summer Institute of Linguistics (SIL), 89, 99, 100

Tamayo, E., 134, 135
Tamburini, Leonardo, 202
Taussig, Michael, 13
Tecpán, 82, 88, 97
tenencias, 34
Tepito, 66
tequios, 55, 56
terceros, 202
territorial autonomy, 16
    Colombia, 107
    Ecuador, 145
    Mexico, 32, 33, 50, 63–7
Territorial Grassroots Organizations (OTBs), 197, 203
Tezaguic Tohón, Fernando, 88
Thoumi, F., 132
Thurner, Mark, 210*n*
Tierra Alta, 123
tierras baldías, 34
Tikal Futura, 100
Tojolabal peasants, 59
Toledo, Alejandro, 11, 17, 171, 172–3, 179, 181, 182
Totoró community, 114
Toye, John, 24, 197
trade unionism
    Ecuador, 134, 148
    Mexico, 45–6, 49
    Peru, 164–6, 168
Training Program for Bilingual Intercultural Education for the Andean Countries (PROEIB), 170–1, 182
Triqui community, 54
Tunubalá, Floro, 109
Tupac Amaru Indian Movement (MITA), 168
Túpac Amaru Revolutionary Movement (MRTA), 160, 183*n*
Turbay, Julio Cesar, 108
tutela right, 110, 118, 122
Tutino, John, 35
Tzeltal peasants, 59
Tzotzil peasants, 59

UCD (*Unión Campesina Democrática*), 51
UCEZ (*Unión de Comuneros Emiliano Zapata*), 47
Uggla, Fredrik, 193, 205
UNCA (*Unión Nacional de Comunidades Aymaras*), 183*n*
UNESCO, 170
Unidad Revolucionaria Nacional Guatemalteca (URNG), 83

Unification Movement of the Triqui Struggle, 62
Unión Campesina Democrática (UCD), 51
Unión de Comuneros Emiliano Zapata (UCEZ), 47
Unión de Organizaciones Regionales Campesinas Autónomas (UNORCA), 49, 57
Unión Nacional de Comunidades Aymaras (UNCA), 183*n*
Unión Patriótica, 108
Union of Regional Autonomous Peasant Organizations (UNORCA), 49, 57
Uniones de Ejidos, 48
United Nations, 84, 85, 93, 169
United Nations Working Group on Indigenous Peoples, 66, 169
United States
    anti-narcotics, 205
    Central American solidarity movement, 102
    Gutiérrez's visit, 148
    as imperial power, 227
    indigenous funding, 84
    Plan Colombia, 115
    race, 219, 226
United Workers Front (FUT), 134
UNORCA (*Unión de Organizaciones Regionales Campesinas Autónomas*), 49, 57
Unzueta, Fernando, 193
Uquillas, J.E., 146
Urban, Greg, 3, 6, 13, 32
Uribe, Alvaro, 108, 113
URNG (*Unidad Revolucionaria Nacional Guatemalteca*), 83
Urrá I hydroelectric plant, 121, 122
Urrá II hydroelectric plant, 121
Urrá S.A. Company, 122, 123
Urrutia, Jaime, 171, 172
USAID, 92, 99, 170
U'wa community, 23, 117–19, 126

VAIPO (*Vice Ministro de Asuntos Indígenas y Pueblos Originarios*), 199, 209*n*
Valle del Cauca department, 126
Van Cott, Donna Lee, 159, 198
    Bolivian elections, 11, 17, 205
    CONDEPA, 195
    democratization, 2, 189, 193
    Goni's reforms, 196, 199
    ILO Convention 169, 169
    Katarista movement, 195
    multiculturalism, 191
Van der Berghe, Pierre, 1, 12
Varas, Augusto, 24
Varese, Stefano, 2, 34, 45, 192
Vargas, María Eugenia, 45
Vasconcelos, José, 37, 38, 86

Index